Effective Leadership
in Policing

EFFECTIVE LEADERSHIP IN POLICING

Successful Traits and Habits

By
Joseph A. Schafer

CAROLINA ACADEMIC PRESS
Durham, North Carolina

Library of Congress Cataloging-in-Publication Data
Schafer, Joseph A. (Joseph Andrew), 1973-
  Effective leadership in policing : successful traits and habits / Joseph A. Schafer.
     p. cm.
  Includes bibliographical references and index.
  ISBN 978-1-59460-803-2 (alk. paper)
  1. Police administration. 2. Police. I. Title.

HV7935.S33 2012
363.2068'4--dc23   2012023678

Carolina Academic Press
700 Kent Street
Durham, North Carolina 27701 Telephone
(919) 489-7486
Fax (919) 493-5668
www.cap-press.com

Printed in the United States of America
2018 Printing

In memory of

John G. Chase
Dallas Police Department
End of Watch: January 23, 1988

&

Jay P. Balchunas
Wisconsin Department of Justice
End of Watch: November 5, 2004

Table of Contents

Acknowledgments

This book would not have been possible without the support of a variety of individuals and institutions.

My access to the FBI Academy and the National Academy program was made possible through a visiting scholar initiative provided by the FBI Behavioral Science Unit (BSU). Supervisory Special Agent Dr. Carl J. Jensen III (retired FBI) worked to establish this opportunity at the FBI Academy to further futures research in the BSU. Carl also played a driving role in creating the Futures Working Group (FWG), a collaborative project between Police Futurists International and the FBI. The FWG was established in 2002 to advance strategic thinking, forecasting, and other futures perspectives in law enforcement. In 2004, Carl asked me to become a member of this group.

In 2006 I was fortunate to be selected as a visiting scholar at the FBI Academy and I served in that capacity until 2008. Carl retired shortly after I began the project that is the basis for this book. His vision and commitment to futures thinking has been carried forward by Chief Criminologist Dr. John P. Jarvis of the BSU. I am indebted to both Carl and John for their support throughout this project and other initiatives we have pursued. It has been my honor to consider Carl and John collaborators, coauthors, colleagues, and, most importantly, friends. "Mistakes were made," but I hope they will not judge this effort to fit that classification.

The FWG and the visiting scholar program were supported by retired BSU Unit Chief Dr. Steve Band. During my time in residence at the Academy, the program was being overseen by BSU Unit Chief Harry Kern and later by BSU Unit Chief Dr. Greg Vecchi. Access to the National Academy students was made possible by National Academy Unit Chief Greg Cappetta. I offer my heartfelt appreciation to the FBI Academy for their support of this project and the collective belief that these questions needed to be studied. It is my hope that this book justifies that support and investment.

I am indebted to the men and women who participated in the National Academy and were willing to participate in surveys, interviews, and informal conversations about leadership and contemporary policing. In the absence of their words and wisdom this project simply would not have been possible. My efforts were also supported by numerous FBI employees working throughout the Academy. During the many weeks I have been fortunate to spend in Quantico, the Academy personnel and the National Academy counselors have continually been gracious, insightful, and generous with their time. Countless hours of data entry and administrative support were provided by BSU interns and staff. The late Ms. Jeri Roberts assisted in many aspects of this project and other FWG efforts; her friendship and efforts will be missed. Though I cannot list and catalog all who encouraged, supported, contributed to, and informed this research effort, know that it is appreciated.

My initial research efforts were aided by a sabbatical leave I received from Southern Illinois University Carbondale. On-going efforts were supported by the Department of Criminology & Criminal Justice (CCJ) and the College of Liberal Arts. My thanks to Dean Alan Vaux (retired) and Dean (and former CCJ Chair) Kimberly Leonard for ensuring I was allowed time to periodically travel to Quantico to collect project data. Many CCJ graduate and undergraduate students assisted with data entry and library research in support of this project. They quietly contributed hundreds of hours to make this project a reality.

Members of the Futures Working Group and Police Futurists International have directly and indirectly contributed to aspects of the police leadership research project and this resulting book. Both groups have served as sources of endless support, wisdom, insight, and collegiality. Both groups continue to challenge my thinking and push me to grow as a scholar and a professional. I have been fortunate to stand upon the shoulder of giants.

Friends from a variety of policing backgrounds provided review and commentary on drafts of the chapters contained in this book. My thanks to Dr. Bernard "Bud" Levin (Waynesboro (VA) Police Department and Blue Ridge Community College), Chief Richard Myers (retired, Colorado Springs (CO) Police Department), Deputy Chief William Maki (retired, Waynesboro (VA) Police Department), Commander Geoff Huff (Ames (IA) Police Department), Dr. Michael Buerger (Bowling Green State University), Dr. Sandy Boyd (College of Marin), Professor Thomas Martinelli (formerly Detroit PD and now a police ethicist and trainer), and Officer Eric Heiple (US Secret Service Police). Melissa Haynes devoted many hours correcting typos, identifying errors, and raising pointed questions; her efforts appreciably improved the quality of the manuscript. These reviewers have often been collaborators in a variety of research and professional endeavors. They kindly contributed their time to help make this book better. It is my honor and good fortune to consider them friends. Much of this book is a credit to their comments and contributions; errors and omissions remain solely my fault.

None of this would have been possible without the love and support of my family. Chapter Five discusses an essay written by Chris Braiden, who writes about the importance of parents being loving enough to instill their children with strong roots and then having the courage to grant their children wings. It is only as an adult that I can realize and appreciate this aspect of how my parents, John and Grace, raised me. I was taught to ask questions and seek answers; as a father, I now aspire to do the same for my own children. Throughout this project my in-laws, Dan and Jodi, were gracious and generous with their time and home, allowing me the opportunity to travel and write. Finally, Shelby, Ellie, and Andrew provided love, support, encouragement, and patience that were essentially to seeing this effort to the end. They sacrificed and endured much throughout this project, including my time out of town, my early morning writing sessions, and my periodic poor mood when the stress and demands of the project were at their greatest. Know that you always were, and always are, in my heart. Thank you.

EFFECTIVE LEADERSHIP
IN POLICING

Chapter 1

Introduction

> Leaders are carved out of morally fallible humans who are put in positions where they are expected to fail less than most people. (Ciulla 2001, 313)

Leaders and leadership are fascinating subjects for contemplation and inquiry. They are the source of both boundless inspiration and endless frustration. In broad society we hear of legendary leaders and their admirable accomplishments with great frequency. Less common, but of equal intrigue, are tales of those leaders who have failed to live up to their responsibilities or potential. Countless books, journal articles, media accounts, movies, internet sites, and other forms of media are devoted to describing those who have sought to lead. The leaders we often see profiled are drawn from the worlds of politics, corporate America, professional and college athletics, or the military. Far less attention has been given to police leaders. The shelves of bookstores and libraries are devoted to the accomplishments and biographies of presidents, politicians, CEOs, coaches, commanders, and soldiers. Few narratives consider police chiefs or sheriffs; even fewer examine police supervisors and officers. This book is an effort to fill part of this void by considering the traits and habits of effective police leaders. What are the characteristics leaders reflect that contribute to their efficacy—to their ability to convince others to follow their direction and vision?

The accounts of effective and popular leaders tend to cast them in a glowing light. We read of the business executive whose risk-taking, intellect, and compassion saved a company and its employees from ruin. We read of the politician whose dedication and commitment to public service has offered new light and hope for struggling communities. We hear of members of the armed services who displayed courage and loyalty in the face of insurmountable odds, sometimes risking or even sacrificing their own lives to protect others and serve their nation. Such accounts are heart-warming and offer us important lessons. Some leadership scholars, however, suggest that we must be careful not to be seduced by the "romance of leadership" (Bailey 1988; Burke 2006; Clements and Washbush 1999; Gardner 1990; Kets de Vries 1993; Mastrofski 2002; Meindl 1990). These glowing tales may reflect our society's love of good stories (Kellerman 2004b) and the proverbial happy ending. While compelling and inspirational, such stories tend to mask the complexities of achieving favorable leadership outcomes.

Ciulla's quote at the beginning of this section paints a more balanced picture of leaders and leadership. Leaders are humans and bring their individual weaknesses, frailties, and predilections to the task of leading others. Leaders make mistakes, sometimes accidentally, sometimes in good faith, and sometimes knowing their actions are improper, immoral, or even criminal. What makes a leader successful in one context or at one point in time can be the same attribute that causes that leader's downfall in another context or time (McCall and Lombardo 1983). For example, self-confidence and a bit of ego can be healthy in a corporate or political leader. These traits give leaders the confidence to be decisive and might help attract followers. When a self-confident leader becomes so absorbed with the notion they are correct, however, they may fail to consider dissenting views at a critical moment (Glad 2002; Maccoby 2000). The self-confidence that previously

3

brought success might result in the leader making a mistake or exercising poor judgment. All leaders have good and bad traits; they are, after all, only human. Perhaps one of the greatest challenges leaders face is recognizing their own dark side and continually working to tame their own shadow—those traits and habits that have the potential to result in their derailment.

The problem with heart-warming accounts of successful leaders and leadership is they make effective leadership seem easy. If we all only showed heart, compassion, a strong work ethic, a dash of ingenuity, and a willingness to take a risk, the world would be at our feet. Several authors have described the "romance of leadership," both in general (Meindl and Ehrlich 1987) and in policing contexts (Kotter 1990; Mastrofski 1998, 2002). This term describes the all-too-common tendency to see leaders as heroic, leadership as being easy under the right conditions, and leaders as being capable of consistently achieving miraculous outcomes under conditions of extreme adversity. Leaders and leadership are framed as the keys to achieving magical transformations within dysfunctional and failing organizations. In characterizing this romance in the context of implementing community policing approaches, Stephen Mastrofski noted that literature has tended to frame the police leader as "a jockey astride a headstrong steed, artfully guiding it around the track" (1998, 193). Despite the strength, power, and will of the "horse" (i.e., police culture, organizational obstacles, entrenched crime problems that defy easy police interventions, and historic animosity between the agency and its public), the leader is framed as being in control, guiding the way to victory (a dedicated and motivated workforce, reduced crime rates, organizational efficiency, etc.).

That is not to say that leaders are not artful, successful, or heroic. But at times leadership is far from the image of the graceful jockey riding to the winner's circle. Rather, at times police leaders may actually be more akin to "the rodeo cowboy who with great skill manages merely to stay astride his bucking bronco until the bell sounds" (Mastrofski 1998, 183). If effective leadership was easy there would not be political or corporate scandals (e.g., Stanton 2003; Swartz and Watkins 2003). Media would not regularly present accounts of how leadership errors or the absence of effective leadership resulted in disasters and failures (Dias and Vaughn 2006; Garrett 1999; Hall 1980; O'Hara 2005). If effective leadership was easy, effective leaders would be plentiful, yet many organizations, including police agencies, struggle to fill supervisory positions with quality leaders (Gardner 1990).

This book approaches effective police leadership as an outcome and accomplishment that can be elusive and difficult in policing. This is not to say there are not effective police leaders or effectively lead police organizations. Rather, policing could benefit greatly if effective leadership practices and effective leaders were more prevalent. To enhance effective leadership in policing, this book draws upon survey data collected from mid-career police supervisors. These supervisors were asked to reflect on their experiences with, and perceptions of, effective leadership (see Appendix A for more details about the study's methodology). The findings are based on the rich experiences and perspectives offered by this large, diverse, and seasoned group of police leaders. Their survey responses are supplemented by interviews, group discussions, informal exchanges, and a review of professional and academic literature on leadership, particularly within policing

The foundation for this book is surveys completed by some 2000 supervisors from around the world who were attending the FBI National Academy. Participants were local, county, state, and federal police officers who had been selected to spend ten weeks attending this prestigious educational and developmental experience housed at the FBI Academy in Quantico, Virginia. During eight sessions of the National Academy students were given the chance to complete a survey addressing aspects of leaders and leadership in policing. In addition, a number of these students participated in interviews and informal conversations that provided additional context and insight to the survey data. The resulting findings provide rich insights into their beliefs about the traits and habits displayed by leaders they considered to be effective and ineffective. The participating police supervisors also reflected on aspects of the very nature of effective leadership, its measurement, and its development.

The book begins with a discussion of the ideas of "leaders," "leadership," and "effective leadership." Though each term has an innate meaning in the minds of individual readers, it is necessary to consider the complexities and nuances that accompany each concept. Of primary importance is the consideration of the traits and habits that contribute to leaders being judged as effective by participants. What were the characteristics and actions of leaders who often achieved their goals? This is not to say such leaders were always effective; rather, they generally did obtain the results they sought and were well regarded by their followers. The majority of the book is a consideration of the eight traits and habits most often identified by the participants as contributing to leadership efficacy. It is also necessary to briefly regard the notion that leadership has a dark side (Burke 2006), can be destructive (Einarsen, Aasland, and Skogstad 2007), can cause leaders to "derail" (Dotlich and Cairo 2003; McCall and Lombardo 1983), and is sometimes "bad" (Kellerman 2004a) or "poor" (Kelloway, Sivanathan, Francis, and Barling 2005). One chapter of the book is devoted to considering the traits and habits of leaders regarded as ineffective by the participants. The final chapter considers how policing might further develop effective leaders and effective leadership practices. As insightfully articulated by Haberfeld (2006), the policing profession has a tendency to do too little, too late to develop quality leaders (see also Howard 2007). One of the keys to advancing the policing profession may lie in creating better systems to develop leaders and effective leadership practices.

Defining Leadership & Leaders

Leadership is a widely understood idea, yet there are not universally accepted definitions of the process (leadership) or those who seek to enact that process (leaders). Every reader has a general understanding of what these terms encompass, but subtle differences could most likely be noted. One of the major reasons so many subtlety distinct conceptions of leadership and leaders emerge is because context matters. Who leads and how leadership emerges in a scout troop may be different from a college sports team or a multinational corporation. The nature of leaders and leadership in that multinational corporation may differ when comparing operations in America with operations in Brazil, Thailand, or Poland. "Leadership is an often misunderstood, nebulous concept, difficult to define and frequently contested, owing to the diversity of contexts in which leadership can be expressed . . . As a consequence there are a plethora of models, frameworks and theories to describe leadership in both academic and populist literature" (Cragg and Spurgeon 2007, 109).

The differences between these varied definitions are often quite subtle, perhaps reflecting the desire of scholars and authors to place their individual mark on this literary and theoretical landscape. After all, what kind of leadership author would fail to provide their own form of leadership by crafting their own unique definition? John Gardner defined leadership as "the process of persuasion or example by which an individual (or leadership team) induces a group to pursue objectives held by the leader or shared by the leader and his or her followers" (1990, 1). Though leadership is often tied to having a vision (a goal or end-state the leader pursues), Ed Oakley and Doug Krug see leadership as more, encompassing "the ability to get the members of the organization to accept ownership for that vision as their own, thus developing the commitment to carry it through to completion" (1991, 19). They term this process of cultivating ownership and commitment "enlightened leadership."

Peter Northouse (2007) points out the definition of leadership varies based upon the dimension of leadership being considered. For example, Gardner's definition above would seem to frame leadership as a group process in which the leader helps migrate a group to a more preferable state or status. This is the approach Northouse takes in his own text. In contrast, other definitions of leadership may consider leadership by evaluating the outcomes of a leader's efforts, such as the achievement of goals, increases in productivity, or increases in capital. Still other approaches might focus on the leader's personality, traits, and characteristics (the approach taken in this book). James Kouzes and Barry Posner, authors of the best-selling book *The Leadership Challenge* (2002), offer a hybrid definition, conceptualizing leadership as "not all about personality; it's [also] about practice" (p. 13). They see leadership as a combination of a leader's effective personality traits (being reasonably engaging and caring about others) and their individual practices, such as leading by example, delegation, and empowerment.

Ralph Stogdill observed that definitions of leadership are almost as abundant as the legion of researchers, consultants, leaders, and authors who have endeavored to address this concept (1974; see also McCauley 2004). In seeking to establish some uniformity across these varied definitions, his collaborator and co-author Bernard Bass articulated several core themes that seemed to weave through many of these definitions (1990). Bass saw leadership as the process of influencing groups and/or inducing compliance through the personality, power, persuasion, and behavior of a key individual or set of individuals (leaders). Such influential and inductive efforts are often intended to organize and/or harmonize group members and their actions in order to achieve one or more desired goals. This conception is quite close to that proffered by Gardner, as well as Oakley and Krug (though Bass' definition lacks the prioritization of vision they emphasized).

Warren Bennis, one of the most influential leadership figures of the 20th century, made an insightful observation a half-century ago. Its truth, it seems, is as valid now as it was then.

> . . . the concept of leadership eludes us or turns up in another form to taunt us again with its slipperiness and complexity. So we have invented an endless proliferation of terms to deal with it . . . and still the concept is not sufficiently defined. (1959, 259)

In other words, though considering these subtly different definitions may seem an academic exercise in semantics, those fine differences ultimately do matter. There is an important distinction between examining what leaders *seek* to achieve, what they *actually* achieve, and *how* they attempt to achieve goals and objectives. The focus of this book is not just on leadership, but specifically on *effective* leadership. What are the traits and habits that allow some leaders to excel in achieving generally accepted aspects of effective leadership (i.e., achieving goals, maintaining a functional workforce, preserving law, order, and civil liberties, etc.)? The traits and habits of effective leaders presumably differ from those of ineffective leaders. Likewise, we might expect there is a difference between effective and ineffective leaders in terms of their personality traits, their individual habits, the outcomes they achieve, and how those outcomes are achieved.

This book does not seek to provide a definitive definition of leadership or a penultimate consideration of the parameters of leaders and leadership. What a half-century of leadership scholarship has failed to achieve will not be solved within the pages of this text. The intent of providing these broad definitions is to offer readers with an understanding of the complexity found in the study of leadership. For the purpose of this book, leadership is conceptualized as the process of moving and/or motivating a group and/or process from a current state to a preferred state of existence/operation. Leaders are those who seek to accomplish this process. In particular, this book focuses on police officers who seek to act as leaders and provide leadership within their organization and community. These officers do not necessarily hold formal rank or positions of heightened authority; as history has demonstrated, sometimes the best leaders emerge from obscurity rather than from positions of overt power and status. The book focuses on the traits and habits of those who excel in leadership, as articulated by mid-career police supervisors.

Also important to this discussion are the notions of followership and followers. Followership is the act of allowing oneself to be lead—to go in the direction a leader has identified, embracing necessary challenges and changes. A follower is an individual who engages in the act of following. Followership and followers are vital within this book, though in an indirect manner. A leader cannot be effective if she/he does not attract and maintain followers. Leaders cannot be effective if they articulate a vision but cannot persuade others to embrace that vision and bring it to life. Equally important, leaders are always followers in some contexts and capacities. A police captain leads a precinct, but follows her chief. A sheriff leads his agency, but follows professors in the classroom and a religious official at church. Leaders require followers in order to be effective and, with very few exceptions, a leader must know when and how to be a follower.

Leadership versus Management

> Leaders manage and mangers lead, but the two activities are not synonymous ... All these management functions can potentially provide leadership; all the leadership activities can contribute to managing. Nevertheless, some managers do not lead, and some leaders do not manage. (Bass 1990, 383)

Though often confused, leadership and management are two separate behaviors. In fact, as elaborated in Chapter Five, many police supervisors encounter problems when they lean toward management instead of leadership. The study of leadership can be dated back to the time of Aristotle, while management emerged as an area of inquiry during the rise of industrial organizations in the 20th century (Northouse 2007). Management is perhaps easier to define and understand, as it is often associated with focusing energy on discrete tasks. For example, Luther Gulick is credited with bringing the notion of POSD-CORB into organizational literature (Gulick and Urwick 1937). POSDCORB was an acronym conveying that corporate managers were responsible for Planning, Organizing, Staffing, Directing, Co-Ordinating, Reporting, and Budgeting. "*To manage* means to accomplish activities and master routines, whereas *to lead* means to influence others and create visions for change" (Northouse 2007, 11, emphasis in original). Managers seek to produce predictability, while leaders seek to effect change (Kotter 1990). Stated another way, "[m]anagers are concerned about how things get done, and they try to get people to perform better. Leaders are concerned with what things mean to people, and they try to get people to agree about the most important things to be done" (Yukl 2002, 5). Though certainly not an easy concept to understand or embody, management tends to be more focused on explicit tasks and, at least on the surface, effective management skills are easier to identify and develop within supervisory personnel.

Though management and leadership might be understood as distinct concepts, they overlap and are inter-related when we consider leaders. Effective leaders must demonstrate some proficiency and capacity to manage and to lead. There are few, if any, aspects of police supervision and direction that only require proficiency as a manager (i.e., there are few supervisors with no subordinates). The very nature of police work, while dynamic and constantly in flux, also embraces stability, routine, and repetition of core tasks in a prescribed manner. In other words, police leaders must be able to lead and to manage. This is not to say supervisors cannot be effective if they lean toward management. In some assignments, a supervisor's efficacy may be enhanced through strong management skills. A police supervisor with responsibility for a routine and formulaic process (the evidence room, the quartermaster, the budget) likely can only be effective if their management skills are quite strong. Some tasks require attention to detail and the management of precise processes. A supervisor might cause undue havoc if they mismanage the chain of evidence, the ordering supplies and commodities, or the tracking of expenses. Police supervisors and executive typically need to have robust abilities to both lead and manage, and to recognize when to do one instead of the other (Stamper 1992).

The nature of police work tends to foster reasonably strong management skills. Officers are trained and socialized to pay attention to details, such as proper protocol and procedure, the nuances of securing a search warrant, and the proper completion of legal documents. Some officers will excel at such detail-oriented tasks while others underperform, whether intentional or not. Problems may arise when supervisors are uncomfortable exhibiting leadership. When this occurs supervisors may default to the comfort and familiarity of bureaucratic management styles rather than expanding their repertoire of skills (Krimmel and Lindenmuth 2001). An over-emphasis on management can create adversarial employer-employee relationships, a rise in unionism, and increased personnel attrition, among other concerns.

In a classic essay examining leadership versus management John Kotter (1990) provided an articulate and informative consideration of their distinct and complimentary attributes. Kotter noted that management is focused on overseeing routine and relatively predictable processes; it brings order and consistency to complexity so an organization can produce quality outcomes. Leadership is focused on guiding change processes; leaders help identify areas in need of change, prepare personnel and the organization, and then help concerned parties cope with shifts to ensure objectives are realized. Kotter refuted the idea that leadership is mythical, mysterious, or the product of rare personality traits. He did not see leadership as something found in only the select few. "Rather, leadership and management are two distinctive and complementary systems of action. Each has its own function and characteristic activities. Both are necessary for success in an increasingly complex and volatile business environment" (1990, 85).

Kotter's essay reinforces the interdependence between leadership and management skills within a given supervisor. Organizations want personnel who can both lead and manage because often those in positions of authority have duties that ideally require competencies with both processes. As suggested above, context is also relevant in the leadership-management balance. A lieutenant tasked with overseeing the property room likely needs to be a strong manager, while leadership skills are perhaps of trailing importance. If that same lieutenant is tasked with revising an agency's deployment system, leadership likely becomes far more germane in shaping the outcome of such efforts. The broader context of an organization's mission and environment can also influence the ideal ratio. Kotter (1990) proposes the military needs strong management during times of peace, but strong leadership in times of war.

The distinction between management and leadership is also important because, though the concepts and their applications have some common elements, being an effective manager does not always equate with being an effective leader. Police supervisors may find it relatively easy to manage, at least symbolically. It is also relatively easy to develop and enhance management skills. Though effective management is not "easy," it may be less elusive than effective leadership. This may be particularly true in the context of American policing, where organizations often focus on developing management skills more so than leadership skills. It is important to not confuse traits and habits of effective management and managers with those of effective leadership and leaders. Though effective management is vital within policing, effective leadership is even more important as organizations seek continuous improvement and development. Though current and aspiring supervisors need strong management skills, it is critical to understand that those skills do not necessarily translate into the making of a more effective leader.

Thinking about Effective Leadership

> Effective leadership is not easy, and there is no easy path to becoming an effective leader. Leadership is in and of itself one of the most complex of human endeavors. (Riggio and Conger 2007, 331)

Defining effective leadership raises some fundamental questions. Can we create a universal definition or typology of an effective leader? Are there traits or habits that an individual MUST display in order to be characterized as an effective leader? Are the traits and habits of effective leaders required of all leaders in all situations or might they be tied to circumstances, contexts, and periods in time (London, Smither, and Diamante 2007)? Do the traits and habits of effective informal police leaders (front line officer) differ from the traits and habits of first line supervisors (sergeants and lieutenants) and top agency executives (chiefs and sheriffs) (see Howard 2007)? The vast writings considering leadership, leaders, and effective leadership could fill a library, yet a thorough understanding of these concepts remains elusive. Though many have sought to describe what it takes to be an effective leader, examples abound of persons who have failed to rise to the challenge and exhibit such behaviors. Surely every reader is confronted on nearly a daily basis with examples of those who have not been able to show the requisite skills and behaviors to be considered an effective leader. Individuals in our personal lives (supervisors, co-workers, community leaders, etc.) and public figures (politicians, corporate executives, pop culture icons, etc.) routinely demonstrate the failings of those who have the opportunity to lead. What do we make of this situation? What lessons might we learn from the failures and shortcomings of others?

Though we might develop broad definitions of leadership, determining what it means to be an effective leader in a given situation is not easily accomplished. A popular adage (sometimes attributed to Abraham Lincoln) warns us that we cannot please everyone in all situations. This is one of the fundamental paradoxes of both police work and leadership. A police officer making an arrest is likely to please the victim of the crime, but is unlikely to secure a similar level of pleasure from the arrestee. A police leader who act in a manner that pleases her subordinates can easily upset her boss or community in the process. Perfect leadership is impossible to obtain with consistency because decisions of any magnitude typically disadvantage someone. Former Los Angeles Police Chief Daryl Gates was considered to be quite popular among his officers (because of his unwavering support of LAPD in the face of criticism), though he did not enjoy the same favorable evaluation from large segments of the Los Angeles community (see Reese 2005). A police executive acting in a manner that secures praise from the public might easily generate harsh feelings among agency employees. Even within an agency it is entirely possible followers will disagree in their evaluation of a given leader or leadership decision.

Contributing to the complexity of defining and assessing effective leadership is that the exact tact and tactic required in response to a set of conditions is often viewed as situational in nature (Hersey and Blanchard 1996). The leadership approach a police executive takes with new officers (who may have a greater tendency to follow without question) may be different than the approach used with seasoned veterans (who may require persuasion or justification). The approach used with police personnel (whom the executive can discipline and fire) may be different than the approach used with members of the city council (over whom the executive holds no formal authority). Effective leaders are often characterized as having a capacity to morph their style to meet a given situation. Leaders deemed less effective may struggle to adapt to changing situations, circumstances, and environments (McCall and Lombardo 1983). For example, Winston Churchill has a strong historical legacy for his leadership and courage during World War II. By some accounts, however, Churchill was a more effective leader in times of war than in times of peace. His style and approach worked well in a time of national crisis, but not in a time of national recovery and growth. Is Churchill the exception or the rule? Was his purported difficulty in being adaptable a rare condition or is this a common struggle?

Part of the challenge in defining effective leadership is determining what exactly is being assessed. Peter Northouse (2007) observed definitions of leadership vary based upon what is being measured, such as achieving desired group processes, demonstrating a charismatic and engaging personality, or utilizing effective traits. A similar complexity emerges when considering effective leaders. Can a leader be effective if she/he fails to achieve objectives, but does so in a good faith manner? Consider the example of Sir Ernest Shackleton, a pioneering Antarctic explorer of the early 20th century. On perhaps his most famous expedition, Sir Shackleton's ship *Endurance* was trapped and crushed in an ice pack. Amazingly, Shackleton was able to lead all of his men back to civilization and safety without the loss of a single life (Lansing 2001). Though he failed to achieve the objective of his expedition (a sea-to-sea crossing of Antarctica via the South Pole), would we label Shackleton an ineffective leader? Preservation of life, by itself, is not a sufficient measure of efficacy.[1] Sometimes achievement of goals may not be the only outcome to consider in assessing a leader's efficacy. Circumstances change and evolve so the original objectives and

---

1. Patrol supervisors would most likely not be judged effective simply because all officers go home at the end of the shift. The Shackleton example further reinforces the notion that leadership efficacy is situational. At the start of his expedition success was making the crossing. When circumstances changed, making the crossing became irrelevant when the very survival of the expedition members was at stake.

goals are no longer considered to be important or take a "back seat" to more pressing demands and obligations.

From the perspective of someone seeking to improve their individual leadership skills and abilities, matters become more complicated when effective leadership is not viewed as something that is fixed and narrow. A rigid definition of leadership efficacy would make it easier to develop a standard approach to being an effective leader. Conversely, a broad conception or definition of leadership makes it difficult for an individual to understand how to actually lead in a given situation. Broad definitions do not support an easy understanding of that definition's application in a tactical, case-by-case setting. How to effectively lead does not seem to be a "one size fits all" process. Different leaders bring their own unique mix of assets and liabilities to a situation. Leadership would seem to be situational and within a given set of circumstances there can be multiple paths to an effective outcome. Two different leaders may be able to achieve desired outcomes through very different approaches. From an outside perspective, neither method may be better than the other, though those being lead may prefer one style over the other.

This reality becomes problematic for those seeking to be effective leaders because it means there is rarely a "right" way to respond to a given set of circumstances. There may be better and "less better" ways to proceed, but which path should the leader select? How does a leader handle the fact that those who are being lead often have divergent (and even conflicting) preferences for how they experience that process? Some followers might respond well to explicit directions, frequent reporting, and clear goals (which they did not help define). Others might prefer to be involved in shaping and defining goals, and then wish to be left to their own devices in achieving those goals. If the ideal outcome in that situation was to see an employee or team of employees achieve a pre-determined goal, can we say one approach is better than the other (presuming both approaches were within law, public values, and agency policy)? The challenges leaders confront are significant.

This overview and discussion of effective leadership seeks to illustrate the many ways in which leadership is dynamic and variable. Effective leaders may have a toolkit of traits and habits they routinely use to accomplish their objectives, while being selective in using those tools based upon their evaluation of what is needed to achieve success in a given situation. Just as a mechanic evaluates what is wrong with a piece of machinery and decides when and how to use specific tools to enact a fix, the effective leader might be seen as using the resources and skills they have at hand to effect an appropriate outcome to a given set of circumstances. This raises questions about whether we can strip effective leadership down to core competencies (communication, team building and networking, ethics, work ethic, etc.) that will almost always translate to success. Is there any one competency that is truly needed to be effective in policing? Even the most virtuous of traits and habits can, in some situations, be framed as something a leader ought not to embrace (see Chapter Three), though such judgments might be subject of vigorous debate.

One of the ways researchers, consultants, and leaders have tried to overcome these types of questions and complexities is to use "consensus" approaches to determine leadership efficacy. Consensus approaches consider efficacy in a broader context, rather than considering efficacy in individual situations. Persons affiliated with a leader (subordinates/followers, peers, and the leader's supervisor) are asked to reflect upon the leader's strengths and weaknesses. The idea behind the consensus model is that rather than looking for objective evidence that a leader is effective, it makes as much if not more sense to ask those surrounding the leader. If followers, peers, and supervisors feel the leader is doing well, at least on most dimensions, this ought to suggest the leader is being effective.

These processes are generally not dichotomous, meaning a leader is not deemed to be either effective or ineffective. Consensus models focus on assessing the ways in which the leader is doing well and the areas in which the leader might show some measure of improvement. Because no leader is perfect, consensus approaches view effective leadership as existing on a continuum. Even a highly effective leader can always find ways to be more responsive, supportive, persuasive, and exemplary in her/his efforts.

The data used in this book mimic the consensus approach to determining leadership efficacy. Participants were not given a definition of effective leadership or asked to evaluate a common individual. Some participants were asked to consider the leaders they knew, select one who was particularly effective (or in some cases, particularly ineffective), and describe what traits and habits made that person effective (or ineffective). Other participants were asked to review a list of traits and habits commonly identified by their peers and assess which are most important in contributing to both leadership efficacy and inefficacy. In other words, this book is not based upon assessments of specific police leaders and what makes them effective based upon objective outcomes. Instead, it is based on themes emerging from a process of asking supervisors to reflect on their experiences and identify what they believe makes leaders particularly effective. This means we cannot be certain the resulting common traits and habits actually result in leadership efficacy. The large number of participating supervisors and their extensive experience should, however, provide reasonable confidence that this list of traits and habits has some broader salience in the context of policing.

A Few Caveats

At the onset it is important that the reader understand the biases and preconceptions about leaders and leadership that shape this book. There is a long-standing debate as to whether leadership is "situational." Are characteristics that make a leader effective universal across time and space, or do they vary based on context and situation? Based on twenty-five years of working for, working with, observing, and studying the police, the author is a follower of the situational perspective. The presumption that there is not a single true way to lead all officers or organizations has likely shaped how the author has reviewed both the broader policing literature as well as the data in this project. The book has not been written to convince readers that there is a single model they should embrace and follow in leading police organizations. Instead, the book seeks to provide current and aspiring leaders with a sense of the main traits and habits they should have in their "tool kit." Individual leaders will need to decide when and how to use these tools in their own contexts.

Situational perspectives on social systems, including leadership, can be traced back more than a century. In the 1880s, British political theorist Herbert Spencer suggested that times produce the person, rather than the contrary (see Heifetz 1994). It was Spencer's position that individuals were shaped by the time and circumstances in which they lived. Advocates of situational leadership have applied Spencer's logic to the study of organizational dynamics. For example, Hemphill wrote "what an individual actually does when acting as a leader is in large part dependent upon characteristics of the situation in which he functions" (Hemphill 1949, v). Fred Fiedler's "situational contingency" perspective (1967) was predicated on the notion that there is not a universal or ideal way to lead. The task at hand and the nature of interpersonal relationships were thought to shape leadership approaches and outcomes. These ideas were further refined in subsequent key works

(House 1971; Vroom and Jago 1988; Vroom and Yetton 1973) that advance the notions that a given leader is not always effective in all contexts and that effective leaders do not always use the same approaches in the pursuit of organizational change and other objectives (Kotter 1990).

In recent decades an array of writers have described and rationalized such situational perspectives on leadership. For example:

- "It becomes clear that an adequate analysis of leadership involves not only a study of leaders, but also of situations" (Stogdill 1948, 64–65).
- "No one leader has the skills, knowledge and behaviour to be effective in all situations" (Cragg and Spurgen 2007, 112).
- ". . . research seems to support the contention that there is not a 'best' leadership style. Successful leaders are able to adapt their style to fit the requirements of the situation" (Zigarmi, Blanchard, O'Connor, and Edeburn 2005, 180).
- "Leadership is far too complex a phenomenon to portray as a commodity that, once identified, can be bottled and distributed to hungry organisations. More to the point, with this paper we emphasise that leadership defies superficial prescriptions for action because it is an emergent, dynamic social process dependent upon numerous variables that are also in a state of constant flux." (Murphy and Drodge 2004, 1).
- "Leader competencies are static markers, while leadership is a dynamic, nonlinear process that defies easy objectification. Competencies may say something about a leader at a given moment in time, but not about leadership because environments ebb and flow requiring different competencies or varying amounts of a given competency to meet the demands of the complex personal and social worlds we all inhabit" (Murphy and Drodge 2004, 7).
- "While the fundamental purpose of leadership remains the same across levels, task complexity varies across levels" (Densten 2003, 401). That is, what works for a leader at one rank may not work at another, either because the behaviors needed to achieve success actually change or the expectations of the leader shift. The leadership approaches that worked for an officer while a sergeant in the patrol unit may not work while serving as a lieutenant overseeing community relations.

These perspectives retain relevance in helping understand the nature of leadership within policing contexts.

The unifying rational supporting situational perspectives was succinctly articulated by Victor Vroom and Arthur Jago (2007), who offered three observations on the role of situations within leadership. "Organizational effectiveness (often taken to be an indication of its leadership) is affected by situational factors not under leader control" (Vroom and Jago 2007, 22). Leadership is situational because leaders attempt to address problems and influence outcomes that are situational. Not every employee wants to be lead in the same way. The issues and challenges that shape organizational dynamics in one agency are not relevant in another (see Buzawa 1984). "Situations shape how leaders behave" (Vroom and Jago 2007, 22). An individual who is a leader within their police department might use different ways to motivate and influence police officers in contrast to how that same leader might operate when seeking to influence players as the coach of a youth soccer team or parishioners as the chair of their church council. "Situations influence the consequences of leader behavior" (Vroom and Jago 2007, 23). A police leader who fails to secure organizational change might contribute to departmental failures costing that leader her or his job. When in the role of youth soccer coach, a lost game or even losing season is less likely to have such dire consequences for the leader.

Skillful leaders have been characterized not as those who use a fixed and rigid style, but as those who can read circumstances and situations effectively so as to select the best approach to achieve a desired outcome (Tannenbaum and Schmidt 1958). That is not to say that leaders are devoid of a moral compass or any limitations on their behavioral choices. Rather, this perspective suggests leaders operate with a degree of fluidity and flexibility to address shifting constraints, differing objectives, and the need to influence people with a variety of needs and motivations. Leaders will also be bounded by their own values, beliefs, experiences, and biases (Meadows 1979). A leader may change, develop, grow, or even regress in terms of these limitations (Kuykendall and Roberg 1988); however it would be unusual to see an individual radically depart from their core beliefs and personality. Finally, position within an organization shapes an individual's priorities, constraints, and perspectives (Cyert and March 1963). A leader once viewed as a "cop's cop" while serving as a patrol sergeant may have a different reputation as a deputy chief or chief executive. The choices, contexts, and consequences confronting that leader will often be quite different, requiring a modification of the leader's style, priorities, and approaches.

This discussion of situational leadership is offered as more than simply a disclosure of bias and belief. A situational perspective should shape how the reader approaches the remainder of the book. It is not the author's intention to suggest that leadership can follow a single magical recipe to ensure successful outcomes. Viv Shackleton eloquently noted "there is much more to being an effective leader than merely possessing a list of traits. While the traits may provide people with the potential for leadership, it is the capacity to create a vision and implement it that turns the potential into reality" (1995, 9). Even the traits that constitute the major portion of this book are neither necessary nor sufficient to ensure leader success. Every successful leader will not demonstrate all of these traits. Every successful leader will not necessarily demonstrate any one of these traits in all situations and contexts.

At times the tone of this text will also seem very critical of police organizations, leaders, and leadership. Any academic working in American higher education should be honest in criticizing police leadership. If there is any profession that is equally problematic and in need of effective leaders and leadership practices, it is higher education. The author has spent most of his adult life in and around colleges and universities, while also working with and studying police organizations. The problems, pathologies, and liabilities of these two professions are often in shocking concert. The author would also concede that as an individual periodically called upon to provide leadership, it is easy to discuss the traits and habits in this book. Successfully applying those traits and habits to achieve effective outcomes (in policing or higher education) is truly challenging.

The Present Volume

The purpose of this book is not to resolve these various controversies or engage in prolonged consideration of these timeless definitional debates. Rather, the intent is to present a consensus model (as identified by a group of police supervisors) of the traits and habits essential to leadership efficacy. These are the traits and habits that National Academy participants felt were the most important to ensure a leader's effectiveness. This does not mean other traits and habits are not important, that a person displaying these behaviors will be deemed effective, or that every well-regarded leader exhibits all of these characteristics. Drawing on the participants' nearly 40,000 collective years of policing experience, these are the traits and habits they believed were most consistent with leadership efficacy. The following analyses and discussions are offered as a starting point for understanding effective leadership and to help aspiring leaders assess their own current behaviors.

The second chapter provides a more detailed overview of the state of leadership research within policing. As is often the case when academics consider a topic, the nuances and complexities of leaders and leadership must be presented and discussed to properly understand the issues this book explores. This discussion is not, however, simply academic navel-gazing. In speaking with police leaders at the onset of this project, it became apparent that even those involved in street-level police operations recognized that leadership, while at first glance a simple notion, is actually multifaceted, nuanced, and, all too often, elusive. Some reflection upon this complexity is necessary to help frame the issues under consideration. The second chapter also explores why traditional bureaucratic approaches to police management generate so many problems for personnel and operations.

Chapters Three through Ten address the eight core traits and habits of effective police leaders that emerged during the two years of data collection. This is not presented as an exhaustive list, but rather as a starting point for considering the traits and habits that participating supervisors felt were associated with leadership efficacy. There was not absolute agreement regarding this list, but the eight themes repeatedly emerged from an examination of the project data. Each is discussed briefly below.

- **Honesty & Integrity.** Above all else participating supervisors felt effective police leaders had to be persons of honesty and integrity. Morality and ethics were considered central to being viewed as a legitimate person whom others (both inside and outside of the organization) might opt to follow. Though this idea seems quite straightforward, Chapter Three provides an argument that honesty and integrity may not always be desirable, depending upon one's perspective and/or situational exigencies.
- **Listening & Communication.** Listening to others matters because it helps leaders recognize when their course of action might be myopic, shortsighted, or just-plain-wrong. Listening is also important because it can help engage and invest followers in the change process, generating commitment and participation that can advance the success of the leader's efforts. If leadership is considered the capacity to move a group, unit, or organization through a process of development and change, communication is clearly a vital element of the leadership process. Effective leaders are able to articulate a clear vision to those whom they seek to influence and to use communication as a tool to motivate, inspire, and secure "buy in" from followers.
- **Delegation & Empowerment.** Though effective leaders must have an eye for management, they must also have a capacity to trust others with select duties. Most leaders are given responsibility over more tasks than they can handle individually—this is why leaders are assigned subordinates. Leaders who delegate responsibilities to their subordinates enhance their efficacy in two ways. First, they free up considerable time and energy to focus on important actions, such as leading. Second, by showing a degree of trust in the judgment of their subordinates, leaders help to convert those subordinates into more loyal followers. Chapter Five

discusses the role delegation and empowerment play in shaping leadership efficacy.

- **Interpersonal Skills.** Much has been written about charisma and leadership efficacy. This notion refers to the ability of leaders to attract followers based on their dynamic and engaging personality, even when leaders and followers might never personally interact. This attribute may be important in large police agencies where personal relationships and interactions are not feasible. In smaller agencies or within a leader's core unit of followers, it can be important for leaders to demonstrate an ability to connect with their followers on some personal level. This is consistent with humanistic perspectives on leadership and organizational dynamics, which emphasizes the importance of securing followership in part by paying attention to the individual needs of those within the organization.

- **Trust & Fairness.** Leaders are expected to make decisions in an appropriate manner, based on consideration of available evidence, and reflecting sound logic. In a way, leaders are expected to behave in a quasi-judicial manner. They are expected to weigh the available information and perspectives regarding a given set of circumstances and identify an appropriate decision. This decision should not be unduly influenced by politics, nepotism, favoritism, or capricious judgment. Leaders who demonstrate the ability to make fair and informed decisions will presumably enjoy the trust of their followers. The latter want leaders who make sound judgments so they can exercise their own discretion in a manner consistent with the objectives of the organization and the leader.

- **Taking Action.** Though it may seem odd to say that leaders must take action (they must lead), this can be what separates a leader from a supervisor. Leaders recognize there is always room for improvements for groups, units, organizations, and individuals. They recognize the need to encourage and nurture groups and individuals to seek out ways to enhance their practices and performance. In policing, this might include the relentless pursuit of enhanced efficacy, efficiency, and equity, even if the pace of change is modest. A supervisor can recognize a need to change something under their control; a true leader will take action in the face of that recognition.

- **Innovation & Growth.** Taking action should not occur simply to say that change is afoot. Rather, leaders seek out the leading innovations and practices within their professional field and seek ways, where necessary, to bring those practices into the operations of their organization. Further, leaders nurture the professional growth and development of their subordinates. They do not stifle the creativity and advancement of their followers; rather, they facilitate those processes. In addition, leaders pursue their own personal growth and development; they recognize that they can always improve their personal practices and performances, and seek out ways to do so. Leaders do not simply turn a critical eye towards others and external problems. They also are willing to be honest about their own performance, mistakes, and shortcomings.

- **Leading by Example.** Leaders live up to their label. They demonstrate the behaviors they seek from their subordinates. They perform their duties in a way that models the behavior they desire to see from others. A leader does not hold others to a higher standard or ask them to work harder than she or he is willing to work. To truly attract followers, the leader must be out in front, articulating a vision, and demonstrating how to embody and implement that vision. This trait is critical in separating those who lead from those who manage or supervise.

This list of traits and habits is not exhaustive, nor is it necessary that an individual excel at all of these traits and habits in order to achieve success.

The nature of these behaviors might be likened to the legs on a stool. A stool with only two or three legs is not a stable platform. It can easily be toppled and the person seated might fall to the ground. Leaders need a foundation of effective tools and techniques. The broader their base, the more stable their leadership and status among followers, peers, and constituents. Simply using authority, power, fear, or discipline is a narrow foundation for leadership success or efficacy. These might initially support the base, but the leader will be easily toppled by circumstances or mistakes. Effective leaders might leverage multiple traits and habits to provide a more stable basis for their influence and status. If one of the traits or habits is not salient in a given situation or fails the leader, there are back-ups to keep the leader's influence and standing on a firm foundation. For example, a leader might not be a strong people person, but she or he can still be effective by leveraging other traits and habits to achieve efficacy.

Chapter Eleven considers the traits and habits of ineffective leaders. Given the earlier contention that leaders must constantly work to overcome and improve their own limitations and weaknesses it is important to explore the traits and habits of those who fail to succeed in leading others. These traits and habits can help effective leaders recognize how their own behaviors might be constraining their success. Barbara Kellerman described leaders as being "like the rest of us; trustworthy and deceitful, cowardly and brave, greedy and generous. To assume that all good leaders are good people is to be willfully blind to the reality of the human condition, and it severely limits our scope for becoming more effective at leadership" (2004b, 45). Leaders must constantly seek to balance those traits and habits that bring them success with those which might hamper or erode their efficacy. Chapter Eleven also seeks to reinforce the notion that leadership is not easy, is not always successful, and can generate unwanted and undesirable outcomes.

The book concludes with a discussion of how policing can improve leadership development processes. All too often, efforts to improve the leadership skills of police personnel occurs well after officers have been placed in supervisory positions. The FBI National Academy, for example, is designed as a leadership and career development experience for participants. Despite this objective, the average National Academy attendee brings nearly a decade of supervisory experience to that program and many are entering the latter phases of their careers. Is this the optimal audience for this type of enrichment experience? Should those advancing policing professionalism be advocating for a comparable experience for those in earlier phases of their careers? In many agencies, there is no formal leadership development process to enhance the quality of leadership or to ensure successful transitions as supervisors are promoted or moved to new duties. Consequently, we know very little about what makes a leader effective and how we can train, educate, and mentor the next generation of leaders to ensure optimal organizational operations.

Conclusion

Though it may seem odd for a scholar to caution readers engaging in the academic study of leadership, such a warning might be appropriate at this juncture. The academic study of leadership tends to look at circumstances, conditions, and traits in a linear fashion . . . doing ABC produces increases in XYZ. What defies easy measurement is the human side of leaders, followers, and leader-follower relationships. There are no silver bullets when considering leadership. Leadership plays out in the context of human systems and interactions, which are messy, unpredictable, dynamic, and nonlinear.[2] This is one of the key reasons successful leadership is not easy and our knowledge of enhanced and effective leadership practices is limited. It is difficult to account for the myriad factors that shape leadership outcomes and how leaders are perceived.

This book is not intended to be read as a leadership "how to." The shelves of libraries and bookstores are laden with texts promising to make the reader more effective, efficient, popular, and wealthy in a few easy steps. This book seeks to avoid making such promises, in part because those assurances are nearly impossible to fulfill. If leadership were simple, we would not lament its recurring absence in our lives and experiences. Leadership is challenging and being an effective leader requires courage, dedication, humility, a thick skin, and a bit of savvy, among other factors. The traits and habits addressed in this book are offered as a set of effective behaviors. Current and aspiring leaders are encouraged to consider whether they truly display these attributes in the normal performance of their leadership duties. Not all of these traits come naturally. This research project was conceived with the intention of providing aspiring and active police leaders with "food for thought"; to provide fodder for contemplation, discussion, and reflection. It is certainly not the final word on what constitutes efficacy in police leadership. This book has been written to provide current and aspiring police leaders with insights into the experiences and perspectives of their peers. It is up to the reader to determine how best to apply that knowledge to his or her individual personality, circumstances, and aspirations.

---

2. My thanks to Mike Farnsworth, Colorado State Police (ret.) for the basis of these observations.

Chapter 2

Police Organizations & Leadership

> The police administrator is a much more important figure in the overall structure of government than is commonly recognized. He is constantly being called upon to formulate policies that require the balancing of fundamental and often conflicting values. His decisions directly affect the quality of life in his community. Moreover, it is the police administrator upon whom we depend most heavily to take the initiative in solving the many problems that plague the police and that reduce their capacity to provide quality services to the public. Responsible leadership of the highest caliber is essential if needed change is to be carried out. (Goldstein 1977, 225)

> Leadership is a process, not a property of a person. (Vroom and Jago 2007, 18)

While there are many good leaders (in the corporate world, in the public sector, in policing) there are few truly great leaders, in large part because achieving true leadership is very difficult. It cannot be easily distilled down to a handful of anecdotes packaged in a 200-page text sold in every major bookstore in the country. It cannot be learned and perfected in a short seminar or executive development program. Instead, true leaders show discipline, vision, self-awareness, and a relentless drive to develop themselves and others, among other attributes. Reading the present book will not make someone a great leader. Hopefully, however, it can raise a reader's awareness of the fact that being a great leader is very difficult. The moment you think you have achieved great leadership is the moment when you are mired in (at best) good leadership (Collins 2001, 2005; Wexler, Wycoff, and Ficher 2007). Leadership principles are often reasonably simple to understand, but divining how to apply those principles in a given context to effectively resolve a given situation is the true leadership challenge.

Despite the centrality of leadership in shaping effective outcomes in organizations of all types (including police departments) developing a cadre of effective leaders still remains elusive in far too many agencies (Angell 1971; Haberfeld 2006; Rowe 2006). This is not a new problem in policing. The five largest commissions charged with studying problems in American policing from 1931–1973 all noted the absence of strong leadership and effective administrative practices contributed to corruption, abuse of authority, use of force, police crimes, and civil rights violations (Pursley 1974). Though failures of leadership have repeatedly emerged as a factor contributing to failures of police organizations (O'Hara 2005) scholars have not given extensive attention to studying this nexus (Dias and Vaughn 2006). Extant literature considering police organizations has tended to emphasize how to control and manage police officers, processes, and agencies. Limited attention has been given to matters of actually achieving leadership in police organizations and by police personnel (Potts 1982).

Scholarly and professional literature considering leaders and leadership in policing has tended to rely upon theories, explanations, and developmental models derived within the corporate sector (Haberfeld 2006; Mastrofski 2002). Given the breadth of policing literature, there is a surprising absence of works that consider leadership using data and insights derived from policing contexts and personnel. Some two decades ago, two prominent scholars of police organizations and leadership noted "we need more broad-based research using a variety of methodological tools and conducted throughout a wide range of police agencies, not simply generalized from management studies conducted in business settings, to understand the current style and status of the police leadership and management." (Sutherland and Reuss-Ianni 1992, 177). Though incremental advances have been made, this observation remains valid and lucid today. There are far too many unresolved questions about the role and function of leadership in policing. Why do we not see more effective leadership in policing? What ideas about leadership might be relevant to rethinking how police officers and organizations are lead? What do we know about leadership in policing? What are we still trying to know and understand about leadership in policing?

This book will not directly address these particular questions, but it does seek to advance the consideration of police leadership. Understanding traits and habits associated with effective (and ineffective) leaders helps to frame future systematic inquiries. This chapter reviews what is known about prevailing structures, models, and processes for organizing, administering, managing, and leading organizations, particularly police departments. It begins by reviewing observations that can be made to describe how many American police departments are structured and operated, particularly those serving at the county and municipal level (which account for nearly ninety percent of all agencies). These observations are followed by a discussion of leadership theories and perspectives most relevant to the research study that generated the data for this book. The discussion also explains key concepts of relevance to the author's presumptions and beliefs in framing a discussion of the traits and habits of effective police leaders.

Next, the chapter reviews literature considering the outcomes and influences police leaders have exhibited in prior studies. Though many questions remain unanswered, there are some key insights to be developed from studies of police leaders and supervisors. The chapter concludes with a short discussion of additional unanswered questions and on-going debates concerning the nature and role of leadership. The focus here is a broad consideration of a range of ideas and issues related to leadership and police organizations. Readers interested in studying these matters more would be advised to consider leading works examining these matters in general (Bass 1990; Hersey, Blanchard, and Johnson 2008; Northouse 2009; Yukl 2009) or within the context of policing (Adlam and Villiers 2003; Anderson, Gisborne, and Holliday 2006; Haberfeld 2006; Ortmeier and Meese 2010; Reese 2005).

Prevailing Administrative Models in American Policing

American police organizations are typically characterized as paramilitary structures (Sandler and Mintz 1974).[1] Personnel are organized within agencies using a horizontal struc-

---

1. With more than 17,500 agencies (Hickman and Reaves 2006) American policing is far from a monolith. There is wide variation in how organizations are structured, how they operate, and how they administer, manage, and lead personnel. This variation will be evident not only across categories of agencies (i.e., federal versus state versus local departments) but also within a given category. The purpose of this discussion is to focus upon the generalizations that have typified American policing (particularly at the local level) for more than a half century. Multiple exceptions can likely be found for each of these general observations. This section is intended to provide a common context rather than cataloging all possible exceptions.

tural design that separates officers based on their assigned responsibilities (i.e., patrol, investigations, or support services) and, in larger agencies, their area of geographic (precinct or division) and/or temporal (shift) responsibility. Prevailing models distinguish between authority and responsibility using an array of vertical elements (ranks and assignments). Sergeants and lieutenants oversee officers and investigators.[2] Captains and commanders oversee divisions, units, and precincts. Majors and deputy chiefs are responsible for broad functions (i.e., patrol, administrative operations, or community services) throughout the agency. At the top of the hierarchy is the chief, who has responsibility and authority over all aspects of an agency, its personnel, its operations, and its communication (Auten 1981).

William King provided a helpful characterization of the prevailing policing model, including this horizontal and vertical distinction.

> The horizontal element includes the number and size of departmental specialized units (such as SWAT) and how tasks are broken down (e.g. does the agency rely on specialists or on generalists?), among others. The hierarchical (vertical) element encompasses the allocation of five organizational resources (authority, skills, rewards, status, and seniority) and it is the differential allocation of these resources which stratifies organizational members into hierarchies. (2003, 209)

Within this framework, leadership is not clearly evident, but can be inferred in aspects of the vertical elements. Formal leaders possess authority in the form of reward (higher pay grades or the assignment of a "take home" vehicle). Informal leaders might be presumed to demonstrate (leadership) skills and would be expected to enjoy a certain degree of status, at least among their peers (Anderson, Gisborne, and Holliday 2006). Though lacking the trappings of formal leaders, those providing informal influence might enjoy considerable status, respect, and deference from co-workers and even supervisors.

These bureaucratic hierarchies emerged in the 1800s as a way to organize workers within factories and other industrial facilities. Advocates believed these types of organizational structures would enhance efficiency and accuracy while ensuring control of employees (Gerth and Mills 1958). It was hoped that by creating orderly and structured work environments agencies could minimize the problems witnessed in the early decades of modern American policing (Walker 1977). Beginning in the late 19th century police reformers began to advocate for bureaucracy as a mechanism to control officer behavior, improve police services, and limit opportunities for corruption and other unwanted outcomes (Schafer 2007). Bureaucratic and paramilitary structures became the gold standard by which agencies and supervisors were judged by the mid-20th century (Wilson 1950; c.f. Buerger 2000; Cowper 2000). The bureaucratic model emphasized clearly defined authority and responsibility, established hierarchy and chains of command, centralized control over front-line personnel, created rigid and limited pathways for communication, and developed rules and policies in an effort to generate consistency both within the workplace and in governing police interactions with the public (Auten 1981; Gray, Stohr-Gillmore, and Lovrich 1991; Sandler and Mintz 1974).

---

2. Exact titles and responsibilities will vary across agencies. The discussion here is offered to illustrate the idea of vertical differentiation, recognizing there are many permutations on the model.

Problems with the Prevailing Bureaucratic Model

On paper and in theory bureaucratic models seem rational and well designed. In practical application such systems have been extensively critiqued based on their inherent limitations and their inability to actually achieve intended outcomes. Such critiques have been leveled at bureaucratic structures and authoritarian styles of police "leadership" both in the US and abroad (Densten 2003). John Angell, who emphasized the tendency for bureaucracy to seek strict control over employees and their discretion, offered one of the earliest critiques of police organizations. Angell observed that bureaucracies treat employees in a fashion "analogous to children in a family—they are expected to obey orders and carry out assignments" (1971, 188). As with traditional expectations for children's behavior toward parents, officers are expected to demonstrate, at least symbolically, deference and obedience to the authority of their supervisors (Cordner 1978; Jermier and Berkes 1979).

The bureaucratic model emphasizes direction and control, which are attributes more properly associated with management and administration. When the terms "leadership" and "leaders" are used in discussions of bureaucratic policing their application is usually a misnomer. Supervisors are not, by virtue of their rank and status, automatically leaders. To the point of the Vroom and Jago quote at the beginning of this chapter, leadership is not a position in an organization, it is a process displayed by an individual. Leadership is a verb (an action) not a noun (a rank). The issue is not simply that an employee holding rank might fail to be a leader. In some situations those in positions of authority might actually be "bad" (Kellerman 2004a) or "evil" leaders (Enter 2006), a situation that is far more destructive and problematic.[3] Arguably the slide toward poor leadership is facilitated by bureaucratic principles and practices (Cordner 1978). Regardless of intent, power and authority are not always wielded benignly in organizations (Clements and Washbush 1999). It should be further noted that poor forms of leadership are not the exclusive problem of those in formal positions of authority. Those with informal influence can also exert a destructive or harmful influence within the workplace, whether intentional or accidental.

In bureaucratic models of organizations leadership is rarely discussed. It is implicitly presumed to exist and operate, but much classical literature on police organizations emphasizes management and administration, with leadership as a small discussion within that broader consideration. Bureaucratic systems explicitly or inadvertently work to suppress real leadership and leaders. The author was discussing this matter with a former Marine and veteran executive in a large state police agency. The executive offered several insightful observations regarding how culture and organizational patterns work to subvert and suppress the emergence of leadership in police agencies. This executive noted that

> Police agencies are largely in-bred cultures that tend to self-select leaders. Many of our academies weed out the independent minds and creative thinkers during the first weeks of recruit school. Those that remain are predominantly conformists and they figure out rather quickly that being a non-conformist is not career enhancing. That is the pool from which leaders are chosen. Those leaders, having

---

3. Examples of bad, evil, and poor leadership behaviors might include being: ineffective, unethical, incompetent, rigid, intemperate, callous, corrupt, insular, and untrustworthy (Burke 2006; Kellerman 2004a). These leaders have been characterized as unable to understand the perspectives of others, insensitive to the considerations and motivations or others, and lacking the social skills to generate and maintain healthy relations and interactions with others (see Hogan and Hogan 2002).

grown up and prospered within the existing culture are usually loath to set about criticizing, disrupting or changing it. There are exceptions to this pattern but they're pretty rare in my experience.

Viewed in this way, bureaucratic policing models exert control (some real, some symbolic) at the expense of fostering leadership. The consequences of this extend beyond simply seeing limited leadership.

Poor and destructive leadership[4] has been linked with a variety of mental health concerns among employees, including stress, helplessness, alienation, anxiety, and depression (Buzawa 1984; House and Podsakoff 1994; Kelloway et al. 2005). Poor or abusive supervisory behaviors can manifest themselves as retaliatory actions, bullying, and abuses of authority. These circumstances can result in decreased job satisfaction, organizational commitment, and professional motivation (Einarsen, Aasland, and Skogstad 2007; Ford, Weissbein, and Plammondon 2003; Kelloway et al. 2005). Anecdotal data collected by Enter (2006) suggests ten percent of police supervisors display what he characterized as "evil leadership" practices. Einarsen and colleagues (2007) estimated that within the corporate world up to ten percent of employees have been bullied in the workplace, with supervisors committing eighty percent of those offenses. In this study, National Academy participants were asked to report how often they observed effective leadership in their agency. Approximately one-third indicated they saw such practices rarely, seldom, or not often enough (Schafer 2010b).

The absence of effective leadership not only influences individual employees, but also creates negative consequences for agencies, such as organizational failures (Dias and Vaughn 2006; Garrett 2004; Hall 1980; McCabe 2005; O'Hara 2005). Among other consequences, the bureaucratic model generates adversarial relationships between the organization and employees, as well as between groups of employees (Reuss-Ianni 1983). Additional problems can include strained community relations, increased unionism, litigation, turnover, and external oversight or control of local police operations (Jermier and Berkes, 1979; Krimmel and Lindenmuth 2001; O'Hara 2005). Collectively these failures of the bureaucratic models generate a host of problems for police personnel, police organizations, and those who use policing services.

Problems for Operations

Bureaucracy emphasizes routinized operations that cause inflexibility within both employees and organizational processes. Operations become rigid and rules seem to serve no purpose other than ensuring compliance with other rules. Independent thought and action are discouraged; creativity and innovation are muted, particularly at the lowest levels of the agency (Cordner 1978). Adherence to the bureaucratic model means there

> are feelings of demoralization and powerlessness in the lower ranks, a conception of top command as arbitrary, a growing cynicism among supervisory and middle-management personnel, and the subsequent development of a we-they attitude toward top management. The organization becomes increasingly rigid

---

4. A valid argument might be made that those who fail to leader or are destructive in their actions are not deserving of the label "leader." The challenge with this point of view is that it frames leadership as a dichotomy. An individual either is or is not a leader. It does not allow for the possibility that someone can lead well in some situations and inadequately in others (see Kellerman 2004a).

as a result, while management wonders about the antipathy toward change among the lower ranks. Ideas are stifled, officers are not confident of the support of top management, and the CYA syndrome takes hold. (Cordner 1978, 30)

Bureaucratic hierarchies impede the free flow of ideas and information (Argyris 1964). Status in the organization is defined by one's position, rather than one's skill at actually performing the core duties of the agency. Line employees are treated like children, who are expected to simply obey directives and carry out assigned tasks (Angell 1971).

Bureaucracy fosters reactive work habits based on attending to routine matters only when specifically directed to do so. In reality, "proactive" and "officer-initiated" activities tend to be constrained to a narrow set of enforcement behaviors (i.e., issuing traffic or parking citations, conducting field stops, or conducting random patrol). Creative efforts focused on solving problems rarely receive attention (Goldstein 1990). Archambeault and Weirman (1983) cataloged the problems bureaucratic models create for police organizations. Productivity, innovation, and initiative are not encouraged or systematically rewarded. Self-interests are routinely placed before organizational interests. Command and control management approaches foster acrimonious and adversarial relations between managers and employees. This strengthens the informal codes, cultures, and systems within the workplace, all of which works against effective organizational change, innovation, and leadership. Where allowed by law, unions and other labor associations can exert strong influence on the thinking, values, and behaviors of front-line personnel.[5] Despite its virtues in exerting control (which is too often largely symbolic), bureaucratic models generate major problems in public sector organizations, particularly when leaders seek to leverage influence and change. Archambeault and Weirman (1983) note with irony that those seeking to demonstrate leadership in police organizations may revert to control and management when they become frustrated with the barriers and resistance they encounter (see also Krimmel and Lindenmuth 2001).

While bureaucratic structures are not ideal within the corporate world (Collins 2001) they may be even more problematic in the public sector. Police executives face appreciable obstacles that are only compounded by the use of bureaucratic models because the context and constraints of public sector organizations are often more complex than those noted in the corporate world (Collins 2005). Police executives are often severely constrained in their ability to deal with problematic personnel. Unions and civil service protections make it difficult to release vested employees for all but the most serious forms of misconduct. Without the incentive of maintaining one's job, there is far less motivation to adapt to and embrace new ideas and innovations proffered within the workplace. This matter is compounded by tendencies of civil service systems to err on the side of protecting employee rights; many agencies have discharged a problematic employee, only to have the officer's job reinstated in arbitration or similar appellate process. Police executives must attempt to make decisions in a way that will satisfy constituents who are so diverse that it may be impossible to please all interested parties. Police as a profession also lacks clear metrics. Measuring success is far more subjective than in the corporate world.

---

5. This observation is not an indictment of labor organizations. It cannot be denied that unions and other groups function to perpetuate their existence and protect the rights of members, sometimes to the detriment of the organization. It also cannot be denied that the majority of labor organizations were established in organizations with rich histories of poor, exploitative, and abusive management practices.

As a result, executives face substantial difficulties because they must confront disagreement not only with their philosophy and methods, but with the very core objectives they are supposed to be pursuing (Wexler, Wycoff and Fischer 2007).

Bureaucratic models can serve to erode trust in the workplace (Douglas 2003; Hennessy 1992). The emphasis on direction and control implicitly and explicitly tells employees they cannot be trusted to judiciously exercise autonomy, be productive, demonstrate integrity, and contribute useful ideas to improve organizational processes. These models implicitly and explicitly tell supervisors their key task is to monitor subordinates through the use of policies, rules, reporting requirements, and discipline. The majority of the supervisor's attention and energy is devoted inward, on the process of controlling employees, rather than being focused outward, on the process of improving the quality and quantity of organizational outputs (Brewer, Wilson, and Beck 1994). Those promoted to supervisory ranks are given too many tasks associated with supervision and oversight and too little latitude to coach, mentor, and develop workers to grow and mature into more skilled and effective members of the workforce.

Problems for Employees

Bureaucratic models have profound influences on all employees and often these influences are less than ideal. Traditional policing systems treat employees as liabilities to be controlled and mitigated. Their actions are seen as being political, legal, professional, and economic risks for supervisors and executives. Communication, decision-making, discipline, reward, and supervisory systems all have the strong potential to generate stress, hostility, attrition, dissatisfaction, diminished organizational commitment, and burn-out among employees (Lambert 2007). Those at the top of the organization are overtly or explicitly placed into the role of problem-solver for all internal issues (Heifetz and Laurie 2001; Wilson and McLaren 1972). Those elsewhere in the organization are not considered viable sources for input or ideas about how to improve aspects of the agency or its operations (Gray, Stohr-Gillmore, and Lovrich 1991).

Police organizations tend to award promotions based on internal politics and the ability to pass through various tests and assessments. The latter emphasize an employee's success in their current position rather than their aptitude for the role into which they seek to be promoted. Excelling as a patrol officer does not mean an employee will make a good first-line supervisor. Police organizations tend to quickly move officers into the top pay scale. Early in their careers officers discover the only way to secure financial rewards beyond cost-of-living raises is to receive a promotion. Consequently, officers seek promotion for financial gain rather than a desire or capacity to lead (Guyot 1979). All too often, success at promotion is based on competently controlling personnel, facilitating prescribed procedures, and reinforcing prevailing traditions and practices (particularly preserving the supervisory status quo). Career advancement is too often assured based on perpetuating traditional directive approaches to supervision, rather than seeking new ways to develop employees, advance the organization, and modernize the methods of service delivery.

An employee's status in the organization is derived from his or her position in the organization (Angell 1971). Authority is based on formal position (rank or duty assignment) rather than skills or standing within the workplace (King 2003). Internal status becomes associated with rank and/or specialized assignments. Generalists (patrol officers) are simply there to triage calls for service and perform grunt work in support of specialists. Front line personnel may become frustrated by inflexible rules and a power structure that minimizes or dismisses their contribution to the organization. These systems create disincentives that dissuade good patrol officers from staying in that assignment because power and greater financial rewards are associated with promotion and/or special assignment. Patrol, as the "backbone" of policing, is subject to constant turnover. It becomes home for those who are still relatively new to the job and those who have not been successful in pursuing promotion/transfer. The former are inexperienced and more likely to make errors in performing their duties. The latter are often less effective and diligent employees. If they have been caught in the trap of internal politics these veterans are likely frustrated, disillusioned, and disenchanted with trying to be good employees.

Employees become frustrated with bureaucratic structures that seek to constrain discretion and decision making. Structured decision making patterns can be helpful in that they reduce bias (intentional or inadvertent) in the provision of policing services. These same structures, however, constrain an officer's ability to be creative in solving problems. The rising educational level of American police officers only serves to exacerbate this problem for personnel (Angell 1971). Employees with more education expect to be able to apply that education in a work environment allowing creativity, innovation, and problem solving. All too often, American policing does not typify these attributes (Schafer 2007). Instead, organizational practices emphasize control via reporting requirements, exhaustive paperwork, and a variety of policies, procedures, rules, and mechanisms intended to regulate and structure the actions of employees. Whether explicitly designed this way or not, organizational structures treat personnel in a way that implies their skills, loyalty, and judgment cannot be trusted (Mayo 1985). It should not be surprising to see bureaucratic approaches serve to limit productivity, initiative, and commitment among workers (Archambeault and Weirman 1983).

Supervisors may shy away from supervisory styles viewed as "risky" (i.e., delegating important tasks to subordinates) in favor of more controlling and directive approaches (Hennessy 1992; Kuykendall and Unsinger 1982). Manipulative, Machiavellian approaches may win out over styles that emphasize collaboration, creativity, and equal contributions from subordinate personnel, a tendency reported not only by American police supervisors, but also their peers around the world (Girodo 1998). Stamper (1992) considered the practices of police chiefs by not only surveying chief executives in large departments (serving more than 200,000 residents), but also their immediate assistants. This methodology provides tremendous insight by demonstrating concordance and contrasts between how leaders claimed to operate and how those around them perceived the executives. In particular, Stamper's work found that while chiefs believed they engaged in behaviors consistent with leadership, assistants perceived the chiefs as operating in a manner more consistent with administration. Rather than inspiring, changing, and elevating their agencies, executives were seen as simply tending to more routine (though not inconsequential) issues of personnel, policy, and budget, which Stamper lamented did not reflect a high degree of leadership.

Problems for Consumers

Bureaucracy is still considered the ideal model for organizing government services. There is little recognition that blind devotion to bureaucratic rules can be inefficient, ineffective, and inequitable. This situation is no different in the context of police bureaucracies. Rules end up trumping providing consumers with the services they want, expect, and need from government officials. This situation is not, of course, purely the fault of blind and mindless bureaucratic thinking. The litigious nature of American society creates incentives for agencies of all types to embrace policies and procedure as presumed protection against liability. Too often, however, the traditional structure and operation of American policing works against the objective of providing consumers with accessible services. Inflexibility, complex procedures, and extensive paperwork frustrate not only officers, but also citizens (Angell 1971).

Bureaucratic models do not provide optimal customer service, at least at the point of service delivery. Broader social clichés about "red tape" are couched in the idea that bureaucracy and formality (particularly from the government) confuse, confound, and frustrate consumers, either by accident or by design. Social theorist Max Weber (Gerth and Mills 1958) was an early advocate of bureaucracy as an ideal form of rational organizational decision making. Yet Weber recognized that bureaucrats should not become blindly subservient to bureaucratic structures. Bureaucracy created the risk of workers becoming hyper-rational by following poor policy, procedure, or decision making chains. Too often bureaucratic systems and their workers focus on means over ends (Goldstein 1977). The core objectives of the organization are downplayed in pursuit of emphasizing adherence to rules and policies. Workers and agencies place greater emphasis and priority upon the pursuit of command, control, and obedience than the pursuit of justice.

Paths Forward

The preceding critique of police organizational structures should not be taken as a call for reforming the structure of police departments. In the 1980s the rise of community policing led to calls to "flatten" or "delayer" police hierarchies to support greater flexibility and discretion for patrol officers. In examining the rationality of these calls in light of broader organizational research, William King (2003) suggests caution in presuming that smaller organizations are inherently better. Simply cutting layers from the hierarchy does not necessarily lead to better policing or more efficient police operations. In fact, reducing levels of supervision can increase span of control (how many people and processes each supervisor must monitor) and lead to unintended outcomes, such as a reduction in rewards, promotions, and raises (Schafer 2001, 2002). Merely revamping structures may not be the most effective way to fix the pathologies seen in police organizations or might result in simply trading old problems for new limitations. The tack taken in this text is that police organizations and personnel would be better served to focus on how we create effective leaders and supervision. Policing should be emphasizing outcomes, not processes. Enhanced operations within American policing will be easier to achieve with better leaders. Seeking to modify organizational systems and processes with ill-prepared staff might evoke aphorisms about rearranging deck chairs on the Titanic.

General Perspectives on Leaders & Leadership

Police leadership is a daunting and difficult task. Leaders have to meet the demands of a diverse set of followers, superiors, external sovereigns, clients, and constituents. The consumers of policing service are often not willing participants in the initiatives and efforts officers and agencies are pursuing. Police leaders are expected to exert influence over organizations and personnel tasked with addressing very complex issues (i.e., crime), in very dynamic environments, while controlling circumstances that they cannot directly influence, such as the degree to which citizens care about their neighborhood. Police leaders in many states have to deal with unions or other entities representing groups of employees. Agencies have no direct control over their assets or budgets, rarely receive a direct share of the financial resources they generate (i.e., fines resulting from citations and arrests), and are routinely asked to bear the burden of unfunded mandates (i.e., state-level requirements to report traffic stop data in the face of concern about racial profiling). In recent decades we have seen the emergence of evidence-based thoughts and practices that have enhanced organizational efficacy, yet often researchers and practitioners do not understand why proven approaches work for some issues or in some areas, but not in others.

The purpose of this book is not to resolve all aspects of police leadership from either a research or policy perspective. It is not intended to be a definitive work distilling dominant leadership theories into a concise package for easy consumption. Other texts do a laudable job providing such a resource (Northouse 2009; Yukl 2009). Nonetheless, a few summary observations need to be made at the onset and a few leadership perspectives germane to the focus of this text need to be reviewed. The following section provides a short overview of leadership perspectives and theories that are of particular relevance to the traits and habits discussed in the text.

Theory X & Theory Y

Douglas McGregor's groundbreaking book *The Human Side of Enterprise* (1960) was a watershed moment in leadership theory and scholarship. McGregor's premise was that there were two basic approaches to managing people. Traditional approaches to management were what McGregor labeled Theory X methods. The presumptions that served as the foundation for Theory X approaches were that: people dislike work and preferred to avoid doing it when possible; the threat of punishment was needed to force people to work toward organizational objectives; people actually preferred to be told when, where, and how to work; and, people were unambitious, avoided responsibility, and desired security. Understandably, adopting this perspective on human motivation and behavior will lead one to embrace management approaches that are directive, authoritarian, and controlling.

In contrast, Theory Y approaches to management were based on an entirely different set of presumptions. In particular, Theory Y methods were grounded in the belief that: work is a natural human pursuit; people can and will demonstrate self-control and self-direction in pursuing organizational objectives (because they find satisfaction in work and work outcomes/outputs); people often seek and accept responsibility; the ability to use imagination, ingenuity, and creativity to solve problems is widely distributed within the population, not a narrow capacity; and, the intellectual potential is under-utilized in most people, not because of self-limitations by the individual but rather because circumstances stifle that potential. Management grounded in Theory Y perspectives is more participative, dynamic, and open. Rather than emphasizing command and control over employees, Theory Y approaches focus on how to create circumstances that allow workers to realize their full potential and contribute to the organization.

Theory X and Theory Y are important concepts in the study of police organizations and leadership. At the time McGregor wrote about these ideas, the corporate and industrial sectors were beginning to shift away from Theory X approaches to management. As conveyed by McGregor's title, he was convinced that leadership and management thinking needed to account for the fact that people were at the core of any enterprise or activity. Prior management thinking had been highly mechanistic, viewing workers as parts of a machine with no feeling or emotion. Research and experience emerging in McGregor's era showed that the human side mattered and that management could be more effective when it considered ways to motivate, engage, reward, and empower workers. In the half century since McGregor advanced his ideas, the private sector has reformulated how it thinks about workers. Unfortunately, much of the public sector, including police organizations, has not fully embraced this transformation in thinking. As a result, police organizations are more often managed than led; the approaches that are used by supervisors are more in line with Theory X presumptions about human behavior and the human condition.[6] Directive approaches to management too often trump achieving actual leadership.

Transactional & Transformational Leadership

Leadership scholar James Burns drew a distinction between "transactional" and "transformational" leadership approaches (1978; see also Bass 1985, 1990). Transactional leadership approaches are more typical of what would be expected in police organizations (Engel 2002). In such systems leaders and followers have relationships based on exchanges or quid pro quo arrangements. The follower performs a defined set of tasks in a specified manner, with the understanding that specific rewards will be delivered. In this arrangement the follower is presumably motivated by extrinsic incentives. These are not simply pay and benefits, but also validation, recognition, awards, and the presumption of future benefits such as raises, special assignments, better vacation options, and promotions. The role of the leader is less to provide leadership, as it is to manage and monitor followers, issuing rewards when earned and discipline when the follower is not achieving outcomes and/or is not using accepted means in pursuit of objectives.

For example, the role of a patrol sergeant would be considered routine and mechanical. They monitor followers to make sure outputs are being produced (i.e., citations, summonses, arrests, reports, and apparent compliance with policies and law). In exchange officers might receive better shift or beat assignments, better vacation days, and recommendations for transfer or promotion. The performance of sergeants might be determined by assessing the performance of their subordinates (Engel 2001). Supervisors use the perks and privileges they control to leverage employee conduct in the desired fashion (Brown 1988; Manning 1997; Rubeinstein 1973; Van Maanen 1983, 1984). The bulk of the supervisor's time and energy is spent brokering the exchanges, monitoring compliance, and issuing expected benefits, though much of this might occur implicitly.

In contrast, Burns described transformational leaders as those who seek ways to improve the organization, its operations, and its personnel, rather than simply maintaining the status quo. Transformational leaders attempt to accomplish this by inspiring employees to embrace a shared vision or set of visions. This further requires that transformational leaders empower those around them. Employees are given freedom to make decisions,

---

6. The tendency of managers in the criminal justice system to embrace Theory X perspectives makes some sense when ideas such as cynicism (Niederhoffer 1969) are considered in the context of the major clientele and work tasks. Much of police work is focused on disadvantaged neighborhoods where poverty is the norm, under-employment rampant, and motivation very limited. Police understandably become cynical about the human condition based on the skewed view of the public with whom they all too frequently interact and this perspective can creep back to the supervisor's orientation within the police station.

develop ideas, and identify their own ways to pursue improvement and innovation. These processes are not simply "lip service" on the part of the leader. Leaders demonstrate through their own behavior how the organization and its employees should operate. They lead by example, showing how to treat others, including consumers of the organization's services. Transformational leaders understand the importance of recognizing accomplishments and contributions within the workplace (Burns 1978; see also Johnson 2006; Kouzes and Posner 2002).

The types of values demonstrated by Burns' transformational leader are very consistent with the traits and habits discussed in this book, though historically they have been sorely lacking among police supervisors (Dobby, Anscombe, and Tuffin 2004; Silvestri 2007).[7] Transformational perspectives require supervisors to see employees as not simply subordinates to be controlled, coerced, or manipulated. Rather, employees are seen as potential followers who, when properly motivated and inspired, can exponentially enhance what can be achieved by the work group. Some recent scholarship has called into question whether transformational leadership is universally superior. The transformational model has tentatively been found to elevate conflict among workers in some situations and circumstances (Kotlyar and Karakowsky 2006, 2007).

Servant Leadership

Servant leadership models shift away from an orientation that emphasizes supervisors existing to direct; instead supervisors are viewed as existing to serve the people in their sphere of influence (Greenleaf 2002). This suggests the "fulfillment of subordinates' needs is the ultimate goal of a servant-leader" (Douglas 2003, 6). Such an approach is considered influential because supervisors can only produce a finite amount of output within the workplace—they are individual employees. If the supervisor can empower others and facilitate their output, a more appreciable gain might be realized. Servant leadership is not a common term in policing literature and discourse, but the underlying ideals have been espoused in visions of policing put forth within the community policing movement. Under this model, supervisors are told their role should be empowering employees to solve local problems and to support improvements within neighborhoods (Trojanowicz, Kappeler, and Gaines 2002) within legal authority and community-accepted boundaries.

Situational Leadership

This text is predicated on the assumption that leadership is situational. Studies of the leadership behaviors of police supervisors and officers demonstrate that there is vari-

---

7. From a research perspective, Burns' transformational leader presents several challenges. These traits and habits are difficult to systematically evaluate within a sample of police leaders to determine whether "better" leadership outcomes are actually achieved. Extant research has not directly tested whether officers prefer transformational leaders or whether transformational leaders are more effective. There is, however, indirect support for the idea that transformational leaders achieve better results in both qualitative (Reuss-Ianni 1983; Van Maanen 1983) and quantitative (Andreescu and Vito 2010; Engel 2001, 2002) studies of police leadership and outcomes, as well as in military (Dvir, Eden, Avolio, and Shamir 2002) and emergency service contexts (Pillai and Williams 2004). Interestingly, Dvir et al. (2002) found transformational leaders were also able to demonstrate a positive influence on the behaviors of indirect followers (those not formally under the reporting authority of that leader).

ability in the models used and preferred (Andreescru and Vita 2010; Cohen 1980; Engel 2001, 2002; Krimmel and Lindenmuth 2001; Kuykendall and Unsinger 1982; Rainguet and Dodge 2001; Vito and Higgins 2010). "What works" is almost never universal, but instead is a function of context, objective, traits and habits of the leader, characteristics and motivators for followers, and the environment within which leadership is taking place. What works in Agency A might not work in Agency B. The approaches used to lead a patrol shift might legitimately be very different than the methods used to lead civilians in the records or communications division. The tactics used by a leader to achieve success as a sergeant might differ from those used when that leader is a deputy chief (Cyert and March 1963; Densten 2003; Kuykendall and Unsinger 1982). The intent of this text is not to suggest every leader adopt all eight traits and habits for applications in all agencies and for all purposes. Rather, leaders should seek to understand how using various combinations of these traits and habits might yield successful outcomes, recognizing that two leaders in identical contexts and situations might both achieve success while employing different methods.

The Police Leadership Challenge

James Kouzes and Barry Posner (2002) frame leadership as a challenging process, yet one that can be learned and developed. Their model is predicated on five core principles about leaders and the practices they use to achieve their objectives. First, leaders set an example by modeling the way; they demonstrate the type of work ethic and orientation expected of their followers. Second, leaders convey a shared vision that inspires those around them. They articulate an ideal state or a vision for the future, and then develop trusting relationships that encourage others to follow and support them. Third, leaders are willing to challenge the status quo by asking difficult questions and imagining exciting possibilities. Fourth, leaders enable others to act by developing and empowering followers; leaders create conditions in which those around them can pursue and achieve the objectives of the leader, follower, and/or organization. Finally, leaders encourage the heart by recognizing and rewarding accomplishments, both of individuals and the group.

This model may seem romanticized and over-simplistic hyperbole. Aspiring leaders should be cautious of characterizations of leadership that suggest success is easy. Though Kouzes and Posner (2002) offer a relatively simple model, the challenge arises in actually accomplishing the five steps. For example, Vito and Higgins (2010) applied this model in a study of police leaders attending the Southern Police Institute. While noting Kouzes and Posner's model had a degree of validity, Vito and Higgins also determined there was a gap between how attendees rated their own acumen in applying the model and how others assessed their performance in their agency. Reinforcing Stampers' (1992) work, their findings suggest that while it might be relatively easy to understand core tenets of leadership in policing, actually applying those principles in a way that is recognized as effective by peers and followers is a true challenge.

The Role of Followers

Though often overlooked in discussions of leadership, followers are central figures that play a role that should be far more explicit when discussing and understanding leadership. Followers are those leaders seek to influence. They may or may not be formally under the authority of a leader; sometimes leaders have no formal authority and in other situations the authority they have does not extend over all individuals. Leaders might also seek to influence those outside of the organization; this is certainly common in policing. Officers seek to influence citizens, which some have framed as a basic form of leadership (Anderson, Gisborne, and Holiday 2006). Formal leaders seek to influence community members, peers and sovereigns in other branches of government, and other leaders within their jurisdiction and beyond.

There is a dyadic relationship between leaders and followers, characterized by an ongoing influence loop between the two. This is a particularly relevant consideration for those who subscribe to situational perspectives on leadership. This reciprocal relationship implies the way leaders act is influenced by the followers at hand, the tasks and goals being pursued, and the constraints and contexts of the circumstances. Leaders do not simply influence their followers; situational leadership suggests that followers influence the approaches and styles used by leaders (Meindl 1990). The constantly shifting social environment in which leaders and followers interact makes the ideal way in which leaders exert influence a malleable path (Murphy and Drodge 2004). A variety of social psychology and leadership theories consider how leaders and followers interact and influence each other through two-way exchanges (Hogg, Martin, Epitropaki, Mankad, Svensoon, and Weeden 2005). Leader-member exchange theory (Graen and Uhl-Bien 1995) suggests that effective leaders should consider followers as unique individuals who will not all respond the same way to the same treatment; some customization of approach is needed. Social identity theory (Hogg 2001) suggests leaders might take different approaches in leveraging influence over groups that have different levels of cohesion and group identity. The culture of the group a leader seeks to influence needs to be relevant in shaping the approaches taken by that leader (Hofstede, Bram, Ohayv, and Sanders 1990; Schein 1990).

The difficult reality of these perspectives is that no single leader can be effective and influential over all groups. A supervisor who achieved good outcomes in one unit of a large organization may be less successful in another unit if s/he cannot adapt her/his style to meet a different group culture and context. A chief executive who achieved major reform in one command may have less success in a new organization. A leader may be quite good at influencing officers, while struggling to engage and secure support from city leaders and citizens. For example, chiefs who are "cop's cops" often have very strong allegiances from, and influences over, employees, while struggling to maintain positive relations with the public, such as Daryl Gates in the Los Angeles Police Department (Reese 2005). In the end, "individuals emerge as group leaders by fitting the shared conception of followers" (Smith and Foti 1998, 148). In other words, successful leaders achieve efficacy when followers consent to be lead. Effective leaders recognize the need to take situational approaches, but seeking to modify their leadership style does not guarantee success in that effort. This is not to say that leaders do not matter—rather, their influence is not always direct or automatic (Hofstede et al. 1990).

The use of the term "followers" in this book should not be construed as a pejorative term. A follower is not an inferior, second-class, or mindless individual blindly obeying the leader. In other contexts and circumstances followers may be leaders themselves. For the purposes of this book, the term "followers" is used to refer to those groups and individuals that leaders are seeking to influence. They might be peers, subordinates, community members, external sovereigns, and even higher-ranking personnel within the agency. Followers are not always subservient, less skilled, less experienced, or less qualified. They are often critical thinking, intelligent, independent, and hard working individuals. Though leaders might aspire to influence them, it should not be presumed or implied that obedience and conformity are easy or automatic. In reality, the leader hopes that "followers" will actually follow, but often that may not be the result of the leader's actions. A leader who approaches followers with an "issue an order and they will obey" mentality will often fail. Effective leaders study, seek to understand, and show respect for those they wish to influence and those whom they hope will follow their leadership.

Good, but Not Great

Experience and research has shown leaders can improve their efficacy and influence by leveraging culture, empowerment, motivation, and social capital, but how to actually do so remains elusive.[8] Jim Collins (2001) reviewed the status of leadership and change in over 1400 companies over a forty-year period. He determined that while the majority of these companies were quite good, less than one percent met his criteria as a great company. He largely attributes the distinction between a good company and a great company to the quality and nature of leadership. Collins believed the truly great leaders shared a common set of characteristics in their own personality and in how they focused the energies and attention of their workers and company. In a later work, Collins applied these principles to the public sector (2005) and worked with a team that applied his ideas specifically in policing (Wexler, Wycoff, and Ficher 2007).

In the context of policing, the "Good to Great" (GTG) principles have identified a core set of attributes and behaviors associated with what leaders do and how they perform. GTG police leaders are "Level 5" leaders who direct their energies on furthering the goals of their organization and personnel; they continually seek ways to build and improve both. These leaders find ways to ensure they can use the right people in the right aspects of the organization. This is far more challenging in public sector organizations, particularly small agencies that typify American policing, but GTG leaders develop ways to maximize flexibility and minimize barriers to ensuring they can develop and use available talent among followers. Leaders who typify GTG principles are not afraid to confront the challenging and difficult aspects of their agencies. They seek to focus organizational operations and individual energies in finite directions. They seek to shape culture in a positive direction, rather than fighting its existence in the organization/unit. None of the GTG principles (see Wexler, Wycoff, and Ficher 2007) are easy to apply in police organizations or any other context. What separates good leaders from great leaders is the ability and will to successfully pursue the very difficult aspects of the job.

Informal Leadership

Informal leaders and leadership are of appreciable importance and influence in police organizations. Rank and file personnel are often fairly stable in where and when they work within the organization. Officers may spend years working with the same general group of peers, while changing supervisors with regularity. In this situation, those who exert an informal leadership influence in that workgroup may be far more influential than formal supervisors. The diffuse nature of policing exacerbates this problem, particularly in larger

---

8. Heifetz and Linsky (2004) discuss these and associated issues in the context of education. The parallels between their observations and the nature of leadership in policing are clear.

organizations. Niche cultures emerged long before the current formal leader assumes command[9]; in most cases those niches will endure long after the current formal leader has promoted or transferred. Front line officers and investigators are workers oriented toward "the job," the task to which they are assigned in the organization. Supervisors and leaders are oriented toward their careers, which means they frequently change duty assignments. Working against many of the positive change efforts described in this book is the reality that front line personnel often view formal leaders as a prison term. The current supervisor must be endured for a period of time, but the employees know they will still be in their unit long after the supervisor is gone. In this situation, though workers might provide symbolic compliance to change and reform efforts, informal leaders may continue to set the pace and tone for actual operations.[10]

What We Know About Police Leadership

As is the case in most aspects of policing research, studies of leadership are almost non-existent prior to the late 1960s. Early studies of police leadership tended to focus on qualitative distinctions and tensions purportedly arising between front line personnel and their supervisors and administrators (Cohen 1980; Engel 2001; Hennessy 1992; Pursley 1974; Van Maanen 1983, 1984). For example, Elizabeth Reuss-Ianni's (1983) study of several precincts in the New York City Police Department highlighted the distinctions and power struggles between "street cops" (front line personnel) and "management cops" (supervisors, administrators, and executives). More recently, Rowe found British police constables were more likely to value supervisors who were seen as having credibility on the street (2006). Though understandably supervisors did not routinely engage in the full range of policing activities, subordinates had more favorable views of supervisors who were judged to still understand the realities of street-level policing.

Though on paper it would seem police supervisors exert clear and direct control over subordinates, the reality of the situation is far more complex. Police officers enjoy a high degree of autonomy and discretion both out of necessity (i.e., the dynamic nature of police work precludes imposing policies that define every choice officers might make) and due to the structure of policing (i.e., policing is a geographically and temporally diffuse job, particularly the patrol function) (Brown 1988; Jermier and Berkes 1979; Klinger 1997, 2004; Wilson 1968). Though "rank in a paramilitary structure confers unquestioned authority, it does not also confer unquestioned obedience" (Reuss-Ianni 1983, 65). Few other government officials have the power and discretionary authority of patrol personnel. Unlike most other governmental organizations, discretion over the most consequential choices made by the agency is concentrated at

---

9. This can even be the case in an entirely new unit or even organization. While attending the annual meetings of the International Association of Chiefs of Police, the author had a chance discussion on a shuttle bus with a chief who had been hired to establish a police department in a newly incorporated community. This chief related that although the officers were a mix of rookie cops and those hired away from other agencies, most of whom did not know each other well, he immediately encountered a culture in the agency. Though his situation should have been "easy" at the onset, he reported the barriers he encountered from culture and informal leaders were as profound as they had been in his prior agency, where he had served as a high-ranking executive.

10. My thanks to Dr. Michael Buerger for offering this insightful (and, unfortunately, very accurate) observation on the dynamics of police culture and organizations.

the lowest level of the hierarchy (Allen 1982; Steinheider and Wuestewald 2008). Patrol officers, not chief executives or even front-line supervisors, are most likely to have to make choices about the use of force (including deadly force) and decisions to deprive persons of fundamental rights and freedoms (via arrest, detention, questioning, stops, searches, etc.). This makes police supervision decidedly different than supervision in most other public sector contexts and elevates the importance of true leadership.

It is also important to distinguish between leadership and organizational effectiveness, as the two concepts are not synonymous with each other (Vroom and Jago 2007). Organizational effectiveness can certainly be influenced by favorable leadership, but there are multiple other forces and factors that contribute to that outcome. Vroom and Jago were writing about the corporate world when making this observation, offering the example that share value (as a measure of organizational effectiveness) can be influenced by such factors as mergers, acquisitions, restructuring, and layoffs. In parallel, a variety of factors contribute to the development of effective organizational outcomes in public sector contexts such as changes in law, public support, personnel systems, and budgets. Those in positions of leadership can shape organizational outcomes in a variety of ways that do not require leadership. It might be argued that someone can demonstrate leadership even if desired outcomes are not achieved in all instances.

Pursley (1974) administered the Leadership Opinion Questionnaire (LOQ) to a sample of police chiefs. The LOQ is a self-assessment tool intended to help managers understand how they relate to those they supervise. Pursley drew a further distinction between "non-traditionalist" (those with a college degree who had moved into their current command from another agency) and "traditionalist" (primarily those with less education who had risen through the ranks of the agency they commanded) police chiefs. He found that non-traditional chiefs indicated a greater willingness to delegate authority and seek input from subordinates before making decisions. Their overall attitudes were consistent with participatory and democratic forms of leadership as opposed to controlling and authoritarian styles of leadership. In contrast, traditionalists reported they emphasized creating a structured work environment that controlled the work-related activities of subordinates. This included de-emphasizing delegation and discretion.

A survey of British police officers found that leadership practices deemed effective supported higher quality services to the public, encouraged stronger personal and professional standards, and provided employees with knowledge, skills and opportunities to exercise independent judgment (Dobby, Anscombe, and Tuffin 2004). In effect, these authors found that officers who felt they were treated more favorably by the organization provided a higher quality of performance and service. Though officers might express such preferences, the type of supervision they receive might differ substantially from the ideal. A study of patrol sergeants in a major Australian police force found variation in the supervisory tactics and techniques (Brewer, Wilson, and Beck 1994). In particular, the Australian data suggested sergeants spent far more time engaging in conventional monitoring than in providing officers with clear feedback on their performance.

When surveyed, police officers report they do not believe supervisor attitudes influence their behavior (Allen and Maxfield; Brown 1988; Mastrofski, Ritti, and Snipes 1994), particularly their productivity. Existing research has produced mixed results in assessing whether supervisors are actually able to influence officers. Such influence is easier to see in incidents where supervisors are present (i.e., arrest is more likely when a supervisor is present for some types of criminal events) (Engel 2002). Johnson (2006) found management expectations were significant predictors of officer productivity in issuing traffic citations and making drunk driving arrests, though this may reinforce that influence is constrained to productivity outcomes that are easy for supervisors to count. In effect, the influence on officer behavior may be as much or more a function of organizational factors (the ability to hold officers accountable to certain expectations) as opposed to true leadership influence (see Klinger 2004).

A study of Dutch police officers found that although leaders were able to influence integrity violations committed by those officers, the impact did vary by offense type (Huberts, Kaptein, and Lasthuizen 2007). They also found that some styles of leadership were more effective in limiting certain forms of (self-reported) integrity violations. Officers working for leaders they characterized as having strict and directive leadership styles were less likely to report engaging in violations such as corruption[11]. Encouragement can be drawn from studies finding that "emergent leaders" applying for employment in policing have been assessed to be high in terms of intelligence, ambition, and likeability (Hogan, Raskin, and Fazzini 1990). Studies of both police leaders (Andreescu and Vito 2010; Burns and Shuman 1988)[12] and police officers (Jermier and Berkes 1979) have tended to demonstrate support for more transformational leadership approaches.

Allen (1982) found more supervision (defined in his study as more supervisor-subordinate contact) did not influence employee outputs. What did matter, however, was the quality and nature of supervision officers perceived they were receiving. Other studies have tended to reinforce the variable and circumstantial influence of leadership in policing. Densten's study of British police found that leadership effectiveness was possible and that it was:

- a function of leader reputation and the followers' satisfaction with job behaviours and activities of their leaders;
- influenced by impression management and image building by leaders;
- moderated by how dependent followers are on leaders giving direction and resources; and
- moderated by how dependent leaders are on followers to complete the processing of the activity for success to occur (2003, 412).

This reinforces that leadership is not simply about the leader. It is also a function of followers' perceptions, predispositions, and orientations.

Unanswered Questions and Unresolved Issues

Despite four decades of inquiry into aspects of police leadership, this area of scholarship remains in its infancy. To date research has tended to rely almost exclusively on self-

---

11. Whether this finding is a function of less misconduct or lower inclination to reporting misconduct is, of course, a subject that might be debated.

12. Interestingly, Andreescu and Vito (2010) find some variation in leader support for transformational approaches based on sex and race/ethnicity; it bears noting that general support among any group does not suggest a universal endorsement of any one approach. Silvestri (2007) found female supervisors in the UK felt they needed to use different approaches than their male peers because of how gender influenced the dynamics of the leader-follower dyad in that cultural and organizational context (see also Hennessy 1992). Engel (2001) achieved similar results in two US agencies, though with a limited number of non-white, male supervisors.

reported behavior or perceptions, without linking those data with tangible outcomes. Studies often have major limitations in their sampling and generalizability. Across the body of literature there are conceptual and operational disparities in how key terms are defined and measured. Too often, "supervision" and "leadership" are not clearly distinct in either data or their subsequent reporting. Much of the empirical literature focuses on first-line supervisors and their influence on traditional measures of productivity by first-line personnel. True leadership is rarely measured and, when it is quantified, studies have tended to measure the influence of directive leadership approaches on narrow aspects of traditional police decision making (i.e., the decision to arrest).

What this means is while it can be noted that studies indicate officers of various ranks prefer leadership styles that are more transformational (using persuasion rather than power, articulating a vision, employing participatory decision making practices, etc.) than bureaucratic and directive, it is unclear: whether leaders actually employ those approaches; whether officers correctly perceive that to be their leader's intended style; or, whether officers subjected to more transformational and/or participatory leadership styles produce better policing outcomes. The data used as the foundation for this book are not immune to many of these criticisms.[13] James Meindl (1990) offered a tempering assessment of the "conventional wisdom" regarding leadership. His essay challenged the way leadership is often treated in literature and professional discourse, contending most research finds leadership's effect on performance to be modest or even non-existent. He also suggested that in reality leadership and its outcomes are very difficult to observe and measure. Stephen Mastrofski (2002) extended Meindl's position into the context of police leadership, contending there has been a tendency to romanticize leaders and leadership. It is not Mastrofski's position that leaders are not influential. Rather, he argues that what leaders do, their level of influences, and their role in the organization is often misunderstood and mischaracterized.

In considering the state of leadership research across disciplines, Hackman and Wageman (2007) identified several key problems in how researchers have posed questions. Their essay lays out alternative questions they believe leadership scholars should be asking to better understand leaders and leadership. The questions they pose include (emphasis in the original):

- "Not do leaders make a difference, but *under what conditions does leadership matter?*" (43). The focus of research is too often misdirected. We presume leaders always have an ability to leverage influence in all situations and that their influence (or lack thereof) is greater than any competing conditions or circumstances. Coaches (not players) are fired when the team is struggling; chiefs (not officers) are fired when agencies have problems.
- "Not what are the traits of leaders, but *how do leaders' personal attributes interact with situational properties to shape outcomes?*" (44). Though this book considers the traits and habits of effective leaders, it seeks to do so in the context of discussing how they function to help leaders achieve desired outcomes.
- "Not do there exist common dimensions on which all leaders can be arrayed, but *are good and poor leadership qualitatively different phenomena?*" (45). There is limited research on this issue, but Hackman and Wageman see evidence that it is not

---

13. Likewise, more conventional academic products associated with this study can be viewed with a similarly critical eye (Schafer 2009, 2010a, 2010b).

that good and poor are opposite sides of the same coin. Rather, they believe that poor leaders "exhibited entirely different patterns of behavior" (45) relative to good leaders.

- "Not how do leaders and followers differ, but *how can leadership models be re-framed so they treat all system members as both leaders and followers?*" (45). In almost any situation, leaders are also followers; analogously, followers are (at least in their potential) leaders (Anderson, Gisborne, and Holiday 2006).
- "Not what should be taught in leadership courses, but *how can leaders be helped to learn?*" (46). If leadership and its instruction were easy, we would not lament the absence of leaders and the general failure to effectively develop them in organizations of all types.

Clearly much work remains to be done in advancing an understanding of the who, what, where, when, why, and how questions associated with leadership in policing and broader contexts. This text seeks to advance an understanding of some of these questions, though it is not the definitive or final word.

Conclusions

The Vroom and Jago quote (2007) at the opening of this chapter framed leadership as a process not a property. Though the book discusses traits and habits of effective leaders, what really matters is when, where, and how those traits and habits are used in pursuit of desired objectives across various groups. Effective leaders understand that there are many ways and approaches to achieve most organizational outcomes. What matters is that leaders are honest with themselves as they seek to apply the right model for a given situation. To be effective over time a leader does not need to reflect all of the traits and habits discussed in this book, but the leader must have a sufficiently broad base of these attributes. A leader who only has a foundation based on personality is no better than the supervisor who seeks to rule by fear of discipline. Short-term success might be realized, but in the long term failure is almost assured.

The focus of this chapter has largely been upon the past. A critique of the current state of police organizations and leadership necessitates revisiting how policing systems reached the current state and what is known about those conditions. Within this discussion it bears noting that recent decades have seen a variety of changes that individually or collectively may mean that some things that have been "known" in the past might be less relevant today. Various forms of hyphenated policing (Buerger 2011) (problem-oriented, community-oriented, intelligence-led, homeland security-based, etc.) have modified more than simply the rhetoric of how the police should operate. Women and minorities have assumed more prominent roles throughout the policing profession (Drodge and Murphy 2002). The relationship and distinction between the police and the military is increasingly blurring, as both entities assume strategies, roles, tactics, tools, language, and culture of the other (see O'Dea and Jarvis 2008). These changes only elevate and accelerate the importance of true leadership in a period of change and uncertainty regarding the future role and function of policing in America.

Chapter 3

Honesty & Integrity

This book opened with a quote from Joanne Ciulla, who remarked on the challenges of creating effective and capable leaders. Ciulla's observation was partly inspired by Immanuel Kant, who wrote ". . . from such warped wood as is man made, nothing straight can be fashioned" (trans. 1983).[1] Consider how often ethics and integrity seem to be the downfall of a leader. President Bill Clinton's legacy will forever be shrouded by his admission of infidelity. Though former Illinois Governor George Ryan is lauded in some circles for his "blanket commutation" of all inmates sitting on that state's death row,[2] he was subsequently convicted on federal charges of racketeering, extortion, bribery, tax fraud, and money laundering. Leaders are drawn from the ranks of average people and bring some level of personal faults and weaknesses to the task of leading others. Their efficacy is tempered by their ability to maintain (at least the appearance of) honesty, morality, and integrity.

In writing about the best practices in leadership ethics, Craig Johnson (2007) noted that leaders often are held to a higher ethical standard. In contrast to subordinates and followers, leaders enjoy greater levels of power and privilege, have access to more protected information, are granted greater levels of responsibility and requisite authority, and must satisfy the interests of a broader range of constituents in carrying out their duties and making decisions. Because leaders have greater power and authority, we expect they will live up to a higher standard. Similar observations are often made about policing and police officers. Because we entrust such tremendous power in the police, it is particularly important that they live up to our expectations. Because of the power and authority they are granted, when the short-comings and mistakes of both leaders and police officers come to light, the response may be amplified. Whether fair or not, a higher standard seems to be in place for those granted greater levels of trust and responsibility.

Public trust is difficult to generate and sustain. When public figures and officials commit acts that violate society's trust and confidence there may be significant repercussions. Theft, dishonesty, infidelity, and criminality are always looked down upon, but they tend to generate an even greater stigma when someone in whom we have entrusted special rights and statuses commits them. In discussing the "warped wood of humanity," Joanne Ciulla (2001) remarks that we struggle to separate the private from the public—it is difficult to

---

1. Kant's writings have been alternatively translated to convey "nothing straight can be constructed from such warped wood as that which man is made of" (Reiss 1970/1996, 46).

2. On January 11, 2003, just before leaving office, Ryan commuted the sentences of all 167 convicted offenders awaiting execution on Illinois' death row; their sentences were converted to life in prison. This action is viewed alternatively as a heroic move in light of growing questions about the reliability of processing capital cases in the state or a diversionary tactic given that Ryan was facing federal corruption charges. Both perspectives have some truth. New evidence was emerging suggestion capital cases were tainted by harsh policing tactics, untoward prosecutorial behavior, improper eyewitness identifications, and sloppy forensics. It was also clear federal officials were preparing to charged Ryan; he was ultimately tried and convicted for a range of offenses.

look beyond the personal indiscretion of a leader when evaluating their overall efficacy. Former New York Governor Eliot Spitzer's legitimacy as a crime fighter was instantly eroded when it was discovered he had used the services of a high-priced prostitute. While private behavior of an "average" citizen is indeed a private matter, leaders and public officials do not enjoy that same protection. When personal lapses in judgment, integrity, and morality become known, they sow the seeds of doubt in the minds of the leader's followers. This doubt may erode the trust and confidence we have in leaders, undercutting their ability to effectively lead.[3]

Ciulla argues that we must be cautious in holding our leaders to higher standards than we hold ourselves. She contends we should not "hold leaders to higher moral standards than ourselves; if anything we should hold them to the same standards. What we do expect from leaders is that they will fail less and succeed more often than most people at meeting those standards" (2001, 314). Ciulla believes the standards should be the same, but that we should observe fewer lapses and failures from our leaders. Similarly, Barbara Kellerman writes we should have a balanced understanding of the relationship between leadership and morality. Kellerman contends, "leadership is not a moral concept. Leaders are like the rest of us; trustworthy and deceitful, cowardly and brave, greedy and generous. To assume that all good leaders are good people is to be willfully blind to the reality of the human condition" (2004b, 45). When we expect our leaders to be perfect, we set them up for failure and may actually encourage leaders to conceal their mistakes, weaknesses, lapses, and errors to avoid the harsh judgment of followers and the public.

As this book goes to press, the National Football League is sanctioning coaches and players from the New Orleans Saints for allegedly operating a "bounty" system that rewarded players for taking opponents out of the game. The starting punishment for Head Coach Sean Payton is a one-year suspension without pay. Prior to the scandal Payton had a positive reputation in the sport and community as a hard working, intelligent, and caring coach who encouraged his team to give back to the community. One justification for his harsh punishment was that he lied to NFL officials when first questioned about the allegations.[4] Though it is too early to know for certain, it is reasonable to question whether Payton's reputation as one of the "good guys" in the NFL might have lead him to be less than forthright. Did preservation of his perceived character and the reputation of his team (a band of loveable underdogs helping rebuild a sense of community and vitality in New Orleans after the devastation of Hurricane Katrina) trump honesty? Similar questions might be asked of the late Joe Paterno's handling of the sex crimes allegations that led to his firing after decades as the iconic head coach of one of the nation's most storied

---

3. This is not, of course, a universal truism. Many prominent social and political leaders have ethical failings and manage to restore at least part of their status and success. Their image might remain tarnished, but their capacity to lead (albeit in new and different ways) can endure. This might be an issue for those holding positions of celebrity status (Eliot Spitzer or Martha Stewart) more so than the "common" leader.

4. An oft-repeated mantra from police executives is "you lie, you die." This phrase is intended to convey to officers that mistakes and lapses in judgment can often be forgiven (though that does not preclude the imposition of punishment or other sanctions). When an officer's actions are questioned, however, she or he is expected to be honest with investigators, including the chief. A minor offense can reach the point of an officer being fired if the officer is not honest when questioned by superiors. Payton's situation would seem to parallel this situation. Though his knowledge and actions might have merited some form of punishment, the magnitude of the sanctions may have been elevated if he was not honest with League officials.

football programs where integrity, accountability, discipline, and playing "the right way" were hallmarks of what "Penn State Football" meant.

This chapter considers the role of honesty and integrity as traits of effective police leaders. The study participants identified these characteristics as leading traits and their comments underscore the importance of a strong ethical bearing to ensure legitimacy and maintain followership. The chapter will also consider the problems encountered when presuming that honesty and integrity are always ideal traits and the problems that arise when police officers and leaders begin to walk down the proverbial slippery slope of accepting less ethical behavior. Where the line is drawn between acceptable and unacceptable conduct is, to some extent, a function of individual judgment and morality. Consequently, some leaders in some circumstances find themselves alternatively decried as unethical and lauded for doing what was necessary to secure desired outcomes.

The Importance of Honesty & Integrity in Policing

Police officers are granted tremendous authority and responsibility by society. It is perhaps not surprising officers participating in the National Academy research project framed honesty and integrity as among the most important traits for a police leader. That honesty, integrity, trustworthiness, and morals matter in policing makes intuitive sense. American policing draws heavily on modern British policing perspectives and traditions, including the notion of "policing by consent." In the late 1820s Sir Robert Peel noted the efficacy of the police was predicated on the willingness of the public to be policed. Underlying this belief was the idea that the efficacy of the police was a function of their ability to maintain the trust and respect of the citizens they seek to police. The police cannot be successful if the public does not consent to be policed and will not cooperate with policing efforts. It is presumed that trust, respect, and honesty are linked to whether the public grants its consent. Police acts deemed immoral, illegal, or distasteful erode their image in the eyes of the public. Though American policing has never explicitly adopted Peelian principles of policing, philosophies such as community policing reflect a parallel presumption about the importance of honesty and integrity in shaping policing outcomes. The position of the police within the legal system only further reinforces the ideal that honesty and integrity are paramount. The police are positioned on the "front line" in society's fight against crime and disorder, but they are expected to combat these problems using tactics and strategies that are beyond reproach.

American police are granted tremendous authority and responsibility. No other agents of the state have the right to use force to secure citizen compliance (Kobler 1975). The decisions made by police officers and leaders have life-and-death consequences for members of the public. This places a great burden on officers and agencies to preserve public trust, legitimacy, and respect. The police cannot be effective if they do not have the support and cooperation of the public (Tyler and Huo 2002). At the same time, we expect the police to control crime and disorder in our communities (Packer 1968). These conditions can result in public support for police operations that are less than honest, ethical, and ideal. For the public to trust the police and view their authority as legitimate (something the police deserve because they are ethical and serve the public good, as opposed to only complying with the police out of fear), operations need to consistently demonstrate high standards of behavior. The result is a degree of discordance between public expectations regarding police integrity and the desire to see vigorous crime control (see Klockars 1980).

Honesty, integrity, ethics, and professionalism have been emphasized to varying degrees in American policing since at least the 1890s (Johnson and Cox 2004; Walker 1977). Recent history has served to reinforce the importance of these ideals within public safety systems. The 9/11 attacks clearly established the need for a policing framework that will enable the nearly 18,000 local, state, and federal law enforcement agencies to efficiently and effectively work to prepare for, prevent, respond to, and recover from myriad critical incidents. The attacks also demonstrated police agencies need to work within the broader frameworks of public safety and intelligence communities. In this way, the interdependence of the police with broader efforts to ensure security and safety (regardless of the cause of a specific event) has expanded. At the same time, questions arise about the civil liberty implications of efforts to ensure information sharing, threat detection, and incident prevention. Groups such as the American Civil Liberties Union repeatedly remind the public that homeland security is only truly achieved when government efforts function within a framework of professionalism and ethics. Answers are rarely easy or universally recognized. The ongoing debate over New York City Police Department efforts to monitor large segments of the city's Muslim population has been endorsed, rationalized, questioned, and vilified (Associated Press 2012).

The public needs to have confidence that public safety and homeland security personnel and agencies are taking seriously the duty to operate in a manner consistent with the public's trust. In terms of both intelligence operations (Carter 2009) and more traditional policing duties (i.e., Los Angeles Police Department 2000; Walker 1977) there are numerous examples of the failures of past generations of police officials and organizations: failures to respect rights; failures to preserve the public's trust; failures to operate in accordance with the law; failures to operate with transparency and accountability, etc. The public has good reason to be distrustful of the police because of past abuses and indiscretions. The public has good reason to hold contemporary police to a high standard given the unique and powerful rights with which the police are entrusted. To be effective, modern officers and agencies need to work to alleviate public suspicions and concerns about the propriety of their operations and the integrity of personnel. Leadership plays a key role in the pursuit of these objectives.

When considering the issue of honesty and integrity in leadership both internal and external dynamics are of relevance. The honesty and integrity of a leader are of internal significance because they speak to the position of that leader within the organization. A leader who is honest and demonstrates integrity is more likely to cultivate trust, cooperation, and followership. Personnel are more likely to believe in the leader's statements, actions, and efforts to enhance and improve the organization. Honesty and integrity have external significance, as well. Ethical leaders are likely to engender trust and cooperation from those outside the organization. Additionally, it would be expected that an ethical leader will set a tone for how operations should be conducted within the workplace. Followers will see the leader's actions and choices as a model (Hueberts, Kaptein, and Lasthuizen 2007; Murphy and Drodge 2004). It would be Pollyannaish to suggest followers will seek to emulate and model their own actions on the example of their leader. More accurately, leaders have to ensure their own conduct and behavior is beyond reproach. Any hint of untoward conduct will be detected and magnified; followers will see the leader as illegitimate, not trustworthy, and inconsistent. It is imperative that leaders set an example and continually articulate to followers the importance of integrity to preserve public trust and compliance.

The ethical dilemmas arising in policing are often related with not only the actions of the involved officer(s) but also the culture and traditions of the employing agency. Too often, an organization's culture allows or turns a blind eye toward corrupt, abusive, unethical, or untoward conduct (Delattre 1996; Johnson and Cox 2004; Klockars et al. 2000). Culture is a product of more than just a leader's vision, direction, and will. Culture emerges from the collective value, beliefs, behaviors, and traditions of all employees including, in some cases, both current and past employees (Crank 1998). Leaders can, however, seek to encourage an organization's culture to value professionalism, integrity, and lawful performance of duties. Perhaps more than anything else, ethics in the workplace can be enhanced by leaders articulating the importance of integrity, reinforcing that ideal in the decisions they make (i.e., investigating potential violations rather than seeking to hide such events), and setting an example for others by carrying themselves with a strong ethical orientation (Hueberts, Kaptein, and Lasthuizen 2007; Weisburd et al. 2000).

This process is broader than a leader simply articulating and reinforcing the importance of ethics within the workplace. "Do the right thing" is a tired and largely ineffective mantra for police ethics (Delattre 1996). Management scholar Rabindra Kanungo (2001) contends that leaders who embrace transformational approaches can maximize their ability to influence the ethical orientation of their workplace's culture. Transformational leaders interact with followers, peers, and external allies in a manner that emphasizes the importance of relationships and reinforces the interdependence of various parties. Transformational leaders focus on both means and ends. Generally they are more altruistic in how they seek to influence others. In other words, transformational leaders seek to be more effective by working well with others, paying attention to interpersonal relationships, and considering how actions and choices affect others (or can be enhanced by engaging others). Kanungo suggests this becomes important from an ethical perspective because seeing this issue emphasized conditions officers to consider how their actions affect and will be interpreted by others. Officers faced with ethical dilemmas would be expected to make the "right" choice more often than not if they are not simply thinking about themselves, but are also thinking about the consequences of their actions for others.

Perspectives from National Academy Participants

The importance of honesty and integrity emerged repeatedly in the descriptions of effective police leader provided by the NA respondents. Effective police leaders "are honest and able to be trusted" (lieutenant large special service agency) possessing "integrity beyond reproach" (captain major county agency). They perform their duties with "[a]bsolute integrity and transparency" (section head major international federal agency). When asked to rank the top five attributes of effective police leaders, NA participants selected honesty and integrity as the most important attribute thirty-five percent of the time. This was one of the top five attributes identified by seventy percent of the respondents. No other attribute approached this level of consistency in the ranking portion of the research project. Throughout the various phases and forms of the research project, respondents frame honesty and integrity as the most important trait of effective leaders. Conversely, questionable ethics and integrity was one of the leading characteristics linked with ineffective leaders.

As recent research has found, supervisors and police executives play a key role in setting a tone of honesty and integrity within their agency. In a national survey of police officers conducted by David Weisburd and his colleague (2000), 85 percent of respondents agreed with the statement that "[i]f a police chief takes a strong position against abuses of authority, he or she can make a big difference in preventing officers from abusing their authority." Nearly 90 percent of respondents agreed that "[g]ood first-line supervisors can help prevent police officers from abusing their authority." Supervisors and leaders play central roles in setting the proper tone within their organization to preserve public trust and ensure organizational efficacy. In a study of previously successful corporate leaders who had "derailed" during the course of their career, Morgan McCall and Michael Lombardo (1983) found one of the key forces "derailing" executives' careers was having betrayed the trust of others. Effective leaders set an ethical tone that contributes to the efficacy of their unit. Effective leaders also engage in honest leadership behaviors in order to establish and maintain the trust of their followers, which pays subsequent dividends in other aspects of their leadership efforts.

Police leaders must be "honest, moral & ethical. This is a 'given' in LE in general & without a clean message from leadership, a department can be doomed (or at least some individuals)" (deputy chief small municipal agency). Leaders practice and maintain good work habits to preserve the integrity of their own conduct and to model the behavior they expect and demand from their followers. Effective leaders "are fair, respectful, honest when dealing with the public and their peers" (deputy chief mid-size county agency). A leader's personal integrity and values might even reflect that individual's perspective on justice and the justice system. They demonstrate a "[b]elief in right and wrong with strong desire to do 'right,' want to improve conditions for others" (sergeant small municipal agency). Framed in this way, the honesty and integrity of a police leader are symbols of the honesty and integrity we want to believe is imbued within our legal system.

Reinforcing the findings achieved by Weisburd et al. (2000), this perspective sees honesty and integrity as important beyond the "policing by consent" vision espoused by Sir Robert Peel. Beyond preserving the public's confidence and cooperation, honesty and integrity are important to the internal dynamics of a police agency. While honesty and integrity might shape the efficacy of the police within the community, they also shape the efficacy of the leader within the agency. Indeed, a parallel to Peel's notion might be seen here- leadership by consent. A police leader's success is shaped by the willingness of others to be lead. Acts that erode or compromise the relationship between leader and follower limit the leaders' efficacy. Leaders need to "be a model to those who you are trying to develop" (lieutenant medium special service agency). Exhibiting honesty and integrity, rather than simply presenting the public with the image of honesty and integrity, demonstrates to other employees that such characteristics are essential and valued. As discussed elsewhere in this book, leadership by example was considered a vital element of effective practices. Front-line personnel cannot be expected to uphold a higher standard than their supervisors.

Consider the case of the Sunnyville Police Department (a pseudonym), a major urban agency that found itself entering into a consent decree with the U.S. Department of Justice (see Schafer and Martinelli 2008). One dimension of this consent decree required SPD to provide first-line supervisors (sergeants and lieutenants) with a 16-hour block of ethics and integrity training. Given a long-standing history of integrity violations and unconstitutional illegal acts in SPD and considering the findings of Weisburd and colleagues (2000) this action would seem rational. Future improvements were unlikely to be realized if first-line supervisors were not demonstrating and enforcing a standard of conduct within SPD. First-line supervisors, as the term implies, were the leaders having the most direct contact with patrol officers and investigators. They were the leaders in the best position to influence the behavior and actions of front-line personnel. Unfortunately, the consent decree did not mandate any training for higher ranking supervisors or the agency's executive staff.

In the course of providing the ethics and integrity training in SPD, Police Ethicist Thomas J. Martinelli would talk with participants about the problems, frustrations, and barriers the agency was confronting. A recurrent theme emerging from these discussions was a concern that the consent decree was creating a higher standard for first-line supervisors than for SPD executives. The message implied through the structure of the consent decree was the long-standing ills SPD was confronting were being blamed on first-line supervisors (the only ones deemed to need training) and future expectations would place a different standard on first-line and executive supervisors. Middle managers participating (by mandate) in the ethics training repeatedly questioned why top executives were not being required to participate in the same or a similar program. Widespread skepticism, cynicism, frustration, and doubts were expressed about the likelihood of future improvements in SPD. First-line supervisors would comment that focusing the training on first-line supervisors reinforced the reality that SPD had a long history of allowing misconduct and corrupt acts among top executives and this was not likely to change through the consent decree. Participating supervisors questioned how they could model proper ethical conduct to front-line personnel when top executives engaged in behaviors perceived as showing favoritism, nepotism, ineptitude, and corruption. They questioned how the consent decree could "work" if officers were told to "do the right thing" while seeing repeated examples of the opposite from their top leaders.

What are the prospects for reform and improvement in an agency such as SPD in light of the results obtained by Weisburd et al. (2000)? Can an agency overcome a history of poor performance when top executives continue to engage in corrupt, abusive, or at least seemingly improper, unethical, or questionable conduct? These pieces of evidence suggest that reform is unlikely when leaders fail to live up to the same standard they seek to impose upon followers. "I believe that honesty and integrity are the two corner stones to being an effective leader. The supervisors that possess these qualities are able to motivate the officers to achieve the agency objectives" (lieutenant medium municipal agency). The concept of leadership by example is perhaps most readily evident in the domain of honesty and integrity. A leader who fails to exemplify these traits will likely struggle in his or her efforts to ensure others emulate those practices. As the preceding comment implies, the benefits of honesty and integrity may span beyond simply ensuring others mirror those traits; it may be the foundation of broader efforts to successfully lead.

Honesty and integrity also tend to imply a certain degree of courage. Leaders may recognize that being honest and truthful is not always in their long-term professional interests. It can be easier, at times, to mislead or hold back one's views or opinions. To be effective, a police leader might have to take action that works in opposition to their career ambitions. Effective police leaders "have administrative courage to offer their opinions honestly" (lieutenant major state agency). They are willing to demonstrate an "ability or willingness to stand for what is right even if it would adversely effect him/her" (lieutenant small municipal agency). They will not "lie to you, for you, or with you" (lieutenant small municipal agency) and "are very grounded in good moral beliefs and have a solid ethical attitude. They base decisions on their ethics and morals without being influenced by political pressures" (lieutenant mid-size municipal agency). These leaders do not fear "telling people the truth about performance . . . accurately describing positives and negatives in a performance evaluation" (deputy chief medium municipal agency).

The political nature of many police departments and government agencies can make it challenging (if not impossible) to actually embody these ideals. Truly being a leader of honesty, integrity, and morality may indeed require a high degree of courage to take unpopular positions, make unpopular statements, and challenge the status quo. This can be difficult in any organization, as evidenced by any number of recent controversies surrounding "whistle blowing" by employees. Viewed in this way, even front-line personnel could demonstrate leadership by speaking out (in appropriate ways and venues) against problematic organizational actions, policies, and protocols. Organizations seeking to foster effective leadership practices will find ways to insulate leaders from negative repercussions for being honest, an action far easier to discuss than to actually instill.

The reality is that police organizations are situated in political environments. Sheriffs are elected and chiefs normally serve at the pleasure of elected officials. Police leaders may be pressured to engage in unethical, questionable, or harmful (though lawful and ethical) actions by the elected officials around them. The best leaders work to preserve and insulate their agencies and personnel from external political pressures. They define the decision making process in the agency as based upon law, policy, ethics, honesty, integrity, and meritorious work behavior. This allows their followers to operate in a world where honesty and integrity are the standard and where officers can exemplify professionalism in their actions.[5] Executives who exemplify honesty and integrity will not be afraid to lose their jobs rather than doing something that violated their integrity. Other leaders must be willing to disrupt their career trajectory rather than doing something that violates their own beliefs and values. Indeed, ethical leadership often does mean doing what is right rather than doing what is easy.

Leaders may also confront periodic dilemmas of whether to seek the preservation of public trust or employee trust. These considerations can be in conflict. For example, police officers often want to use force early and often to avoid injury to themselves and their co-workers. In contrast, the public wants the police to use force as a last resort. When used, the public wants accountability, particularly in more serious applications of force. This can suggest agencies should document, audit, and investigate the use of force, at least in some instances and when complaints are filed. The public needs to be confident that officers are acting with restraint and only using force when other options have been exhausted. Officers, understandably, do not like to feel they will be continually second-guessed. It can be difficult for a leader to determine how to balance the preferences of officers and the needs of the public to create a just use of force system that grants officers latitude, ensures accountability, and preserves employee and public trust.

Honesty and integrity are also related with the extent to which followers believe they can trust their leader. Trust in one's leader is particularly important in higher risk settings, such as policing. A group of officers being led through a tactical situation need to have confidence they can trust the judgment and decisions made by their leader. Even in more routine contexts, followers need to be confident that a leader is making appropriate decisions regarding equipment acquisition, staffing, and deployment. One of the core traits of ineffective leaders was appearing to be arbitrary or capricious in making decisions—in other words, leaders were perceived to be ineffective when followers could not trust in their capacity to understand the leaders' motives and core beliefs. This trust did not, however, move in only one direction. Effective leaders know "when to trust their subordinates" (sergeant medium municipal agency); the trust moves in both directions. Part of

---

5. My thanks to Deputy Chief William Maki (retired) of the Waynesboro (VA) Police Department for providing a clear articulation of this and several other points in this section addressing ethical police leadership.

being a leader of honesty and integrity is cultivating the trust of followers. Part of preserving that trust is to reciprocate by showing a willingness to trust followers, their judgment, and the propriety of their actions.

Leaders exemplifying honesty and integrity could be trusted by subordinates; trusted to make appropriate good-faith decisions, trusted to keep their word, and trusted to support employees acting in a good-faith fashion. Leaders exemplifying honesty and integrity could be trusted by the community, its residents, and its constituents; trusted to hold sacred the authority and responsibility granted to the police by the public, and trusted to support the ideals of justice and equity. Leaders exemplifying honesty and integrity could be trusted by those they followed; trusted to follow the orders they were given, to be model employees, and to treat their charges and duties with respect. That honestly and integrity were highly valued among the National Academy participants was evident in a number of ways. Some consideration must be given, however, to contrasting points of view. Are there situations or circumstances in which honesty and integrity might be viewed as working against a leader's efficacy and their ability to achieve desired outcomes? The next section considers this possibility.

A Contrasting Perspective

Are honesty and integrity absolute? Is it always in the best interest of an effective police leader to act in a manner reflecting strong core professional ethics? Does that course of actions always benefit the leader, his followers, his organization, and his community? In an ideal world there would presumably be no reason for a leader to behave in anything less than an honest and forthright manner. The world of policing and bureaucratic police organizations is far from ideal. There are numerous situations, both hypothetical and real, in which it might arguably be understandable and perhaps appropriate for a leader to display less than untoward judgment. Whether these arguments hold merit or not will be filtered through the lens of individual readers and their personal judgment. Less-than-absolute honesty and integrity can be viewed as necessary to achieve results within an imperfect system or can be viewed as an excuse to avoid living up to challenging and high standards.

The idea that front-line police personnel might engage in unethical or questionably ethical conduct in the furtherance of organization or community interests is often referred to as "noble cause corruption" (Caldero and Crank 2009). One extreme example of this was well articulated by Carl Klockars in his treatment of "the Dirty Harry problem" (1980). Clint Eastwood's classic movie character "Dirty" Harry Callahan uses a variety of morally questionable means in the pursuit of morally good outcomes. In his quest for his subjective interpretation of justice, which he seeks within an imperfect justice system, Callahan is able to rationalize a variety of illegal acts. Seeking to save the life of a kidnapping victim, Dirty Harry breaks a number of laws and engages in abusive practices; his actions ultimately result in an inability to convict the offender. Dirty Harry is a fictional embellishment used to present an engaging story in a movie. His conduct, however, is hardly different from the officer who, while on a traffic stop, conducts an illegal search, locates a weapon or contraband, and lies on her/his report about finding those materials in a lawful manner. Dirty Harry is hardly different from the officer who falsifies an evidence tag to preserve the image of a seamless chain of custody. Dirty Harry is hardly different from the officer who raises her/his hand, takes the stand, and lies about seemingly inconsequential aspects of a case to ensure a conviction.[6] Might there be parallel circumstances where dishonest behavior by a police leader can be rationalized in the pursuit of justice or other objectives?

Even setting aside "noble cause corruption," deceptive practices are an integral part of modern policing as a whole (Barker and Carter 1994; Manning 1978, 1997).[7] Though this reality is not ideal and advocates for police integrity may wish this were not the case, dishonest and deceptive practices might generally be considered elements of "good" police work. Once again, the writings of Carl Klockars (1984) are insightful in this respect. An officer policing a demonstration might lie to a passively resistant citizen in order to secure their compliance and avoid the possible use of force and/or injuries. An officer questioning a suspect may over-state the strength of the evidence or witnesses in order to convince the presumed offender to confess to the crime. An agency representative may appear before the media and deny that a suspect has been identified in a major criminal incident in order to keep that suspect off-guard in the furtherance of an on-going investigation. There are myriad situations in which being less-than-forthright or even outright dishonest (though not to the extent of violating the law) can be viewed as necessary or even ideal to achieve broader agency or individual interests.

The point of this discussion is not to argue for or against absolute honesty and integrity in policing. Rather, the objective is to illustrate that complex realities complicate achieving the ideal of high ethics and morality in policing. Stepping away from absolute integrity and justifying light forms of misconduct does, however, set us on the proverbial "slippery slope." If our society is willing to accept lying on the part of police officers that are questioning a viable suspect in an investigation, when does that lying "cross the line" and become unacceptable, even if no laws are broken? Is it acceptable for an officer to make misleading statements? To lie about the existence of witnesses? To lie about a witness's statement? To lie about the existence of other implicating evidence? Answering such questions becomes further complicated by the fact some acts may not violate the law, but may be contrary to our norms and expectations for the police. While an officer might not break the law when misleading a suspect by stating a witness's account links the suspect to a crime scene, this action may be counter to our beliefs of what is "right," "just," or ethical. The situation becomes a catch-22 for the police. Society as a whole is likely to support a bit of Dirty Harry tactics, but it can be impossible to know when some actions have gone beyond what the public will allow until after a scandal emerges and the damage has been inflicted.

This extended discussion does, in fact, have a real bearing on consideration of honesty and integrity on the part of police leaders. Just as arguments can be made to legitimize and justify the less-than-absolute honesty of a police officer seeking to achieve an

---

6. This act is sometimes referred to as "testilying" (Cunningham 1999; Slobogin 1996) and it may often occur in less serious criminal matters. For example, an officer testifying in court against a motorist in a disputed traffic ticket may have no recollection of a traffic stop made months earlier. Rather than admitting he or she does not recall the details of the traffic stop, the officer might lie under oath in order to ensure a conviction and/or preserve face in light of the inability to recall the incident.

7. To be fair, officers will vary in their comfort with using such tactics (i.e. Muir 1977). Some officers will routinely use deceptive approaches and/or repeatedly push the lawful boundaries in their use of deceptive approaches. Others will be far less comfortable with such practices, recognizing that once deception is embraced as a tactic, it can become difficult to determine when actions go too far beyond what law, culture, and social norms would or should allow. As noted by one of the police leaders who reviewed this chapter of the text "an organization that has lying as an integral part of their policing system is broken and needs repair."

admirable objective, arguments can be made to legitimize the less-than-absolute honesty of a leader pursuing a laudable organizational outcome. Consider a chief investigator for a county agency being interviewed by the local media regarding an on-going investigation into a series of auto thefts. If the agency's investigators are nearing the point of being able to make arrests in the case and have suspects and/or high-risk areas under active surveillance, does the chief investigator undercut her efficacy if she lies in the interview? Disclosing that arrests are imminent might cause suspects to flee or alter their offending patterns, delaying or denying justice altogether.

Consider a more nuanced example that actually occurred in several regional police forces in another country. Mid-level leaders (unit and precinct commanders) within the agencies in question were under pressure from top executives, politicians, and the public to increase drug enforcement. Mid-level leaders could employ limited tactics, however, because the agency had few covert vehicles for use by drug enforcement officers. The few available covert vehicles were well known to local offenders. Several mid-level leaders began to falsify aspects of overtime budgets and payments to skim salary money into an internal "slush fund." These soft monies were used to purchase beer the police leaders and officers gave to area auto dealers. In exchange, the agencies were able to borrow vehicles off the car lots for short-term covert use in drug investigations. Leaders displayed dishonest behavior to cope with a budgetary and bureaucratic obstacle in an effort to support legitimate, lawful, and desirable enforcement operations. In the case of this foreign agency, leaders engaged in unethical and potentially criminal conduct to address an organizational pressure and public expectation.

Is this behavior appropriate or not? Does it represent creative and adaptive leadership, or does it reflect corrupt acts that will only encourage emulation among subordinate officers in the form of noble cause corruption, or worse? Individual readers undoubtedly will differ in their views. Leaders can only exercise so much influence and virtually every leader must also act as a follower in some contexts. The mid-level leaders in question had to follow the rules and restrictions set forth by their leaders (agency executives and political leaders that determined the agency's budget). Were these leaders better off exercising absolute integrity and operating with the available resources, even if that limited their capacity to pursue organizational objectives (drug enforcement)? Should they be considered better leaders because they innovated and adapted in the face of a dysfunctional situation? Did they hamper the long-term efficacy of the agencies' drug enforcement efforts by indirectly communicating to top executives that modified budgets were not needed to achieve successful drug enforcement (after all, the drug units made many arrests . . .)?

Stepping Onto the Slippery Slope

In considering the role of honesty and morality in leadership, F.G. Bailey argued true leaders are never saints; they are never immaculate and most engage in poor moral action on at least some occasions. "Certainly there are degrees of defilement; but . . . no leader can survive as a leader without deceiving others (followers no less than opponents) and without deliberately doing to others what he would prefer not to have done to himself. Leadership and malefaction everywhere and at all times go hand in hand" (1988, ix). Bailey's view might seem cynical or jaded, but is it far from the truth? In the process of bringing about change in an organization, does not the effective leader often have to manipulate, coerce, and compel others to do that which they would rather not do? Are all of those actions morally proper or do they, in fact, necessitate that the leader step onto the proverbial slip-pery slope of dishonesty, questionable ethics and integrity, and, perhaps in some cases, criminality? Is the leader engaging in such conduct in the furtherance of what is best for the agency much different from the officer who legitimizes noble cause corruption in pur-suit of a conviction and what the officer subjectively believes is best for the community?

In an ideal world these types of ethical dilemmas would not confront police leaders or officers. Life is, however, far from ideal. In the international example, agencies and local funding authorities were failing these leaders, their officers, and their communities by not providing drug enforcement officers with the basic tools they needed to perform their duties. Given that reality, were the police leaders better off being "ethically ineffective" or "unethically effective"? Was it better to uphold protocol and administrative policies, even if this would greatly limit efforts to target local drug markets? Was it better to seek cre-ative ways to address drug markets within administrative limitations, even if doing so re-quired leaders to break administrative rules and laws? Did the supervisors only ensure the continuation of this problem by showing funding authorities that effective drug en-forcement was possible, even in the face of insufficient resources? Such questions could be debated and argued from either perspective, though many readers might find it diffi-cult to support a given side of the argument. The point of presenting these examples and questions is not to resolve this particular controversy, nor is it an endorsement of noble cause corruption on the part of leaders.

Instead, the example is provided to point out the many ways in which absolute in-tegrity might be viewed (in at least some perspectives and circumstances) as working against the interests of a leader or her/his subordinates, peers, agency, or community. Whether it is appropriate or understandable to take the less ethical and honest road could be vigorously debated. Perhaps Bailey is correct and a certain degree of manipulation and dishonesty is an integral part of being a leader. Perhaps completely honest and moral leadership is not feasible; perhaps ethics are not always unambiguously virtuous, partic-ularly given that leaders are only human. The problems associated with police officers stepping onto the proverbial slippery slope of dishonesty and unethical conduct is well-trod ground. Similar concerns and questions arise if we advocate that effective police lead-ers must or sometimes should do the same. It may be impossible for a leader to never cross into this dangerous area. If we accept this to be true, what are the limitations sepa-rating appropriate and inappropriate actions? Can there be such a thing as "noble cause leadership" and, if so, when does it cross beyond a noble act into the realm of dishonest, unethical, immoral, and even criminal leadership behavior?

Conclusions

That honesty and integrity were identified as important attributes of effective police leadership is hardly surprising. Strong ethics have been considered of critical importance in policing for the past century. The authority society grants to the police is predicated on the assumption that police conduct will not violate the underlying social trust, ex-pectations, and rights. The police are important and prominent actors within our crim-inal legal system and the perceived integrity of their testimony is of substantial importance. It makes sense that leaders ought to exemplify these traits and model them for followers. Leaders need to demonstrate the value of trust and honesty by epitomizing these behav-iors to their followers. Leaders need to earn the trust and respect of their followers by showing they are honest and trustworthy. Leaders need to hold sacred the authority they are granted by society and their followers, avoiding actions that would maliciously, capriciously, or foolishly damage those relationships.

Despite the fact honesty and integrity have clear importance in policing, their presence may be taken for granted in some contexts and by some leaders. Though the profession emphasizes ethics in various ways much of the attention given to ethical conduct is concerned with its presence among front-line personnel. The Sunnyville situation is but a single example of an agency that was heavily focused on integrity among front-line officers and supervisors, while turning a blind eye to the behavior of mid-level and top leaders. The ethical challenges faced by officers likely vary by rank. Front-line officers are more likely to be given opportunities to violate operational policies, accept bribes, and engage in conduct that violates citizens' rights. As an officer rises through the ranks in a typical agency she or he will spend less time engaging in routine street-level policing, but ethical questions still exist even if they take a different form. Perhaps the profession presumes that someone who was apparently ethical early in their career will maintain that bearing when confronted with new ethical dilemmas. Whether this presumption is valid remains unclear.

Even if leaders demonstrate a strong level of personal ethics and integrity that may not, by itself, be enough to ensure an appropriate level of ethical conduct among their followers. Management scholar Edward Aronson addressed this issue, noting that:

> Ethical behavior on the part of the leader would appear to be a necessary condition for the establishment of an ethical organization, but this alone is not sufficient . . . Leaders must establish the spirit, set the ambience, and determine the boundaries of acceptable behaviour. Difficulties arise when leaders' attention is diverted by operational issues and they neglect the provision of an effective ethical infrastructure. (2001, 245)

Ethical leadership is not simply a function of how the leader carries her/himself and the decisions she/he makes (Johnson and Cox 2004). Ethical leaders ensure those around them are carrying out their duties in the desired fashion. The leader asks difficult questions, holds a high standard, and does not turn a blind eye when productivity, output, or accomplishments seem questionable or too good to be true. It is alleged that one of the reasons Los Angeles Police Department leaders allowed the CRASH (Community Resources Against Street Hoodlums) Unit to operate with minimal oversight was because of its high productivity (Los Angeles Police Department 2000; Reese 2005). A leader's personal ethics are necessary, but not sufficient, to create an appropriate environment of honesty and integrity.

Are honesty and integrity absolute virtues? Though not every reader might be convinced by the examples provided in this chapter, it is clear there are situations and circumstances where less honest conduct might be alluring for a leader. Some readers may feel effective leaders recognize when those matters arise and find appropriate ways to pursue maximum honesty and integrity within imperfect realities. Other readers may believe the hallmark of a true leader is a willingness to maintain honesty and integrity, even in the face of challenges and adversity. In a broader sense, many of the traits and habits discussed in this book can be considered situational and circumstantial. The challenge faced by prospective leaders is how to embody idealized traits and habits within imperfect systems and dynamic circumstances, while bearing the burden of being a fallible human. That challenge is, at times, considerable and perhaps is most evident as leaders seek to embody and model the importance of honesty and integrity in leadership and policing practices.

Chapter 4

Listening and Communication

> Under the guidance of an effective leader, an agency thrives and changes. All personnel who work for the agency understand the goals of the organization, feel valued for their work, and believe that the lines of communication are always open for both new ideas and the resolution of complaints.
> —Lieutenant, large municipal agency

> Without the ability to communicate you cannot lead.
> —Detective, small municipal agency

The abilities to genuinely listen and to communicate clearly are central to leadership efficacy for a variety of reasons. This includes being able to truly listen to others and hear their concerns, input, ideas, and messages, as well as being articulate in written and verbal forms. Though police officers routinely engage in written and verbal communication, concise and clear radio transmissions and the ability to write a strong incident report do not directly translate into efficacy when briefing the city council, addressing a community group, or writing a memo. As a front-line officer, a leader may have mastered the ability of feigning the act of listening or providing others with the chance to "vent." As a leader, symbolic listening will be an ill-advised tactic in the long term. Listening means doing more than simply engaging in the physiological process of hearing sound; it means that effective leaders actual understand and internalize the concerns, suggestions, feedback, advice, and other messages expressed by those around them (peers, followers, supervisors, external constituents, etc.). Leaders recognize when and how to use these contributions to identify problems and solutions, inform decisions, and exert their influence as a leader.

The art of communication is not simply the acts of speaking, writing, or listening. When and how a leader engages in acts of communication influences how others receive that message and perceive the leader. Well-timed and clear messages can reinforce the leader's intentions and can mollify resistance to a controversial decision. Legitimately listening to the input of others can improve a leader's decision making ability and enhance a leader's standing and power among those she or he seeks to influence. Communication is a vital tool and a potential stumbling block in many aspects of organizational dynamics, change, and management. Leaders who can effectively communicate provide clarity, increase acceptance, and improve motivation of those around them. The specifics of the communication processes (what, when, how, and why) leaders use vary with context. A sergeant may use one process to communicate with and motivate patrol officers assigned to his shift. A sheriff seeking to communicate her rationale for a policy change to deputies and staff throughout a large, multifacility agency is likely to use a different process in the pursuit of the desired outcome.

Effective leaders have to demonstrate strong communication skills. They are "not only . . . excellent speakers, but they are also good listeners" (captain small municipal agency). Sometimes people simply need to "vent" and express frustration, complaints, anger, anxiety, or other emotions. A leader needs to recognize and respond accordingly. As well, a wise leader realizes when to seek the input of those with more knowledge of, or investment in, a decision. Listening to others can both inform the leader's choices and create buy-in from those who will have to abide by that decision. Effective leaders provide "good communications [in both] written & oral" form (lieutenant large county agency). These communication methods are not exclusively oriented toward any one audience. Efficacy requires that leaders use their skills to listen to and communicate in ways that are both "customer and employee oriented" (director medium county agency).

As with the other traits and habits discussed in this book, good communication skills by themselves are not enough to generate effective leadership outcomes. Many persuasive and compelling communicators are poor leaders. What sets effective leaders above others is an understanding of how listening and communication can amplify the efficacy of other leadership approaches. There are various permutations on the popular aphorism that people have two ears and one mouth. The implication of this observation is that good communicators listen more than they speak. They pause before they open their mouths or press the "send" button. They understand when and how to seek the input of others to enhance their understanding of situations, options, and potential outcomes. Good leaders think about how they receive and transmit information and are intentional in both processes. They continually seek new ways to gather information and convey their message, which is especially important in a society of changing communication modes and patterns (i.e., the rise of text messaging, social media, and wikis). Effective leaders also recognize communication is not simply a one way process; it is not just about how leaders reach out to followers, but also about how followers can be heard by their leaders. The burden is on leaders to communicate in the times, places, and manners that are preferred by those the leaders seek to influence, engage, motivate, and inspire (Kidd and Braziel 1999).

Communication is a multifaceted process. It is about seeking, receiving, and absorbing the comments and concerns expressed by others. That input may be face-to-face, by phone, electronic, or facilitated through some other medium. It can be synchronous (in real time) or asynchronous (delayed). It might be an ongoing process or a one-time event. Communication can occur in a single direction (a leader providing orders or a leader asking for input) or multiple directions (a leader asking for input and explaining how that input was used in making a decision). Listening is one of several sub-components of communication. It is a form of communication, but communication involves more than just listening. This chapter addresses listening in particular because the National Academy participants repeatedly mentioned the importance of listening within the umbrella of communication by leaders. Consideration is first given to the context of why listening and communicating matter in shaping leadership outcomes in policing. Next, the chapter considers why listening matters and how leaders can leverage technology in the pursuit of greater efficacy. Then, communication is reviewed as a tool that can enhance a leader's ability to articulate, sell, and reinforce a message.

The Context of Listening and Communicating

It is evident why strong communication skills would help top agency executives to be more effective in performing their duties. Communication skills are equally important for front-line supervisors and informal leaders when one thinks about the flow of information in a police agency. Personnel work in temporal (different shifts) and often geographic (different precincts, substations, or units) separation from agency executives. Supervisors, such as shift sergeants, function as an important communication link between department administrators, front-line personnel, and the community the agency serves. Effective organizational operations and the achievement of outcomes are frequently predicated on the ability of supervisors to articulate the chief's vision and expectations to officers and investigators performing core policing tasks (Trojanowicz 1980). It is also important that supervisors have an ability to recognize and understand questions and concerns generated by front-line personnel in order to provide explanation and, when needed, seek clarification from those higher in the organization's structure (Van Maanen 1983, 1984). Communication skills are important for informal leaders, as well. A field training officer (FTO) can only be effective if he or she can successfully interact with a trainee. The FTO must be able to provide informative feedback, understand and answer questions, and communicate both formal and informal agency expectations, norms, and standards. FTOs and front-line supervisors need strong communication skills because they play a key role in socializing young officers (Trojanowicz 1980).

The dynamics of communication will be variable across tasks, personnel, and organizations. When the task at hand is clear and easy to measure, such as the expectation officers will increase the issuance of parking citations or conduct more traffic stops for suspected drunk driving, it is quite easy for a leader to articulate the expectation and assess whether it was achieved (Engel 2002). Modern policing seems to increasingly invoke a range of circumstances and demands that are far less explicit than traditional objectives such as citing, arresting, and filing reports. Community policing and homeland security are two prominent examples of policing tasks that are difficult to articulate and assess (Trojanowicz, Kappeler, and Gaines 2002; Oliver 2009). When ambiguous or nebulous tasks are at hand, it can be both more challenging and more important for leaders to effectively communicate with personnel to ensure there is clarification and understanding as to the goals, objectives, preferred means, and metrics to measure success in the pursuits of those tasks (Schafer 2002).

The importance and mode of communication will likely vary based on personnel and across organizations. Some employees might prefer more directive styles of leadership where communication travels in one direction (Jermier and Berkes 1979), while others might prefer a workplace dynamic that is participative. Younger employees might be more comfortable with electronic methods of communication in contrast to their older peers, who might prefer to engage in face-to-face dialog. Organizational culture and norms can influence when, how, and about what employees and leaders wish to communicate. Effective communicators understand this reality and adjust to suit the preferences of the audience(s) they seek to reach.

Though it perhaps seems straightforward, every reader can undoubtedly think of supervisors, teachers, politicians, and others they have known who lacked one or more of these abilities. There are leaders who listen but "do not hear" those who are speaking. There are FTOs who are extremely effective in interactions with citizens, but who cannot write clear incident reports. An academy instructor may be regarded as a brilliant expert on criminal procedure, but cannot effectively convey that expertise to a class of recruits. All of these individuals are in a position to be an effective leader, but may fail at one or more elements of being an effective communicator. The inability to listen and communicate might not negate the ability to lead, but it will normally represent an impediment to that outcome.

Leaders cannot be everywhere across space and time. This situation becomes increasingly acute in larger, more complex organizations, as well as when a leader rises within an organization. A patrol sergeant has responsibility and authority that are generally restricted to a shift or squad of officers working during a fixed period of time and/or working to address a narrow set of tasks. The sergeant's responsibility does not usually extend to incidents or situations that occur while those officers are off duty or when the incident is outside of the squad's assigned responsibility. As a supervisor rises within an organization, broader authority and responsibility will usually accompany each promotion, though the nature of this will vary across organizations and based on specific assignments. For example, a sergeant who is promoted to patrol lieutenant may now have responsibility for all actions occurring on her assigned shift, regardless of whether the action happened on her day off or she was not physically presence at the event in question. A lieutenant promoted to patrol commander might have a degree of accountability for everything happening within the patrol division every day, around the clock, even though he might only work a standard forty hour week.

This situation extends upward in the organization. A chief or sheriff is generally held accountable for all aspects of the organization's operations and all actions taken by its personnel. This is why chiefs and sheriffs often find themselves out of work when a major scandal or incident emerges in an agency, even if she or he had no direct knowledge of or involvement in the wrong doing. Holding people to this high level of responsibility makes sense and is certainly not unique to policing. Living up to such an obligation, however, is difficult even in small agencies. Chiefs, sheriffs, and other executives are physically present only a fraction of the hours in a work week and rarely find themselves on the front-line of the agency's operations. The matter becomes more challenging as an agency increases in size (both number of employees and geographic coverage) and/or the executive comes from outside the ranks of the agency they lead.

Given this daunting situation how does the chief executive or any other leader fulfill their obligations to the organization? How does a patrol commander working Monday through Friday on the day shift develop awareness that there are problems on the weekend and/or the night shift in the agency? How does the new sheriff or chief derive awareness of the challenges confronting an agency for which she has not worked, perhaps even in a state in which she has not lived? How does the supervisor who has always worked in the patrol division gain an understanding of the issues existing in the investigations division or records bureau, having no prior direct knowledge of those units? One of the answers to these and associated questions is listening and communicating. Everyone in a police organization enjoys some degree of discretion, freedom, and authority; they have the right to exercise judgment (within set parameters) in the performance of their duties. Effective leaders will want to ensure employees are making appropriate and wise use of their judgment in furtherance of the organization's goals and objectives. To do that, the leader must communicate values, preferences, and edicts. The leader must listen in order to recognize problems and ensure overall compliance. Though methods and modes of listening and communicating might vary, the importance of these behaviors is universal for effective leaders.

Listening: Why it Matters

At the onset effective communication is about clear articulation. It is a one-way process in which the leader seeks to "give clear guidance and direction" (lieutenant large special jurisdiction agency) to potential followers. In its optimal form, however, communication is a two-way interaction in which the leader takes the time to "listen to the people they supervise" (lieutenant mid-size county agency) and demonstrate they "have mastered the ability to listen to people at every level" (assistant commander major county agency). This may not be a task the leader can achieve in all circumstances and times, but the leader recognizes the value of seeking input. In all but the most critical events, leaders do have the time to listen to trusted advisors and knowledgeable personnel, those performing the core tasks of the organization, and those directly affected by the decision at hand. Whether a leader opts to do so is another matter, though effective leaders will capitalize on the opportunity more often than not.

A leader who believes he is an expert on all aspects of the personnel, tasks, and operations he supervises is assured to fail in the pursuit of effective outcomes. Even informal leaders performing the core tasks of an organization or unit will benefit from hearing concerns, experiences, and insights from peers. Listening is a vital component of being an effective leader. The effective leader will ask questions, solicit opinions and suggestions, and create mechanisms to generate input from others in the workplace and those affected by the actions of the unit or agency. They will have "the ability to communicate effectively with staff, public and superiors. Being able to listen, identify and rectify or respond appropriately to the situation at hand. Also being able to 'put yourself' into a situation and see how it is perceived by others" (chief small municipal agency). Listening helps leaders recognize problems with processes, understanding, compliance, or perception. Listening helps leaders realize there might be better ways to do the job. Even the most effective leader does not have sole possession of an understanding of how a unit works, how others view its operations (workers and those receiving the unit's services), and how its operations might be improved. Effective leaders listen to others so they can maximize the efficiency, efficacy, and equity of their efforts.

Even those with direct knowledge of the unit/organization and its operations should consider how listening is used as a leadership tool. Too often police organizations suffer from poor communication. The layers of bureaucracy, as well as ego and personal politics (Cordner 1978; Cowper 2000; Enter 2006), result in leaders who are reluctant to solicit input, either because they view it as unnecessary or a sign of weakness. Likewise, supervisors and executives falling into this behavioral trap may feel they do no need to justify their choices or explain their actions. All too often the result is a divide between leaders and those they seek to influence (Reuss-Ianni 1983; Van Maanen 1983). The leader is seen as distant, arrogant, and locked into a particular way of thinking. Followers and others are viewed as malcontents, trouble-makers, argumentative, and unmanageable. Small problems spiral into major issues. Innovation and transformation are stifled. Morale sinks and cooperation disappears (Cordner 1978).

Effective leaders are said to be strong communicators because they "listen to the problems of subordinates" (inspector major international federal agency), as well as those within and outside of the agency. At times this listening is simply a gesture on the part of the leader. Sometimes employees do need to "vent" and there is no need to do anything other than facilitate that process. Leaders must be able to recognize when a rant is actually the manifestation of a problem in need of a solution. Effective leaders ensure that two-way lines of communication remain open so that feedback can be received without excessive layers of bureaucracy (which often distort the message), too much inconvenience, or the passage of too much time. These leaders can set aside their personal egos to hear the message being expressed by others, even if the crux of that message is that the leaders made the wrong decision or are failing in some aspect of the job. Not every complaint needs to be brought to the attention of a top leader in an organization; however, when stakes are high, mechanisms need to be in place to allow input to be received by decision makers without distortion, delay, or impediment.

Listening and Enhanced Decision Making

The secondary value of listening is that it allows a leader to make better decisions. In reality, even those who might like to think they have strong direct understanding of an agency, unit, or issue, including associated problems and pathologies, may be more removed than they wish to believe. Patrol sergeants in all but very small agencies do not routinely perform the full spectrum of core tasks conducted by the patrol division. Though they might spend time on patrol, backing officers up on calls, and making traffic stops, they also spend considerable time supervising, attending to administrative tasks, and providing information and answers to followers. Paperwork and other administrative processes are often handed off to subordinate personnel, even when the supervisor initiated the contact or was the first officer on the scene. Sergeants might often "cherry pick" the calls to which they respond. Even a chief or sheriff coming up through the ranks of an agency has probably not made more than a handful of arrests or traffic stops, written more than a handful of incident reports, or defused more than a handful of volatile incidents (on the street) in a considerable period of time.

This does not mean a sergeant, chief, or sheriff never engages in core policing tasks or never handles the paperwork associated with a traffic accident, but the frequency with which most supervisors engage in those tasks is low. Laws change, communities evolve, reporting requirements shift, new technologies emerge, and other changes occur that modify the realities of operations the leader once understood intimately and personally. Over time, the very nature of the tasks and any associated underlying problems evolve. A supervisor not performing a core task on a routine basis may slowly lose the ability to independently recognize difficulties and complications. Equally important, the leader may miss the cues suggesting that an opportunity exists to improve aspects of the agency's operations and service delivery. Listening is not only about identifying problems and solutions—it is also about discovering opportunities and avenues for positive change. This is not to say the leader lacks understanding, awareness, or insight; however, others may have a more current appreciation for the particular problems and circumstances at hand. Leaders realize their own experiences, education, and training has engendered them with the ability to exercise good judgment. At the same time, the leader's position with the organization also creates a duty to listen to those with direct expertise and familiarity. A commander might have once been a highly effective patrol officer, but as her career advanced and she developed new domains of expertise, she must realize that others may have more current and valid expertise. This is not an admission of weakness or limited knowledge; this is a sign of wisdom on the part of the leader.

There must be an element of earnestness when a leader is engaging in listening to those around them, both inside and outside of the organization. The process of listening can enable the leader to achieve multiple goals. In addition to receiving good input and information to guide the decision making process, listening can help the leader show he or she "cares about other people's opinions" (sergeant mid-size county agency). Does this mean the leader always follows the advice of those with whom they communicate? Certainly not. If, however, the leader consistently tends to not heed the input and recommendations of others, the process becomes pointless. People want their voices to be heard. Listening provides people the chance to offer input. It validates their knowledge, expertise, and insights. A leader recognizes that listening "to your men helps develop good leadership. This shows that you are willing to take advice and use it to do what you think is best" (lieutenant large county agency).

Effective communicators are "able to listen to others and make them feel that their ideas are considered" (lieutenant small municipal agency). This process is not merely symbolic. Recognizing the value of listening means that leaders realize the ideas of others can contribute to the leader's own knowledge and growth. Leaders have a "genuine respect for others [sic] opinions and experiences" (lieutenant mid-size agency). Leaders may undermine their own efforts if they are perceived to be providing subordinates and others with a chance to voice their views, but never truly hear and act upon those recommendations. This does not mean that a leader avoids taking decisive action in favor of obtaining consensus opinions, nor that a leader always does what others desire. "Leaders must be good listeners and allow members to participate in decision making processes when applicable" (director medium county agency). Though police officials of all ranks periodically are required to make split-second judgments, the reality is that most decisions made in police organizations allow officers and leaders to seek information and input before taking action.

Earnest listening can lead to both better decisions and improved employee satisfaction, both of which help a leader build her ability to leverage influence in the workplace. When leaders show followers they are willing to listen and can recognize and act upon good suggestions regardless of from where they originate, it can enhance the leader's prestige and image. As noted by a lieutenant in a large municipal agency:

> Effective leaders have a vision and guide their people in the direction to accomplish their vision or goals. Leaders look for input from others to gather the best information to help them make informal decisions. Leaders keep people motivated and looking ahead to improve the organization and themselves.

As discussed in the next chapter, delegating tasks and empowering employees are important traits leaders use to leverage their influence and enhance outputs and efficacy. Listening and communication are habits that help support the success of these traits in the workplace.

Listening: Leveraging Technology

Leaders recognize that listening is as important as (and in some perspectives more important than) speaking or writing. Strong communicators listen to constituents, whether they are superiors, peers, followers, or those outside of their unit or organization. This means truly listening, not simply being quiet to give the impression of listening. Leaders demonstrate they "are willing to listen to peers and subordinates and incorporate good ideas" (captain mid-size municipal agency). This certainly does not mean leaders and strong communicators do not exercise independent judgment or select a course that is contrary to the advice they are being given. Leaders recognize when they need to seek and internalize the advice of others in making an appropriate decision. The rise of social media technology has created powerful new ways in which this process can be enacted.

The Department of Defense has shown initial signs it recognizes weaknesses in conventional way of creating doctrine, which is a form of policy detailing how troops should perform their duties and carry out mission-specific objectives. Historically army field manuals were written by the few for consumption by the many. In the summer of 2009 the Army charted a new course based on an understanding that traditional ways of approaching the creation of doctrine, policies, procedures, and manuals might not ensure the best information was being communicated to personnel operating in the field. Historically, those leaders tasked with writing a military field manual detailing how troops should handle given matters may not have seen combat in a long period of time (if ever) and perhaps in a context that was less than salient to current military operational environments, missions, and objectives. A commander might have spent the early years of his career securing perimeters and guard posts along a static boundary between Western Europe and the former Soviet Bloc countries. In those types of operations, environments, locations, and resources were fixed, the enemies were from clearly defined nations, and the task was important, but generally routine and predictable. Is that commander ideally suited to write doctrine for troops seeking to establish new political order in highly dynamic areas of the Middle East, where culture, religion, ideology, and historical conflict may all trump fixed geopolitical definitions, and where enemies are defined by belief systems, rather than nationality?

In the summer of 2009 the U.S. Army began to "wikify" some elements of its doctrine (Cohen 2009). Rather than having content created by a few distant commanders, the Army placed their policies on a wiki, a website that allows any authorized user to edit, modify, add, or delete content. Explaining the rationale behind this change, a Department of Defense official remarked, "The soldier or development worker on the ground is usually the person best informed about the environment and the enemy. Moving up through levels of hierarchy is normally a journey into greater degrees of cluelessness" (Flynn, Pottinger, and Betchelor 2010, 12). Allowing doctrine, policy, and manuals to be directly influenced by those with recent and direct understanding of tasks, objectives, contexts, opportunities, and challenges was predicted to result in more useful and relevant guidance for personnel preparing to enter a new operational environment. In the case of the Army this wiki was secure (so only active personnel could access the materials) and contributors were tagged to connect them to any additions or changes.

These same general approaches led to the rise of the online encyclopedia Wikipedia .com in the early 2000s. Rather than creating an encyclopedia written by a few subject matter experts (in a fashion that was hierarchical, bureaucratic, slow, cumbersome, and expensive) Wikipedia sought to create content by relying upon the contributions and edits of any user. This allowed for the collective generation of knowledge. The digital nature of the resulting content ensured entries could be modified at any point in time. This "real time" aspect of Wikipedia allowed content to be continually improved, updated, and corrected, a vital consideration for fluid topics where circumstances, environments, and experiences continually evolve. The digital format also enabled the creation of an encyclopedia with almost limitless content. Entries could be very long, could link readers to additional information, and could cover a range of topics too obscure for conventional encyclopedias. The "footprint" of this online volume quickly reached millions of entries in hundreds of language at almost no expense to the creators.

Since Wikipedia created the first large-scale demonstration of how this process could work, western societies have begun the creation of myriad forms of content. Knowledge, media, and materials generated by large numbers of users change when, where, how, and by whom ideas and insights are developed, expressed, and refined. Are there ways to unite the expertise, ideas, and insights of disparate individuals? Can allowing those at the bottom of the hierarchy to generate and "own" the content create a better product? Can diverse people who do not know each other be united to create documents and media that exceed what they could have achieved as isolated individuals? Might the resulting product be as good, or better, than what might have been produced through conventional modes and methods? Wikipedia and its progeny believe the answer to these and associated question is "yes."

How does this relate to police leadership and effective communication? Wikis challenge conventional thinking about who has the expertise to contribute to the creation of content and knowledge. The underlying presumption is that collective generation will, in the aggregate, lead to better outcomes. To be sure, this presumption will not always be correct and there are many reasons why we might suspect the Army's experiment might not achieve the desired results (not the least of which are culture and fear of being "tagged" to content those in charge view in a negative fashion). But it is also reasonable to question whether "top down" creation of knowledge produces information that is more often "better" than a "bottom up" approach. As this book goes to print, wikis and related tools remain as much a curiosity as a proven tool for effective governance. Wikipedia created a good, but imperfect, encyclopedia. Whether this means similar thinking can create better, though perhaps still imperfect, doctrine, policies, ideas, and media is not clear. Time, experience, and experimentation still need to define when and how wikis might be used in various contexts, such as police operations. Yet it is reasonable to ask whether an agency might achieve better outcomes by providing officers not with "top down" created mandates, but "bottom up" generated policies and procedures.

What these examples convey is an important idea within the context of communication. Effective communicators are willing to listen to and accept the ideas of others, even if they are followers or those external to the organization. Effective communicators are open to the reality that those in unconventional positions can provide keen ideas, important insights, and better ways to engage in routine practices, even if they are not police officers. This does not mean that police officers and police commanders are not also valid sources of ideas and information. This does not mean leaders should cede decision making authority to those below them and/or external to the agency (for a variety of liability concerns this would often be a poor decision). Wikis and other forms of social media and communication technology have the potential to enhance the ability of leaders to listen to others, to capture the wisdom of groups, and to make better decisions. At the end of the day, it may be the leader who does make the final choice, who does approve the final policy, and who, at times, acts against the recommendation of many others. The potential of emerging technologies is not to allow leaders to be perfect in making their decisions; rather, the potential is to help leaders make the right decision more often than they do using traditional methods and techniques.

Communication as Articulation

A significant reason why communication is important for effective leadership is reflected in general definitions of leadership. If leadership is the act of guiding a group or process into a preferred state, that act normally requires communication. Leadership implies change. It implies a modification of policies, procedures, goals, objectives, and directives. It requires that followers and peers understand the leader's vision of a preferred state. To understand and internalize that preferred state, others must be able to comprehend the leader's message, be it written or verbal. Leaders can use power, fear, coercion, and discipline to bring followers into compliance with changes; however, this aggressive style requires constant vigilance and supervision by the leader. In dynamic and (temporally and geographically) diffuse professions such as policing, it is difficult to monitor follower behavior. In many situations police leaders are likely to be more effective in bringing about change and influencing followers through the use of effective communication that articulates the value of change, helps followers understand how to operate in a manner consistent with that change, and persuades followers that supporting that change is the right thing to do.

Effective leaders are able to convey their vision, values, beliefs, rationales, and expectations. They are able to communicate clearly, ideally in both written and spoken modes. In some cases, that communication is closely linked with listening. To be effective a leader must engage in ongoing two-way dialog with followers, superiors, peers, and members of the public. Being able to effectively communicate in two-way dialog is a helpful attribute for front-line personnel. A patrol officer needs to be able to understand and defuse a tense situation, ideally without resorting to violence. An investigator needs to be able to interview a reluctant witness or question a potential suspect. Similarly, an effective leader is able to engage in productive dialog with citizens, officers, other government personnel, or members of other agencies. This communication can help ensure problems are resolved, crises are averted, and proper decisions are made.

Effective leaders not only have goals, but they also have the "ability to communicate those [goals] to the organization" (undersheriff, medium county agency). Communication by itself may not be sufficient to effectively lead. What is communicated also matters. Memos, meetings, advisory groups, and other forms of verbal and written communication are wonderful. Leaders need to be able to use these and other ways of communication as a part of their "ability to communicate clearly the objectives a particular task" (captain mid-size municipal agency). In the end, however, if these modalities do not advance followers' understanding of what the leader/organization is trying to achieve, less is gained. Communication is not just about delivering a clear message that is received and understood by others. Communication is also about helping others comprehend values, beliefs, preferred behaviors, goals, objectives, and desired outcomes. "One of the most important principles is the ability to be a good communicator. A leader must be able to relate the mission of the group to the group members in terms that are understood by everyone" (lieutenant large municipal agency). When, what, and how leaders communicate may not be the same for every audience. Strong leaders have the "ability to communicate effectively up and down the chain of command" (detective small municipal agency). They realize the ways they communicate with the public may differ from how they communicate with their superiors or personnel.

Effective leaders are able to leverage communication as a resource and tool to achieve desired outcomes. Leaders are responsible for articulating the function and mission of a unit or organization, which becomes even more important when the leader is an outsider to the unit or agency, or is seeking to bring a new vision or approach into the workplace. This includes ensuring both followers and relevant outsiders have a clear understanding of what the agency is seeking to accomplish, how those objectives are to be pursued, how outcomes will be assessed, and the potential consequences for either failing to achieve desired outcomes or using unacceptable methods. In policing contexts, leaders need to articulate:

- Desired outcomes: a reduction in crime; a modified use of force policy; or a change in personnel allocation.
- Preferred or required methods of achieving outcomes: a problem-oriented policing approach; the introduction of conducted electrical devices; or a move to ten-hour patrol shifts.
- How success will be measured: reported crimes or citizen surveys; fewer injuries to officers and arrestees; or more staffing during periods of peak demand.
- The parameters of acceptable conduct: within agency policy and applicable law; not to be used on minors or the elderly; or officers cannot sleep on the job.
- And, the consequences of failing to operate within those parameters: for these examples, internal disciplinary action and potential civil and/or criminal sanctions in extreme circumstances.

Communication is vital to articulate the who, what, when, where, why, and how questions regarding any group or organizations.

The role of communication as a tool for articulation can perhaps best be seen in Victor Vroom's Expectancy Motivation Theory (EMT) (1964). Vroom proposed that individual actions are predicated on motivation to behave in a specific manner. Motivation does not exist within a vacuum and its presence cannot be presumed. Vroom articulated that even a motivated person has to: understand the task they are expected to achieve; have the capacity (the skills) to perform the task; have the opportunity (time and resources) to perform the task; and understand both the rewards for performing the task and the punishment for failure. Within the EMT framework, when all of these elements are present, Vroom proposed most employees would perform the desired task. Communication is vital to ensuring the first and last of these four conditions; good listening skills are needed so leaders can understand if the employee believes the second and/or third conditions are not being provided. Employees cannot be expected to adapt new ways of performing their duties if they do not understand what they are being asked to do and why they are being asked to perform their duties in the prescribed manner. Even if they are willing to adapt how they perform their duties, employees need to have the necessary skills and opportunities.

A brief real world example illustrates how listening and communication intersect with EMT. In the mid-1990s the author worked on a research project with Motor City Police Department[1] (MCPD), an agency of about 200 officers located in the Midwest. The agency was undergoing a massive reorganization and realignment; the specifics of that effort are not wholly relevant to make a point in this discussion (see Schafer 2001, 2002 for more details). What the executives of the MCPD were attempting to do fundamentally altered how officers approached persistent community problems in the neighborhoods they policed. The reorganization also changed how patrol officers were expected to interact with peers working other shifts and those working other assignments (community policing, traffic, canine, and investigations). The approach combined elements of community-oriented and problem-oriented policing in a team based system.

The core problem driving the MCPD reorganization was a valid issue that needed to be corrected. The idea developed by MCPD was created with input from personnel throughout the agency. The leaders were honest, diligent, and intelligent. They were operating

---

1. A pseudonym.

with the best of intentions and were not pursuing change simply for its own sake. But one of the key problems that stymied the effort was a fundamental lack of communication and articulation (Schafer 2002). The executives had a somewhat-cloudy vision of how MCPD would work under the reorganization. Front-line personnel and first-line supervisors (sergeants and lieutenants) had a very murky understanding of what, when, how, and with whom officers were supposed to perform their duties. Officers believed they lacked sufficient training to operate in this changed environment and to satisfy new occupational expectations. Agency executives disagreed vehemently with this point, insisting officers had been given the tools and resources to engage in this new problem-solving strategy. Problems arose because regardless of who was correct, those charged with carrying out the modified duties believed they were not trained to do so. First-line supervisors reported they lacked sufficient rewards and punishments to bring personnel into compliance with the envisioned change. Officers and supervisors believed patrol officers lacked the time to engage in elective problem-solving efforts on a routine basis. In the end, the effort failed on all four elements of EMT: officers did not feel they understood what they were supposed to accomplish under the revised system; officers felt they lacked the skills to operate in a non-traditional manner; officers and shift supervisors believed the patrol division lacked the opportunity to engage in elective problem solving; and, first-line supervisors felt they did not have the ability to reward officers who adopted new work patterns or punish those who made no efforts to modify their habits.

Though the failures experienced in MCPD are a bit more complex than related here, motivated officers were not able to comply with the new directives, even when they had the desire to do so. With only a handful of exceptions, officers continued to engage in traditional policing operations, albeit in a slightly different organizational structure. When a new chief was hired the fundamental elements of the innovative approach were gutted and even the symbolic trappings of a more innovative approach to policing were stripped away. The failures in MCPD were not a failure of imagination, good intentions, or intelligent, dedicated personnel. They were, in large part, a failure to effectively listen and the failure of top leaders to articulate an understandable vision to core personnel, even after being clearly told such articulation was needed. Executives stubbornly maintained officers were being unnecessarily obstinate and had the clarity, training, and time to succeed in the new system. The executives failed to listen to the persistent and vocal calls from every quarter of the organization that more information, more training, and better communication were needed. The vision of MCPD executives was potentially a viable approach to policing. Where the efforts faltered was in execution, communication, and articulation. EMT is one of several theoretical perspectives that seek to explain and understand how articulation and communication influence outcomes within the workplace. Tests of this theory within policing contexts have produced mixed findings (c.f.,DeJong, Mastrofski, and Parks 2001; Johnson, 2006; Mastrofski, Ritti, and Snipes 1994), though this may be as much a function of the complexities of measuring social science theories in policing as a reflection on the veracity of Vroom's ideas.

Communication as Selling

At times the communication between a leader and various audiences is more akin to "selling" an idea or a vision. Within the context of Vroom's EMT it is important for individuals to understand what they are being asked to do, to have the resources and skills to comply, and to be rewarded or punished based on the level of compliance they demonstrate. In addition, there is something to be said for a leader who is able to convince followers that there are fundamentally valid reasons why they should embrace the leader's vision or request. Sticks (punishments) and carrots (rewards) are powerful motivators, but so is the belief that a leader is correct. Sticks and carrots require leaders to closely monitor follower conduct and output to ensure compliance. When followers are following because they believe the leader is correct, the leader can spend time and energy on advancing the vision rather than being wrapped up in supervising, disciplining, and rewarding followers.

This notion was richly articulated in American policing during the late 1980s and early 1990s as community policing began to influence at least the rhetoric of police operations, organizations, and leadership. Arthur Lurigio and Wesley Skogan (1994) aptly described the need for leaders to win the "hearts and minds" of personnel to bring about the implementation of community policing in an agency. In using this description Lurigio and Skogan suggested that leaders needed to follow the first principle of Vroom's theory (though they did not use that exact reference) by helping officers understand what community policing meant for the way they performed their duties. This was the process of winning over officers' minds; "an effective leader is one who is able to motivate his or her subordinates to achieve the objectives of the organization" (lieutenant medium municipal agency). This act was not, however, sufficient by itself. Lurigio and Skogan also contended that leaders needed to win over officers' hearts by convincing them that community policing was a better way to serve the jurisdiction and to bring about law and order. Explaining change or vision so officers understand a leader's intention is not enough. What is also needed is the ability to convince officers to comply not out of fear or motivation based in self-interests (rewards), but because officers fundamentally believe the change or vision is just, right, and effective. To accomplish the latter, a leader needs to be able to sell their vision to others.

What this means is that leaders must sometimes use communication to not only develop comprehension but also to develop "buy in" by those receiving a message. A follower can fully understand a leader's message, but may not believe in that message. The follower might still comply with the message out of fear or coercion. Compliance helps avert discipline and might pave the way toward favorable workplace outcomes, such as awards, promotions, and better duty assignments. This is less preferable in policing because the diffuse nature of police work means supervisors have a limited capacity to ensure subordinates follow out of fear of punishment or desire for rewards. There are too many chances for followers to engage in symbolic followership and to manage appearances that they are compliant, while they continue to do their jobs the way they wish (see Manning 1997). Securing followership not through fear but through persuasion is preferable. Effective leaders embrace this reality and use communication to both convey changes, visions, goals, and objectives, as well as to sell others on the idea of moving in the direction described by the leader. Leaders are able to "communicate expectations clearly and are able to motivate their people to produce or complete tasks" (lieutenant large county agency). They have "communications skills that are persuasive [in demonstrating] that the goals are 'right' and worthwhile" (lieutenant medium municipal agency).

To accomplish these objectives leaders not only express answers to who, what, where, when, and how questions (the mechanical aspects of a situation) but also "why" questions (see Sinek 2009 for a helpful discussion of this process in corporate contexts). They help followers understand why change is being pursued and sell followers on the idea that change is desirable, something that should be supported, and worthy of pursuit. When and how leaders sell an idea may vary based on the audience. The way to sell an idea to the public might differ from the way to sell an idea to a squad of detectives or a shift of patrol officers. This does not mean leaders are disingenuous with how they communicate, but rather that they recognize the sales pitch must differ based on situation, context, and audience. What matters, however, is that the leader understands that successful outcomes often begin with anticipating and addressing the "why" questions of those they seek to influence. Even though followers might not always agree with those answers, having that explanation at the onset might be a powerful way to enhance the likelihood that followers will generally adapt their behavior in the desired manner.

Communication as Reinforcement

Listening and communicating allow leaders to bring about more effective change and leverage greater influence. By listening to superiors, peers, followers, and constituents, a leader can understand their perspectives and concerns. That input guides the leader's decisions or actions. It allows the leader to better understand the perspectives, experiences, concerns, and beliefs of members of those groups. It allows the leader to identify problems, solutions, and opportunities. It enables followers to have a clear understanding of what outcomes they are expected to pursue, how to do so, why those outcomes matter, and what benefits will accrue to the follower and organization. As aptly characterized by a lieutenant from a small municipal agency, an effective leader

> is a person with clear vision and direction of purpose. Clearly communicates his/her vision and everything (ie budget, personnel, staffing, etc.) reflects direction and commitment to vision/purpose. No one in the dept. should be unable to understand and articulate. Just what we are trying to accomplish.

Whether the leader thinks the message has been articulated is far less important than whether potential followers agree with that assessment.

Even if leaders' actions are contrary to the wishes of a group or individual, understanding that differences of opinion exist ensures more favorable outcomes. First, leaders need to have listened enough to know that an action or choice is going to be upsetting to some people. Second, leaders need to understand why that is the case; they needs to have insight into why a group or individual will have an adverse reaction. That knowledge enables the leaders to make necessary modifications in the process of implementing change. Third, communication directed back toward constituent groups can help them to understand the leaders' actions and choices; "communicating with those being led [allows the leader] to explain (when appropriate), listen, and educate" (lieutenant large county agency).

Communication is a tool to reinforce a leader's values, mission, goals, and preferences. The work of followers can be validated when the leader uses communication as a method of "recognizing/rewarding . . . success" (captain major state agency). Even simple verbal or written communiqués can be used to let a follower know the leader recognizes and appreciates performance, assistance, or support. Special accomplishments can be noted with "atta boy/girl" memos. More significant and public forms of communication (memos sent not to just an employee and her/his supervisor, but to larger portions of the workforce; public awards ceremonies recognizing exemplary performance) expand the audience that is aware of the recognition given by the leader. These types of reinforcing messages have the potential to serve a dual purpose as a leader seeks to influence and change an organization or practice. The communication has a specific validating effect by letting recipients know their work is recognized and appreciated. This helps ensure at least temporary motivation for that employee. Messages can have a general validating effect when a larger portion of the workforce receives them. Seeing the recognition and rewards directed at a co-worker can provide other employees with validation, reinforcement of the mission, and clarification of organizational priorities and preferences.

These communication tools do not assure the leader of successfully providing either specific or general validation within the workforce. In some instances even well-meaning leaders will be viewed as pandering, patronizing, or playing favorites. The audience observing the recognition being directed at another employee may not be persuaded to change their performance or priorities. By themselves these tools are likely insufficient to ensure change efforts succeed. Used in concert with other approaches, however, leaders hope to ensure their desired change is achieved in the long-term aggregate level. Leaders cannot use principles such as Vroom's EMT or the idea of winning over "hearts and minds" if they fail to clearly communicate with their employees. Listening and communication are at the cornerstone of effective leader-follower interactions. They serve to help the leader express a vision or plan, articulate why followers should follow, receive feedback and concerns, and reinforce the salience and viability of their objectives.

Conclusions

Taken as a whole, communication is a process for gleaning knowledge from anywhere it can be found inside and around the organization. Listening is learning for a leader; learning about problems, learning about challenges, learning about opportunities, and learning what followers and constituents feel they need. Communication is not just about listening and speaking, but also integrating what is heard. It is a process of recognizing problems, identifying solutions, capitalizing on opportunities, engaging followers, and ensuring that visions are understood and embraced by those performing the core work tasks of a unit or organization. Leaders use communication as a set of tools and practices that create methods by which input can be received when needed, even if it was not sought (i.e., open door policies, real or virtual). Communication can also assist leaders in endeavoring to encourage, engage, influence, and learn from followers while minimizing resistance to the leaders' ideas and messages.

Though on the surface communication would seem straightforward and easy to achieve, it is often a point of failure for police leaders. Police executive and trainer Jack Enter (2006) notes that all too often, police organizations (especially larger agencies) primarily communicate when there is a problem. Officers receive fewer explanations of "why" they are being asked to change; the message is simply to change. Enter challenges leaders to think about ways to improve lines of communication throughout their organization in creative ways. He provides helpful ideas that even executives of large agencies can use to create more personalized contacts with personnel. Finally, Enter challenges executives to communicate with all personnel in the organization, not just sworn officers. Civilian support staff have important ideas and needs which require good communication. Throughout the organization, communication is a tool leaders can use to demonstrate their care, compassion, and accessibility, though of course those traits must genuinely exist.

Effective leaders understand that communication is dynamic. The ways in which leaders listen to and communicate with followers is variable and situational. Younger audiences will prefer technology-assisted methods of communication (i.e., text messaging, social media applications, the use of blogs and wikis, etc.), while older audiences are likely to prefer face-to-face interactions. This may require separate or redundant communication modes and methods depending on when, where, how, and with whom leaders seek to communicate. What likely sets effective communicators aside from others is the recognition that the burden is on the leader to adjust his or her method of communication to the audience he or she wishes to reach (Kidd and Braziel 1999). A chief taking command of a large agency or an agency employing a large proportion of younger officers will need to be comfortable using technology to receive and send information to her potential followers. If she is not comfortable with using such approaches and refuses to learn about the power of these new technologies, she is likely limiting her efficacy at the onset.

In some situations it is not what leaders communicate, but how they communicate, that shapes follower reactions. In an essay describing servant-leadership approaches to supervision, Max Douglas (2003) encouraged leaders to become active listeners in order to develop relationships based on trust and respect. Douglas contended that effective leaders are effective stewards of their organizations who find ways to involve others in decision-making processes and to develop favorable relationships. Receiving a message more often than sending one is instructive; though not scientifically precise, the ratio of two ears and one mouth might serve as a helpful guide in considering the dynamics of communication. Accomplishing these objectives requires that leaders listen and communicate. These acts help leaders unify workers and external constituents (i.e., community members). They also reinforce a vision for change in a way that can help leaders encourage people to do what they otherwise might not do (Murphy and Drodge 2004).

Effective leaders recognize that being clear in how they articulate their vision, values, orders, and other messages (verbally or in writing) is not in and of itself sufficient to ensure complete communication. Every reader has likely observed the problems that arise when a leader is effective in communicating to followers, but fails to truly listen. Listening does not mean leaders always do what others request. Likewise, listening is not an empty process where the leader allows others to speak, but then acts in a unilateral fashion. Effective leaders are effective communicators and understand that others have important opinions, insights, ideas, and observations that can guide the leader's decision making process. Whether those "others" are inside or outside the agency, above or below the leader, they may offer keen insight to guide the leader's decisions. In some instances listening is not a tool used to inform the leader's decisions or understanding; rather, sometimes listening is about providing others with a voice and a chance to vent their frustrations and opinions. Those addressing the leader may not be looking for anything other than validation that someone in a position of authority is hearing and respecting them. Effective leaders understand the power of listening and the importance of developing and maintaining two-way communication with those they seek to influence.

Chapter 5

Delegation and Empowerment

The best leader is the one who has sense enough to pick good men to do what he wants done, and self-restraint enough to keep from meddling with them while they do it.

—Theodore Roosevelt

Effective Leadership involves getting goals accomplished with the resources you have in an efficient manner and in a way that everyone involved has ownership and accountability for the issues and also share in the success of the mission. Effective leaders encourage participation and risk taking and are willing to let subordinates make mistakes.

—Major, large municipal agency

In Chapter One a distinction was made between the act of management and the act of leadership. Both activities have their time and place and an effective leader must have at least moderate skills as a manager. Among the many tasks, patterns, and styles leaders must balance is the distinction between creating a democratic workplace and exhibiting control when situations and circumstances necessitate a more directive leadership style (Tannenbaum and Schmidt 1958). Employees often want to have a voice in their workplace, to be consulted on issues within their area of expertise, to provide input in major decisions, to be recognized for having experience and education of relevance in the workplace, and to work for supervisors who lean toward consultative and autocratic leadership styles (Harrison and Pelletier 1987; Steinheider and Wuestewald 2008).[1] As discussed in Chapter Four, leaders can benefit by involving followers in the decision making process; employee empowerment is often expedient both in terms of achieving better decisions and fostering a more motivated, engaged, and satisfied workforce (Argyris 1964; Gray, Stohr-Gillmore, and Lovrich 1991; Steinheider and Wuestewald 2008). The acts of delegation and empowerment are frequently discussed under the umbrella of democratic leadership—approaches that provide the governed with a chance to shape and direct how they are led and to what ends.

Delegation is the process of granting others the authority to make choices and take action. Delegation and direction are similar, as both tend to involve asking followers to achieve specific outcomes. The general distinction between the two is that a directed employee is told how to achieve that outcome, while the delegated employee is given license to make choices on his/her own (though often within defined parameters of law, policy, resources, etc.). Empowerment is the process of allowing followers the right to exercise greater

---

1. These statements certainly do not describe all employees and workplaces. Some employees will prefer very directive forms of leadership in which they are told what to do and are expected to carry out a task with precision and consistency. It is widely accepted, however, that most employees, particularly younger and more educated employees, prefer organizational dynamics that provide them with a role in making decisions and a voice in operations (see generally Conger and Riggio 2007).

degrees of authority and independence. Democratic leadership styles are not used to "pass the buck," avoid making tough choices, or foist potential blame on others. Likewise, participatory approaches cannot be symbolic actions on the part of the leader (c.f., Pfeffer 1981; Tannenbaum and Schmidt 1958). They must be genuine attempts to hear the ideas, opinions, expertise, and input of others. On the latter issue, Tannenbaum and Schmidt insightfully wrote that

> If, for example, he [the leader] actually intends to make a certain decision himself, but the subordinate group gets the impression that he has delegated this authority, considerable confusion and resentment are likely to follow. Problems may also occur when the boss uses a "democratic" façade to conceal the fact that he has already made a decision which he hopes the group will accept as its own (1958, 98).

To an extent, empowered subordinates are allowed to lead themselves and, in some cases, others. Kenneth Blanchard and Paul Hersey aptly noted "leadership is done *with* people, not *to* people" (1996, 44, emphasis in the original). Leaders who delegate and empower do not simply lead others, they lead *with* others by providing chances for followers to participate in decision-making and the very process of leading the organization. Leadership may work best when it is a mutual process. This does not imply the leader is not in a position of greater power, but rather that power ought to be wielded in a restrained, benign, and cooperative manner.

Engaging in delegation and empowerment requires that supervisors focus on positive and good behavior exhibited by employees. This is an all-too-unusual emphasis in police organizations. Policing as a profession tends to focus on the negative. Officers are conditioned to notice violations, offenses, unusual circumstances, and that something is wrong with a situation. This may easily carry over into how a new supervisor approaches his or her duties (Heifetz and Laurie 2001). The effective beat cop who was skilled at controlling the public now seeks ways to control subordinate personnel as a first line supervisor. Because bureaucracy is focused on control of people, processes, and behavior, it tends to result in supervisors using "sticks" to regulate actions over the use of "carrots" to motivate and reward (Angell 1971). Bureaucracies also overemphasize the use of policies to instruct personnel what to do, rather than limiting policies to defining what personnel should not do and allowing the use of structured discretion (Wilson 1968). Both individual (supervisor predisposition) and organizational (bureaucracy) forces work against the widespread use of delegation and empowerment in police organizational environments.

Delegation and empowerment work best when supervisors emphasize potential and capacity in their workforce. To the point of the Roosevelt quote at the start of this chapter, leaders need to have the wisdom and courage to recognize one of the best ways to leverage influence and maximize outcomes is to point followers in the right direction, grant them the proper resources to do good things, and then allow them the freedom to do good work. This is not an easy task or a common practice (Witte, Travis, and Langworthy 1990) as it requires that leaders trust followers, a mindset in complete opposition to traditional ways of supervising police personnel and administering police organizations (Angell 1971; Enter 2006). Police organizations, like most public sector bureaucracies, create structures, policies, and protocols that treat employees as if they are risks to be controlled rather than educated and informed workers who can be trusted to use their skills to achieve organizational objectives (Wilson 1968).

Three examples illustrate the concepts of delegation and empowerment by detailing their opposites. First, a shift supervisor exercises the authority to direct officers in the use of discretionary patrol time. At the start of each shift, the supervisor instructs officers what areas (parks, school zone, housing complexes, and business districts) and issues (prostitution, speeding, loitering, and rowdy youth) need particular attention and focus. Second, a police chief decides the shift assignment process needs modification within her agency. In the past, officers in this agency participated in an annual bid for shift assignments based on seniority. Officers have complained they do not like committing to working a shift for an entire year and they are requesting change. The chief unilaterally revises the policy based on her belief the correct solution is to bid on shifts every quarter. Third, in response to a highly publicized and controversial incident, a sheriff's department implements changes in its use of force policies and reporting requirements. Any time officers make an arrest they are required to document whether force was used and/or resistance encountered. It is an election year so the sheriff is quite concerned about compliance. He begins to follow up with deputies when they report force was not involved in an arrest to determine if the report is factual. Historically, shift supervisors and the chief deputy for patrol operations were charged with ensuring deputies were compliant and accurate in filing all paperwork and reports.

The three examples here are intentionally black-and-white. Certainly nuanced modification to these vignettes could create channels for delegation and empowerment. As presented, however, the fictive supervisors and executives demonstrated a high degree of management and centralized control in their decision making. Subordinates were directed where to patrol and what to enforce. Officers were informed of the new policy for shift selection. Deputies faced extensive scrutiny from the agency executive, circumventing normal monitoring protocols using intermediate supervisors. The subordinates in these examples were allowed no substantive delegation and empowerment. They were not allowed to exercise discretion, provide input, or demonstrate professional judgment. They were not treated as a resource from which solutions to problems might be derived. They were not trusted to be compliant with departmental policies in the absence of evidence to the contrary. They were presumptively guilty until they demonstrated their innocence. The consequences of a low degree of delegation and empowerment can be profound within the workplace (Harrison and Pelletier 1987; Steinheider and Wuestewald 2008; Wycoff and Skogan 1994).

Traditional Police Bureaucracies, Delegation, & Empowerment

The traditional hierarchical model observed in police organizations is intended to create centralized control, consolidated decision making, tightly regulated discretion, and a high degree of accountability. Agencies appear highly structured, bound tightly by rules, and emphasize vertical, horizontal, and interpersonal power relationships (King 2003; Mastrofski 1998; Sklansky 2007; Steinheider and Wuestewald 2008). This vision of police professionalism emerged in the early decades of the 20th century when there was a legitimate need to reform police organizations to address widespread and systematic corruption and abuses of authority (Uchida 2010). Police leaders and executives attempted to implement policies, procedures, and protocols to regulate behavior, discretion, and decisions made by officers throughout their agencies, particularly those working the front line. The geographic and temporal nature of policing has always made it difficult to effectively monitor and supervise personnel working patrol and other assignments within the community (Walker 1977). This situation has improved with the proliferation of the automobile, two-way radio, cell phone, and GPS technology, but the challenges endure. Policing remains a relatively low-visibility occupation (Brown 1988).[2]

The police professionalism movement of the mid-20th century provided a number of desirable and favorable improvements for the law enforcement profession. Unfortunately, the movement also created an emphasis on means over ends. Police procedures were increasingly standardized, despite the fact that the problems officers confront vary considerably across space, time, citizens, and situations. Agencies continued to emphasize reports, procedures, and protocols over efficacy, equity, equality, outcomes, relationships, and community betterment (Wilson 2000). A major factor driving the rise of community policing rhetoric and practice was the realization that bureaucratic imperatives had trumped improving American communities (Goldstein 1990; Trojanowicz, Kappeler, and Gaines, 2002). Officers and agencies were focused too much on how duties were being performed at the expense of considering what ends and objectives were being achieved. In reality, the hierarchical model never yielded the intended level of control (Crank 1998). Officers still enjoyed (and do enjoy) a wide range of discretion and autonomy in performing their duties, particularly matters that are of low visibility and are less serious, which still characterizes a majority of the matters handled by patrol personnel (Brown 1988).

Given this historical trajectory and the reality of control and discretion in American policing, delegation and empowerment make logical sense. Even where supervisors seek to exercise very tight control, most officers (particularly those working field assignments) can find numerous ways to circumvent edicts, imperatives, policies, and directives intended to control discretion. Officers may learn to manage the appearance of compliance in order to avoid being sanctioned by their micromanaging or controlling supervisor, while still being able to perform many duties as they see fit (Manning 1997). Though officers can learn to manage appearances and negotiate what they perceive to be "bullshit" policies, procedures, and directives from departmental executives and supervisors, those processes do invoke a degree of stress and aggravation (Crank and Caldero 1991). Some argue it has contributed to cynicism and other unhealthy aspects of the culture of American policing (Crank 1998).

The Acts of Delegation and Empowerment

Public safety organizations routinely confront situations where leaders and personnel must make split-second decisions (Blanchard and Hersey 1996). It is not feasible to mobilize a committee charged with making decisions about specific uses of deadly force, vehicle pursuits, or searches conducted in exception to routine evidentiary and legal standards.

---

2. One reviewer correctly noted that policing is increasingly a high-visibility occupation that is simply difficult to effectively supervise. The increasing prevalence of small, portable, and networked recording devices is changing the level of visibility and transparency in routine police operations. Recent court rulings have strengthened the rights of citizens to record and distribute public encounters with the police.

Both legal and practical standards necessitate that all levels of public safety personnel must routinely make decisions. Leaders must make tactical and operational choices, and followers must be willing and able to act on those orders without questioning the decision. Recognizing this reality, too many police organizations and leaders cling to antiquated and centralized decision making about matters that could involve and engage a wide range of employees in support of a variety of leadership objectives. These circumstances were aptly characterized by Steinheider and Wuestewald, noting that "modern police organizations remain largely centralized in their decision-making, structurally vertical, rule bound, and mired in power relationships . . . These limitations are seen as impediments to the development of adaptive, learning organizations capable of leveraging their human assets and appropriately responding to the dynamics of modern social expectations" (2008, 145).

Effective leaders engage in delegation (assigning tasks to others) and empowerment (granting followers with the authority to make independent decisions) for two key reasons. First, those charged with making decisions often have incomplete information and perspectives on an issue. Involving others in decision making processes ensures communication is used as a positive tool to facilitate the use of relevant information in support of better outcomes. Second, many employees derive satisfaction and increased morale when they are given the opportunity to contribute more than just manual labor. Early leadership scholarship and inquiry was largely focused on leaders; who they were and their habits and attributes. By the middle of the 20th century, leadership research began to look not only at leaders, but also at organizational dynamics, the operations and functions of work groups, and employee morale (Levy 2010). Scholars shifted their focus to include consideration of what motivates and satisfies followers and what practices create more functional organizational dynamics. Emerging from this research effort was the realization that allowing employees to assist in making decisions and exercise some degree of personal judgment and freedom results in employees who are more satisfied with the job, work more diligently, and are less likely to separate from the organization.

Nothing in this discussion ignores the fact that in any organization (particularly police agencies) there are decisions that must be made decisively and authoritatively with little or no consultation. These can include decisions with short time-horizons (i.e., a leader needing to make an immediate decision in a tactical situation) or decisions that will clearly be against the preferences of employees (i.e., when a leader is hired to reform a unit or organization). A large number of decisions made by police leaders do not, however, fall into these categories. One of the greatest challenges leaders confront can be determining when and in what ways to allow followers latitude to perform duties within the organization. That employees want discretion and latitude to perform their duties in the manner they deem most appropriate is well established (Conger and Riggio 2007), particularly in occupations where employees consider themselves to be professionals. The nature of civil liability as it relates to policing makes this situation even more challenging than in other types of organizations and industries. Supervisors may be concerned that allowing employees the right to make unilateral decisions will create liability for the leader or organization. This liability could take the form of citizen complaints or legal action against the agency, but more centrally supervisors might be concerned with creating a threat toward their professional standing within a bureaucratic entity.

Beyond street-level concerns with operational discretion, leaders also wrestle with how much input and involvement followers should have in shaping organizational and unit-level decision making. To what extent should employees be allowed to shape policy, budgeting, and strategic planning? How deeply should the leader solicit and utilize the input and ideas of their followers? When should the leader make decisions unilaterally or using minimal input, when should leaders seek broader input, how broad should that input be, and when should a leader partially or fully allow groups of subordinates to make key decisions? There are numerous permutations to how a leader can allow varying levels of delegation and empowerment to involve and engage employees. Responses from the National Academy participants consistently suggested effective leaders were able to take a balanced approach in the degree to which they directed, managed, supervised, and guided their followers. Effective leaders were cast as those who were able to delegate tasks to their employees and empower their followers to work within defined parameters in making decisions, solving problems, and achieving desired outcomes.

Respecting that leaders must be allowed to ultimately make some decisions, followers may value and appreciate situations in which their leader "allows others to have ownership in the task and results" (lieutenant large municipal agency). Delegating responsibilities and empowering employees serves a number of important purposes. It can ensure various perspectives and input are received to inform the decision making process. It can provide followers with a sense of satisfaction and engagement in the workplace. It can also maximize unit or organizational outcomes by allowing those doing the core work to attend to those work tasks. Leaders may enhance their efficacy through this step by creating employees who are more engaged, satisfied, and committed to their employing organization, their assigned unit, or specific types of change and innovation (Ford 2007; Ford, Weissbein, and Plamondon 2003; Wycoff and Skogan 1994).

National Academy Perspectives

Effective leadership delegates rights and responsibilities to subordinates. Though leaders might define objectives, parameters, and limitations (i.e., time, resources, and constraints) others are allowed to make key decisions about how to reach the desired outcome. An analogy can be drawn to this process by considering a trip and a map. The delegating and empowering leader articulates the objective (get from our present location to a defined destination) and defines the limitations and parameters (the four boundaries of the map) that might include financial and resource limitations, legal and policy restrictions, and broader objectives. The leader delegates planning the trip to others and empowers them to carry out the journey. The leader or supervisor defines the "direction they want the dept/unit to go, but allow subordinates to get there using their minds and ideas" (sergeant mid-size county agency). Empowering leaders "are flexible . . . allow employee to do it there [sic] way if it is within guidelines." If there are "5 ways to do [a task] & they [the employee] do way 3 & the boss likes way 1, [the boss] lets them do it way 3" (captain small municipal agency).

An effective leader has a "vision of what needs to be done and where an organization needs to go empower" personnel (captain mid-size municipal agency). To bring this vision to fruition they are willing to empower others "to lead a group of individuals or [the] organization from point A to B." The "leader points the way and his people are the ones that take them there" (commander medium municipal agency). Delegation and empowerment is not being lazy. This approach concedes that a leader cannot monitor everything and everyone within their span of control. When leaders are willing to allow subordinates to exercise educated and professional judgment it is presumed that better results are achieved. Delegation and empowerment can also mean that leaders involve others in the decision making process, even if the leader remains in control of a particular process. An effective leader will "seek input of qualified subordinates" (lieutenant small municipal agency) and "allows for input from subordinates . . . in making decisions" (sergeant mid-size county agency).

A leader who is willing to "relinquish decision making to the subordinates below" him or her (lieutenant medium municipal agency) demonstrates a degree of trust in others working in the organization. The sheriff in the earlier example circumvented normal modes of supervision and oversight. By individually following up with deputies to question them about incidents and their reports, does this sheriff demonstrate trust and confidence his employees, including shift supervisors and the chief deputy? "Effective leadership is leadership that creates an atmosphere of trust and confidence within the agency" (sergeant small municipal agency). Leaders must trust in order to be trusted. Leaders must be trusted in order to be effective, particularly when they seek to bring about more substantial change within the organization. Leaders recognize preferred outcomes can often best be achieved when they allow "personnel to be independent thinkers and take chances" in the pursuit of goals and objectives (lieutenant small municipal agency).

To truly be effective, delegation and empowerment cannot be symbolic or ceremonial events (Tannenbaum and Schmidt 1958). This parallels the need for listening to be a legitimate and genuine process. Leaders may not always follow the advice and input from any given group of followers or constituents, but it needs to be clear the chosen course of action was informed by and formulated with the input derived from others. Participatory systems only work when they are perceived to be genuine in shaping decision making within the organization. Leaders engage in delegation and empowerment in order to achieve their objectives and advance the organization. Their personal standing and advancement should not be a central motivation in using these systems. "Effective leaders are willing to do the right thing for the organization by getting employees involved and giving the credit to them instead of taking all the credit" (captain large municipal agency).

A supervisor from a large federal agency gave credit to President Harry Truman for having an insightful observation on this issue. President Truman is commonly credited with expressing that "It is amazing what you can accomplish if you do not care who gets the credit." It is not about individual glory, it is about organizational success. It is not about the leader, it is about the organization and personnel. Leaders may realize that efficacy is achieved by "giving your officers some freedom to accomplish the stated goal or mission" of the unit or organization (captain mid-size municipal agency). A leader cannot be everywhere at all times within the organization. Delegation of tasks and responsibilities allows him or her to achieve goals, objectives, mandates, and mission. This does, however, require a degree of trust in followers and other personnel. In reality, every leader does some measure of delegation. A shift sergeant cannot be at every call handled by her squad. A detective supervisor cannot personally be involved in every investigation carried out by his investigative staff. The question becomes where the supervisor draws "the line" between exercising no oversight and doing the job him or herself. How much latitude are detectives allowed in deciding how to conduct their own investigations in the way they see fit? How much discretion are patrol officers allowed in determining whether and how to address persistent problems in their community or precinct?

Delegation & Empowerment in Policing Applications

Traditional hierarchical structures noted in policing tend to inhibit the empowerment of employees (Skogan 2004). Beginning in the 1970s, police organizations began to experiment with ways to overcome the historical limitations and pathologies associated with the preva-lence of excessive control, micromanaging, and directive leadership styles. One of the more common alternatives subject to experimentation since the 1970s were approaches that fall under the umbrella of participative management (PM) systems. PM systems "bring together the major stakeholders in police organizations in collaborative decision-making" (Steinheider and Wuestewald 2008, 146). In addition to improving organiza-tional operations and decisions, PM models are utilized with the intention of improving "labor-management relations, building employee commitment, improving public service, and reducing rank-and-file resistance to police reform initiatives" (146).[3] Dr. Brigitte Steinheider and Chief Todd Wuestewald (2008) have documented efforts to create a PM and shared leadership system in the Broken Arrow (Oklahoma) Police Department (BAPD), one of the most prominent PM efforts in policing in the past decade. Broken Arrow is a community of 95,000 residents in the Tulsa metropolitan area and BAPD employs around 175 personnel. BAPD had been structured with a traditional top-down autocratic hier-archy for making decisions, which tended to alienate employees from management deci-sions and fueled tension between the administration and various labor organizations. Chief Wuestewald rose through the ranks of BAPD and assumed his command in 2003, taking charge of an agency with a documented history of low morale, perceived poor communications, and officers who resented upper administration.

Shortly after Wuestewald was sworn in as chief, BAPD created a "representative employee steering committee . . . to assist senior management in running the agency" (Steinheider and Wuestewald 2008, 149). The Leadership Team was comprised of 12 individuals rep-resenting the patrol officer union, management, and an assortment of divisions, ranks, and functions throughout the agency. The Team was empowered with the authority to make policy and direct the activities of the various elements of BAPD; the team was given the authority to "make binding decisions on a wide range of policy issues, working condi-tions, and strategic matters" (150). The Chief is only allowed to override the Team if a decision violates labor laws, is outside of budgetary restrictions, or creates the potential for civil liability; in effect, the Chief is largely subservient to the decisions of the Team. The BAPD system does allow the Chief to decide on the Team's agenda, thus issues referred to the Team for consideration (any employee can refer an issue or item through assorted mechanisms) do not always receive attention. Once the Chief refers a matter, however, he is bound by the Team's decision. The Chief did not craft this gate-keeper restriction to rel-egate the Team to a symbolic gesture. Rather, it is a concession to reality. Though the Chief opted to share leadership and control, he remains ultimately responsible for the agency and its operations. If decisions go awry, the job of the Chief, not the jobs of mem-bers of the Team, would be vulnerable.

Through 2008, the Team's focus had largely been on policy matters, not routine and daily operational concerns. For the latter, BAPD does still rely on a more conventional chain of command and hierarchical division of labor. Likewise, while the Team had re-vised aspects of the agency's disciplinary system; when violations occurred supervisors still retained control over determining sanctions within the parameters of that revised system. In 2005 BAPD replicated a 2002 study of employee attitudes and perceptions in

---

3. Steinheider and Wuestewald provide a helpful and concise summary of experiential and re-search evidence regarding the use and benefits of participative management and shared leadership approaches, both in general and in the context of policing (2008, 146–148).

an effort to determine how sworn personnel in BAPD perceived the Leadership Team (and by extension, participatory management). The results were quite favorable. In contrast to the 2002 data, in 2005 BAPD officers were more likely to report:

- the chief and the agency's majors were attentive to officer needs.
- officer input received serious consideration and officers were being recognized and rewarded for good work.
- qualified applicants were being hired, promotions were fair and equitable, discipline was handled impartially, and there were incentives to encourage good performance.

Additional data reported by Steinheider and Wuestewald (2008) paint a cautious, but favorable picture of PM in the form of the Leadership Team.

The BAPD experience is a single agency observed over a relatively short period of time. It cannot be assumed the Leadership Team or other PM systems would achieve the same results in other agencies, though limited scholarship in PM in policing has been favorable (Adams, Rohe, and Arcury 2002; Fridell 2004; Gray, Stohr-Gillmore, and Lovrich 1992; Skogan and Hartnett 1997; Wycoff and Skogan 1994). It also is not yet clear whether the Leadership Team will sustain positive outcomes in BAPD. As officers acclimate to the system, the "halo effect" of a new and radically different leadership approach might wane or generate new forms of discontent. Despite these limitations, the BAPD experience builds upon a body of research literature that suggests delegation and empowerment can have profound and positive influences on police personnel and police organizations.

Why Delegation & Empowerment Matter

In a democratic society the police play important roles both protecting the rights citizens enjoy and reflecting the idealized vision of the relationship between government and the governed. To achieve the latter, clear boundaries and restraints are imposed upon the power and authority of the police. Citizens accept these restrictions will mean some guilty parties might go free, but those "false negative" errors are deemed more palatable than the risk of making over-zealous errors that infringe on the Constitutional rights of the innocent (false positive errors). Within this situation, police organizations themselves operate in a curiously paradoxical manner. The police uphold and reflect democratic values, but police organizations often operate in a fashion that is decidedly non-democratic (Silverstri 2007). Writing about reformation efforts involving the South African police, Marks and Fleming observed "external democratization on the part of the police can only be expected to come to light if internal organizational democratization is manifest" (2004, 800). If a society expects its police to protect the proper balance between government and the governed, police agencies must first demonstrate this balance in their own operations (i.e., relations between the organization and supervisors, and those who perform the core functions of the agency).

In addition to this symbolic value, delegation and empowerment are acts of simple expedience. Police supervisors cannot be present in all places and times when personnel make decisions. Though policies, procedures, reporting requirements, and recording devices can all help to ensure employees are held accountable for performance standards and expectations, discretion is necessary in police operations (Klockars 1985). The British policing system is built in part on the ethos of "policing by consent," which holds that if policing is carried out in a manner the public finds acceptable, the public will cooperate with the police—they will consent to be policed. If the public finds the tactics and role of policing to be objectionable, the police will have to use force, coercion, and heavy-handed tactics to exert control over citizens. Parallels might be seen with leadership in policing. Police officers consent to be led. Where they approve of the philosophy, vision, tactics, and standards of those in charge, officers will generally be cooperative followers. When officers do not embrace or approve of a supervisor and/or his/her style of leadership, the supervisor is likely to have to use greater control, coercion, discipline, and authority to secure basic levels of cooperation (Villiers 2003).[4]

Just as citizens who do not consent to be policed are likely to cooperate in public, while subverting in private, the supervisor who leads by coercion is likely to appear to have tight control over their subordinate personnel. Whether those officers actually behave in the desired fashion when carrying out their duties outside of scrutiny and oversight is far less likely. Leadership by consent is a desirable and pragmatic approach because officers can circumvent, subvert, and sabotage even the most iron-fisted and strong-willed leader. A supervisor who leads with the consent of subordinate personnel can focus on actually achieving their vision and goals, rather than spending inordinate amounts of time focused on compliance. The leader can focus on achieving desired ends in the workplace, rather than excessively monitoring the means with which personnel carry out assigned tasks. The leader can actually lead, rather than focusing energy and attention on control, direction, management, and supervision that do little to advance the achievement of individual and organizational objectives.

Consider the Field Training Officer (FTO) model that has become standard in most police departments. The FTO is a leader for his or her assignee. A rookie officer on their first day out of the academy is not likely to be delegated tremendous responsibility. That officer has "book" intelligence, but may be viewed as lacking "street smarts." The new officer may not be familiar with even basic matters such as the topography and geography of the area he is patrolling. He may not yet know street names, compass directions, and various routes he might take from point A to point B in order to avoid traffic and vehicle choke points (bodies of water, interstate overpasses, railroad crossings, etc.). At the onset, the FTO may delegate little authority and power to the rookie officer. The latter might be expected to ride in the passenger seat and passively observe much of what transpires during the shift. Very quickly, however, a competent and dutiful FTO is likely to start delegating tasks. The rookie is expected to operate the radio, computer, emergency lights, and other equipment. The rookie might soon be expected to drive, provide navigation information, and even be the point officer on routine traffic stops or minor calls for service.

As a new officer proceeds through the Field Training process (with the same or a successive series of FTOs), he or she is normally delegated increasing levels of responsibility as time passes. As the rookie demonstrates mastery of basic tasks, additional responsibilities are allocated to ensure she or he has the competence to perform the core of police

---

4. Even these approaches will not guarantee officers perform the expected duties in the desired fashion. One of the chapter reviewers related the challenges of a lieutenant who "had a veteran officer do nothing for 2½ months, then in the final two weeks of the review period, write the minimal amount of tickets, make a cursory misdemeanor arrest, and got his 3 out of 5 grade, for the period, 4 times a year, making him immune to counseling or re-training." Smart officers can learn to "game" any system. Nothing in this book should imply it is easy to motivate or influence recalcitrant officers who do not wish to perform.

patrol work. Being the lead officer on a traffic stop for speeding evolves into taking the lead in stopping a suspected drunk driver. Being responsible for taking a vandalism report evolves into being in charge when handling a call for a neighborhood dispute. Why is the rookie delegated increasing responsibilities? Because other officers need him or her to mature into a fully functional and competent officer. They cannot "babysit" that officer through her or his career. Many FTO systems end with a "shadow" phase in which the rookie officer, now months separated from the Academy, works with an FTO who is in street clothing. The rookie is now the sole police officer in uniform so the public will turn to this officer with the expectation he or she can solve any situation and have all the requisite answers. The FTO is there as a safety net and resource, but has now delegated the majority of the discretion and work tasks to that new officer. The FTO is no longer there to model or mentor for the new officer; rather, the FTO is primarily there to evaluate whether the delegation has paid the expected dividends. Over time the FTO must grant the trainee the freedom to take the lead in doing the job; organizationally this is a necessity to ensure the safety and well being of the trainee, other officers, and the community. Supervisors must do the same with their employees.

Effective leaders might realize that this same model and mentality is the way they will maximize the efficacy of the unit or organization for which they are responsible. Delegation can initially be uncomfortable because it often means asking people to do things they have never done. Their reactions and performance can be difficult to predict. FTOs working with rookie officers fresh from the academy does not know exactly how those rookies will perform on their first traffic stop or first fight. Will the rookies remember their training and respond accordingly or will they panic? In the same vein, a leader may not know how a follower will respond when tasked with a new duty, such as organizing a community meeting or working with the mayor's office to address a community problem. Sadly, many supervisors fail to be leaders because they will not delegate. Often this occurs despite ample evidence that followers simply need to be allowed to do their jobs with a measure of freedom and independence. Supervisors fail to stand back and let competent individuals perform the duties for which they have been trained and at which they have repeatedly proven their capability.

The Avoidance of Micromanagement

This chapter opened with a quote from Theodore Roosevelt regarding the need for leaders to "keep from meddling" by allowing good employees to do the work for which they were hired. Supervisors who fail to heed Roosevelt's imperative are often characterized as "micromanaging" their followers. The term micromanagement has been widely used and subject to some variation in definition, but generally refers to a supervisor who fails to delegate and empower, among other short-comings. A micromanager second guesses employees, requires extensive reporting from followers, checks every last detail of the work and products of their subordinates, and is often viewed as obsessing over trivial issues, such as font selection in a document (White 2010). Harry Chambers likens micromagement to "managing by hovering and hounding" and the habit of not trusting "your people to do the jobs you hired them to do" (2004, 10). Those who exhibit these types of supervisory behaviors undoubtedly believe the approach is right and even necessary. Micromanagers might not trust employees, overestimate their own judgment and expertise, believe their workers lack competence, or believe the world will end if they do not pay attention to every last detail of operations within their responsibility and authority.

Contrary to the micromanager's presumption that this approach leads to better outcomes in the workplace, this style has been judged to result in: employees who are frustrated; low morale among workers; employees who feel harassed; and workers who are less productive, more likely to use sick time, and more likely to separate from their employing organization (White 2010), among other problems and pathologies (Chambers 2004). Micromanagement is, in many ways, the antithesis of leadership. Rather than allowing followers to exercise their professional judgment and expertise in making decisions, micromanagers find the need to review and exercise oversight for an assortment of tasks and duties. Supervisors who fall into the trap of micromanagement are often far removed from the idealized nature of delegation and empowerment. Micromanagers are relegating employees to a much lower level of functioning by not granting workers needed or helpful autonomy to perform street-level and tactical duties.

Hallmarks of a micromanager could include creating excessive policies and procedures that minimize employee discretion in performing routine tasks. Admittedly, notions such as "excessive" policies are highly subjective and, in policing contexts, become hazy when policy, policing, liability, and law intersect (Sklansky 2007). For example, is a detailed policy governing the collection and handling of physical evidence excessive or a necessary step to minimize liability and ensure criminal cases result in successful prosecution? Effective communication should assist leaders in demonstrating to followers why certain procedures and policies are in effect (and hence why they are a necessity and not an act of micromanagement). In some situations restrictions are clearly unrelated to any such justifications. For example, a supervisor might require officers secure permission or authorization before engaging in certain enforcement actions, leaving their assigned patrol area, taking meal and personal breaks, or other routine circumstances.

Supervisors who avoid micromanagement allow employees to exercise professional judgment and discretion in performing regular duties. New policies and protocols are not created simply because of a single incident where discretion was misapplied. This can be a pathological problem in police organizations. How many policies or procedures in the typical police agency bear a single officers name, at least informally, denoting the one officer who "screwed it up" for everyone else? How many were written because of a single incident, often involving a mistake or misdeed by one officer, often outside of the agency in question? Agencies tend to focus policies on specific mistakes made in the past, rather than focusing on core principles and values that should govern actions in the future. Effective leaders recognize when a problem in the unit represents a fundamental issue in need of formal resolution. When does a problem require a solution that imposes restrictions on the entire workforce? Ideally, the answer should be "rarely."

As a supervisor rises through the ranks in an organization, avoiding micromanagement means empowering and delegating to front line supervisors. The chief or commander of the patrol division cannot be present twenty-four hours a day, seven days a week. Those executives have to trust that sergeants, lieutenants and other shift supervisors can and will effectively supervise personnel. This includes monitoring front-line officers, ensuring those officers are doing their job appropriately, and invoking needed discipline or corrective action, when warranted. An agency executive who is an effective leader "depends upon front line supervisors to provide day to day guidance, but will step in & correct problems immediately before they become major events or issues" (chief small federal agency). Avoiding micromanagement is not simply about allowing front-line personnel to have discretion. It is a process of a leader allowing their followers (regardless of rank and position) to have the latitude and freedom to perform their assigned tasks and responsibilities. A leader should "state the end state desired, empower others to get the job done, and allow others to carry out the mission . . . without micromanaging" (lieutenant major state agency).

Anyone can be a micromanaging supervisor. It is easy to attempt to hold tight control over the choices and decisions made by subordinate personnel or at least to believe one has such control. It takes courage, wisdom, and trust to delegate tasks to followers, to empower them to use their discretion, and to believe in their competency. This situation was succinctly conveyed by an extended description of an effective leader offered by a sergeant in a large state agency, who wrote:

> Effective leadership in policing is defined as a particular leader being proactive with his subordinates, but not a micromanager. Further, some of the best leadership in policing may not come from the "Boss" it may come from within the ranks and should be utilized so much as possible. The differences in a "Boss" and a "leader" is the difference in night and day. In the short term a Boss can thrive in the police world because of regimented policies and procedures. However, this is short lived. A Leader is someone who can work within policies but is someone who has vision, can take care of his people, and also finish the mission of his particular agency.

A captain from a mid-size municipal agency offered a similar characterization, defining effective leadership as:

> having a vision for your agency, casting the vision before your personnel, and then generate enthusiasm and shared commitment toward your vision. It is being able to surround yourself with capable staff, and then giving them the authority to make the day to day decisions that help move you further towards accomplishing the visions. It requires a combination of high energy, intelligence, communication skills, compassion and dedication, among many other things.

Policing invokes many situations where delegation and empowerment are not practical. But too often those in a position to lead fail to do so because they lack the insight or courage to realize when and why delegation and empowerment might lead to better outcomes. Much as the parent must realize when to take training wheels off a child's bike and later trust that child to ride a few blocks alone to see a friend, a leader must have the wisdom and courage allow followers to exercise judgment.[5]

Benefits of Delegation & Empowerment

The use of delegation and empowerment offers several potential benefits for police leaders. Most centrally, these approaches reflect the reality of decision making, authority,

---

5. This process is not always easy or nor is it always fully within the control of the leader. In many situations, the ability of an agency executive to delegate and empower is at least partially predicated on that executive's supervisor (typically a city manager or mayor). If that city official is not willing to trust and allow the executive to operate in this fashion, the executive may do little more than hasten his or her exit from the organization by using delegation and empowerment. This reality, sadly, is all too true and has played out repeatedly in agencies across the country.

autonomy, and power dynamics in modern police organizations. Using these tactics demonstrates to followers that the leader trusts them. It shows the leader has faith in the education, training, experience, and judgment of followers, which can be a reinforcing realization for workers. "They trust the person they are giving an assignment to complete the task. The employee, wanting to maintain this trust, performs in the best way as to represent future trust" (lieutenant medium municipal agency). Delegation "allows others to have ownership in the task and [its] results" (lieutenant large municipal agency). Delegating and empowering employees to make independent choices about the path or course to take in a given situation can help invest that employee in the outcomes of that situation. One way to win over the hearts and minds of officers is to help them develop a sense of ownership over the outcomes a leader is trying to achieve (Skogan and Hartnett 1997). This can be an important benefit by granting officers a sense of control over their jobs (Noblet, Rodwell, and Allisey 2009) and generating commitment to new initiatives and efforts (Fridell 2004).

Consider the role delegation and empowerment play in the context of an effort to change a substantial aspect of a police department or its operations. When those involved in the change effort delegate key tasks to employees and empower followers to make important decisions in the context of that change, "buy in" and support can be improved. "By giving the subordinates the necessary authority to accomplish the desired goals, and the subordinates accept the authority, they will rise to the required level of expectation and have an increased sense of job satisfaction and higher morale" (lieutenant major municipal agency). Change becomes more than just a task the leader asks followers to accept as employees. Followers empowered to exercise independent judgment about how to achieve that change should become more invested in working toward success when they have helped define the path forward. In many circumstances, followers who have enjoyed the opportunities provided through delegation and empowerment develop a great commitment to seeing the change result in successful outcomes (see generally Gray et al. 1991).

Employees cannot effectively learn new tasks and develop new skills (including the skills associated with being a better leader) if they are not given independence. Accepting that leadership is at least partially situational (e.g., not every follower, situation, or circumstances is responsive to the same leadership style and approach) prospective leaders need the freedom to experiment and learn how to understand and respond to the circumstances at hand. This means effective leaders will allow followers to make mistakes within certain limitations. A leader should not permit an error when it is likely to result in appreciable expense, liability, injury, property damage, or fatality. There are many situations, however, where the consequences of an error are far less appreciable. Though the follower may be embarrassed, suffer a temporary loss of standing (possibly including with the public), and endure some good-natured ridicule from co-workers, this will pass. What hopefully remains is a valuable lesson; mistakes can be instructive when we are willing to accept and learn from the lessons they offer.

As a leader rises higher in an organization and has more subordinate personnel reporting to him or her, delegation and empowerment may become more important tools, as well. In an ideal form the effective leader delegates and empowers supervisory personnel under her/his control. In turn, those supervisors delegate and empower their subordinates. Delegation and empowerment do not mean the leader takes a "hands off" approach to every situation. While a top executive may rely upon "front line supervisors to provide day to day guidance" that leader must also be willing to "step in and correct problems immediately before they become major events or issues" (chief small federal agency). To follow with the mapping analogy used earlier in the chapter, this means a leader might entrust followers to plan their route from point A to point B. If, however, the leader is aware the planned path will lead the followers off of a proverbial cliff or into a dead end, corrective action may be warranted. When and how the leader intervenes would presumably vary. Sometimes lessons can be learned by allowing followers to take controlled risks and make acceptable errors; where injury, damage, or liability are concerned, intervention by the leader may become a necessity.[6]

Delegation & Empowerment as Challenges for Followers

Delegation and empowerment are not traits pursued by a leader in order to be lazy, avoid work, or shed responsibility for undesired tasks. It is important that leaders demonstrate a willingness to complete any task within the organization, but to be effective they must not actually do so much of the time. Effective leaders "don't ask their people to do what they would not do themselves. Unfortunately many administrators forget where they came from" (lieutenant mid-size county agency). The commander of a large county agency wrote that effective leaders are always willing to work, "but they also delegate when appropriate." Though leaders might "lead from afar and delegate authority, they must roll up their sleeves and work with the troops on occasion" (lieutenant small municipal agency). True leadership is hard work. It challenges the leader and requires bravery, integrity, and a sense of self (a moral compass—guidance by knowing one's principles, values, and objectives).

Delegation and empowerment are not easy tasks, either for leaders or those charged with additional rights, responsibilities, and duties. When properly enacted, delegation and empowerment demonstrate the challenges of leadership to the affected employees. This furthers the objective of developing employees through the use of these approaches. In reviewing the leadership experiences and biographies of a group of prominent leaders, Robert Thomas identified the importance of crucible moments. Thomas (2008) described how these crucible moments forced leaders to determine their core values and beliefs. Consider the Leadership Team members in BAPD who revised the agency's disciplinary system. Those members could not engage in that task with competence and good faith if they did not first consider what they valued as employees including the performance and standards the agency should expect of its personnel. To craft an array of penalties for common disciplinary infractions should have required that those team members carefully reflect on the challenging considerations leaders would face in meting out actual punishment. Should leaders take into account mitigating and aggravating circumstances when deviating from the standard punishment? If so, when, why, and how should such deviations be allowed?

Delegation and empowerment are not soft approaches to leadership and are not always comfortable for followers, particularly if they are used to more directive forms of supervision. Heifetz and Laurie suggest that "[f]ollowers want comfort, stability, and solutions from their leaders. . . . Real leaders ask hard questions and knock people out of their comfort zones. Then they manage the resulting distress" (2001, 131). Some followers might be more comfortable showing up to work, being told what to do, performing those duties as

---

6. An important caveat on this statement is that a lesson must be learned. It should not be implied that leaders will allow others to make the same mistake repeatedly. To do so is not facilitating learning—it is perpetuating incompetence.

they have been trained, and then not thinking about their job once they are off the clock. Being delegated new tasks can challenge the status quo and create discomfort, particularly among more senior employees who are more locked into certain routines in performing their duties. Being empowered and given freedom and discretion can be uncomfortable for someone used to applying judgment in narrow circumstances using prescribed rules. Employees unaccustomed to the new roles, relationships, values, and approaches to work brought forth by participative management approaches can find the experience distressing. "They often look to the senior executive to take problems off their shoulders. But those expectations have to be unlearned" (Heifetz and Laurie 2001, 132).

Delegation & Empowerment as Challenges for Leaders

Delegating and empowering employees runs counter to the approaches many supervisors experienced earlier in their careers. Applying this trait often requires that leaders not only change the habits of followers (to receive directive supervision), but also their own habits. Police officers are problem solvers. They spend their professional lives being asked to bring order from chaos, to impose orders that others will accept. It is natural that new supervisors will approach their job and provide supervision in the form of solutions. Recognizing a problem, the supervisor will seek to identify and implement the correct solution. Many supervisors reach positions of authority because they have demonstrated competency in taking responsibility for solving problems in the workplace (Heifetz and Laurie 2001). Those who have risen through the ranks because they have a reputation for solving problems may find that delegation and empowerment are not intuitive processes. It may take training, experience, and time for a "hands on" leader to learn when, where, and how to be more "hands off" with personnel.

Delegation and empowerment can also become a weapon used against the leader by followers. Once these approaches have taken hold employees may become resistant to accepting situations in which they should be following a directive order issued by their leader. Employees can use the mantra of delegation and empowerment as a rational for why they should not have to comply with an unpopular policy, procedure, or order. Delegation and empowerment are not a panacea. When successfully implemented, empowered employees will want to have their "why" questions answered. Leaders and followers might disagree as to when and how delegation should be employed. The road will not always be smooth. What leaders need to consider is whether this approach (including the burdens it invokes) are preferable to traditional police management approaches (and the burdens they invoke).

Participative approaches, however, are predicated on the belief that solutions to organizational challenges are most often found in the collective wisdom, experience, intelligence, and insight of employees throughout the organization. Leaders need to have the wisdom to recognize this fact and have the courage to trust that they (and their peers and superiors) do not have all the answers. Police officers and supervisors often express support for participatory approaches (Hoover and Mader 1990; Witte, Travis, and Langworthy 1990), yet most report low levels of actual participation in the ways in which their agencies are administered (Witte, Travis, and Langworthy 1990). Research demonstrates more participative decision making styles yield multiple benefits. Officers and supervisors express support for such leadership models. But despite being discussed in policing literature for more than thirty years, these ideas continue to remain the exception more than the rule in the majority of police organizations.

Delegation & Empowerment as Developmental Tools

A good leader pays attention to the development of personnel (see Chapter Twelve). That developmental process is focused on ensuring followers are growing their competence and skill set related to the duties they currently perform. It may also include helping that follower develop competence and skill sets related to future tasks and duties. This means allowing a newer detective (who has been working property crimes) to assist on a violent crime case to expand his or her repertoire as an investigator. The detective presumably might learn new forensic techniques, new approaches to questioning victims and witnesses, and new areas of law. Development means allowing a patrol officer who has an idea for initiating a bicycle patrol unit to prepare a proposal articulating why that unit would be useful, when/where/how it would be deployed, how it would be staffed, and how much it would cost to establish and maintain the unit over time. Development means allowing the first officer who arrives at the scene of a call to "run" that situation, even when more experienced officers and supervisors arrive to provide assistance. All of these actions help employees learn more about leadership, their core job, new tasks they have not performed, and how to influence people, affect change, and bring new ideas into the organization.

Leadership development is perhaps the clearest example of the importance of delegation within the workplace. One of the most fundamental tasks a leader might attend to is the development of future leaders in the organization. A leader who does not delegate authority and responsibility is not cultivating capable future leaders. Some leaders do this intentionally, fearing they may end up being usurped or surpassed by a more competent employee who is currently a subordinate. The decision to not empower others is conscious so the leader still appears to be the most knowledgeable, capable, skilled, and experienced person in their unit. In other cases, the failure to delegate and empower emerges out of ignorance. Leaders do not realize when and how they can help others develop leadership skills in the workplace, perhaps because they never saw such behavior modeled by other leaders and supervisors.

Done properly, leadership developmental systems can work in a fashion similar to an FTO program and with minimal effort and resources. A subordinate can be exposed to "classroom" or textbook knowledge about leadership and associated issues (communication, organizations, development, etc.). The Commandant of the U.S. Marine Corp has a standing tradition of issuing recommended reading lists for Marines of various ranks that reflect core knowledge (not exclusively about leadership) believed to be associated with top performance. This is done to reinforce the importance of preserving life-long learning and mental fitness, as well as to expose Marines to ideas of relevance as they rise through the ranks of the Corp. How many police agencies do anything similar with their personnel? Once officers have been exposed to classes, recommended readings, and other developmental experiences, they can be delegated increasing leadership responsibility in the workplace. As confidence and competence grows, a follower becomes a better leader or, equally valuable, may demonstrate the limits of their leadership competence. The intention of such a process is not to set an employee up to fail. Rather, the process is intended to help maximize the efficacy of the unit/organization (and by extension, the formal leader) by increasing the capacity of the workforce.

Former Edmonton Police Superintendent Chris Braiden wrote (1992) about police leadership and employee development being akin to parenting. He describes how he and his wife attempted to provide their children roots and wings. The roots they sought to instill in their children included a set of values, beliefs, and skills. In a policing context, this might mean providing an employee with basic and advanced training on job-related tasks, but also less tangible socialization emphasizing matters such as integrity, a sense of public service, and an orientation toward doing what is best for the community. The wings Braiden and his wife sought to provide referred to having the courage as parents to allow their children to make decisions, even when they could see the child was making a mistake. Knowing that a child understood the mechanics of riding a bicycle, as well as rules of bike safety, a parent has to then have the courage to stand in front of their house, watch their child ride around the corner or over the horizon, and trust the child has the skills to safely return home from a journey to see a friend, go to the library, or ride to the local grocery store. The only way the child can grow into a strong adult is to have roots to guide their conduct and to be given the wings (the independence and autonomy) to apply those values and that knowledge. The parent must have the courage to let the child mature and develop into an adult, knowing that mistakes will be made and poor judgment will be exercised, but that in the end the child will be better for those experiences.

Delegation by leaders might be considered a parallel process, though it should not be implied that leaders are akin to parents and followers akin to children. The leader and organization must provide the employee with strong roots. They must provide a solid basis of legal and operational knowledge, a foundation of ethics, an orientation toward the ideals of public service, an understanding of community norms and expectations, and socialization into the culture and values of the jurisdiction, organization, and profession. Once this has been done the organization must have the courage to let the new officer spread his or her wings, knowing mistakes will be made and that some outcomes will not be ideal. Once it has been determined rookie officers have sufficient roots in the performance of their duties the agency must allow them to patrol without an FTO. Leaders realize that within accepted parameters (i.e., law and policy) followers must be given the wings to "perform their duties without being told 'how' to do it" (sergeant small municipal agency) by their leaders, peers, and partners. The only way to develop new leaders is to allow followers the experiences that will improve their judgment and skills.[7] Tasks must be delegated and followers must be empowered.

This development approach does not mean that parents or supervisors never step in to avoid a catastrophic error, but it implies that at some point children and officers have to be allowed to select a course of action and live with the consequences. Sometimes parents and supervisors will discover that while the decision was not the same one they might have made, it is not necessarily a wrong choice. The process of providing roots and having the courage to grant wings is not just a task for parents or the supervision of new front line personnel. This model is not simply a process suitable for patrol officers and can extend all the way up an agency. As supervisors rise through the ranks they need to be exposed to increasing areas of responsibility, new challenges, and different aspects of the process of leading at successively higher levels. An effective leader "takes an active role in developing others" (lieutenant medium county agency) through the trajectory of the fol-

---

7. Leaders (parents, FTOs, or anyone else) must have confidence that the person being empowered is ready to accept that responsibility. Regardless of the metaphor, the individual being empowered is often less certain that they are ready to "leave the nest." The rookie officer might have some trepidation about patrolling and handling calls without oversight. The new or aspiring leader might be concerned about taking on a task with unfettered authority. Hopefully this fear is turned in a healthy direction and leads to vigilance, hard work, and attention to detail, resulting in a favorable outcome.

lower's career. A chief or sheriff must have the foresight and courage to make sure mid-level supervisors and executive staff are being afforded the chances to grow and develop, regardless of how experienced and educated the follower. Even followers with decades of experience in their role and rank should be viewed as a work in progress. Leaders should view their own leadership competence in the same way. Roots can always be made deeper and even experienced "fliers" can find new ways to develop their skills by being granted the wings to assume new challenges, experiences, and responsibilities.

Conclusions

Delegation and empowerment offer many potential advantages for enhancing police leadership efficacy. These approaches allow supervisors to truly lead and avoid the dreaded trap of micromanagement. They recognize the reality that supervisors cannot control everything done by employees. In general, it might be expected that if employees are treated as responsible and creative adults, they will act as such. If they are treated as petulant children and risks to be managed, it should not be surprising when officers engage in subversion, sabotage, and circumvention. Delegation and empowerment should, over time, result in making better decisions that will be supported and embraced by employees. These tools can improve decision making, increase buy-in, and ensure greater outcomes. That is not to say they are easy for leaders to embrace and utilize, particularly in policing, which is dominated by concerns over liability and a long-standing tradition of directive management styles. Some supervisors may legitimately have no professional exposure to systematic models of delegation and empowerment. It is difficult to advance the use of a particular leadership tool when supervisors have no framework to understand and implement such approaches. Ultimately, effective leaders delegate and empower for a variety of reasons, not the least of which is that it advances their commitment to develop leadership throughout the workplace. If current supervisors are not focused and committed to developing the leadership and professional skills of those in their command, the prospects for appreciably advancing an agency are greatly constrained.

Chapter 6

Interpersonal Skills

Leadership is not just about writing correct and clear policy, making good decisions in a decisive manner, delegating, engaging, or empowering. Efficacy and success as a leader or as a manager is always about people. Fundamentally, policing is a "people" business; the overwhelming majority of tasks and issues agencies and officers confront are done with or to people. Police supervisors interact with subordinate officers, peers, their own supervisors, constituents, partner agencies, communities, and offenders, among other populations. A true leader endeavors to effectively communicate, manage interactions, and maintain relations with all of those groups. Simultaneously, effective leaders need to develop and maintain genuine trust, respect, cooperation, and engagement with these groups and their members. This is where the leader as a person comes into play. A leader may be at an advantage if she or he has a warm and engaging personality, is friendly, has a sense of humor, and is comfortable speaking with people of diverse backgrounds and experiences.

That said, simply having charisma is not, by itself, sufficient to ensure long-term efficacy.[1] Many elected officials find themselves in office because they convey a "winning personality" to voters. Charisma might help them earn their office, but being able to be effective as an elected leader will generally require an ability to work with others and to be viewed as someone who is compassionate, approachable, and cares about individuals. The National Academy participants frequently used the term "charisma" in defining effective leaders, but exploring how they used this term in greater depth suggested they were not using it in the conventional narrow sense. Charisma was not characterized as being about leaders having white teeth, nice hair, a proper wardrobe, a winning smile, and a repertoire of good jokes. Style did not trump substance when the leader's personality was being considered. Being a charismatic leader in policing is showing genuine compassion, concern, care, and a human side. It is a process of earning the trust and respect of those the leader wishes to influence. The leader's experiences, accomplishments, and past record serve to instill confidence in those who are current or potential followers. Charismatic leadership is about winning the "hearts and minds" of others by convincing people the leader and his/her ideas are worth following (Lurigio and Skogan 1994). This conviction has to ultimately be based on a belief that the leader is doing things for the right reasons and has the best interests of the organization and its personnel at heart.

A leader with strong interpersonal skills "understands personality and accepts the fact that people are different" (lieutenant small municipal agency). These leaders appreciate the way they treat followers has a situational element. This does not mean the leader is vapid, patronizing, condescending, or disingenuous. Rather, it is recognition that the leader must

---

1. Jim Collins (2001) discusses this same point, contending that a leader whose main pillar of support is charisma and popularity cannot provide sustained greatness. Eventually the charisma fades as followers realize there is not real strength and capacity behind the cult of personality. The successes the leader achieved will fade with their popularity in the organization. Though charisma or strong interpersonal skills can be an important element of leadership efficacy, they cannot be the sole or even primary basis of long-term leadership greatness and success.

temper their own personality to best engage individuals and groups. For the purposes of this chapter, charisma will also be considered in a broader sense in light of this last point. Charisma is not an act or a "game face" worn by the leader. For leaders who are effective, charisma is the process of engaging people on a personal level and making individual connections. It is a process through which leaders show compassion and care for the human needs of their employees. This can mean spending the time and energy getting to know and recognize personal details about followers, such as births, weddings, birthdays, graduations, and academic and athletic accomplishments of children. It can also mean difficult tasks, such as taking the time and being vulnerable by mourning with followers over the loss of a loved one.

Transformational leaders may have an advantage over transactional leaders when considering the role of interpersonal relations in shaping efficacy. Transactional leaders operate from a relationship foundation based on rewards, discipline, and short-term exchanges (Burns 1978; see also Zigarmi, Blanchard, O'Connor, and Edeburn 2005). The transformational leader emphasizes trust, care, interpersonal connections, and loyalty, all of which may generate stronger and more sustainable followership. Such ideas may, of course, run in contrast to dominant organizational cultures often observed in policing (Murphy 2008). It is worth noting that employees who realize the importance of interpersonal relationships may be able to leverage greater influence within the workplace, even when they are not formally in positions of authority (Anderson, Gisborne, and Holliday 2006; Murphy 2008). This chapter examines the way effective leaders use interpersonal relationships to achieve better organizational outcomes.

Personality

Police leaders who exemplify strong interpersonal skills "have excellent 'people skills,' which is what this business is all about" (lieutenant small municipal agency). Being competent while interacting with others could be seen as a necessary element to ensure success as a front-line officer or investigator, yet many officers are not optimally proficient in this area (see Muir 1977). Though it might initially be presumed all police personnel have strong interpersonal skills and the personality needed to successfully engage others, the reality is this is not a universal skill among potential leaders. Where this skill is present, it can be an important condition of leadership efficacy, but personality is not, by itself, enough to sustain leader efficacy over time. Officers routinely interact with a wide range of people whom they seek to influence and an engaging, charismatic personality can be an asset in the pursuit of that outcome. Officers and leaders might both use coercion, threats, intimidation and punishment to assert authority over citizens or subordinates, operating in a transactional manner with "sticks" and "carrots" to influence behavior. Though this might ultimately allow the leader to achieve desired objectives, it does not necessarily equate with efficacy.

In contrast, transformational leaders may demonstrate how personality and charisma can contribute to leadership efficacy. Getting others to comply voluntarily, rather than through fear, can be more powerful and desirable among leaders. Transactional leaders have to create supervisory mechanisms to know when to use sticks (punishment) and issue carrots (rewards). Such mechanisms take time and attention. The transformational leader's personality helps ensure subordinates become followers, rather than risks to be managed. Why does the distinction matter if desired outcomes are achieved? If people only comply through fear, what do they do when the leader is absent or not looking? Do they continue to comply? Are they loyal to that leader? Will they support and defend that leader and his or her objectives and priorities? Followers recognize and are motivated by a leader who engages, encourages, and empowers. The base of that leader's legitimacy and influence is respect, admiration, and a drive to satisfy the leader and his/her expectations. A leader employing a transformational style creates a group of followers that "wants to do the right thing because it is the right thing, not because they fear punishment" (sergeant mid-size county agency). Rather than imposing fear, asserting control, and invoking their authority, the charismatic and transformational leader has the "ability to interact with others in a positive manner . . . [and the] ability to motivate others" (captain large county agency).

The leader's personality would ideally have a reasonable degree of charisma, but ultimately the leader needs to be more than a dynamic, gregarious individual. Leaders need to be able to engage people. There needs to be substance, knowledge, and experience underneath an ability to connect with people on some level. Leaders with sufficient interpersonal skills "can motivate people (police & community) to make their community a better place. Someone who . . . mentors [and] praises" (commander large municipal agency). Leaders who exemplify this trait "are charismatic in a way that 'draws' people to them- oftentimes a leader will be the one officer who has the ability to change people's behavior before it becomes a disciplinary problem" (sergeant large county agency). Charisma ideally engenders others with the confidence that the leader is competent, capable, and makes good decisions. Implicit in this situation is the notion that technical competence, by itself, might not be sufficient to ensure efficacy. Leaders need to be effective and have the ability to convince others that is the case. Absent the latter, efficacy may be compromised, at least to an extent. Furthermore, charisma and personality do not imply idol worship on the part of followers or a cult of personality surrounding the leaders. Followers may realize the leader is not perfect, but believe the leader is competent and worthy of trust, respect, and followership. This might mean the leader's personality not only conveys some level of charisma, but also that the leader is stable, reliable, and makes decisions using appropriate information and processes.

In recent years the subject of "emotional intelligence" has received appreciable attention in the realms of leadership, management, personality, and interpersonal relations. Much like leadership, emotional intelligence does not have a universal definition, but those discussing this concept describe it as having an ability to interpret and act upon emotions displayed by others. Those with high emotional intelligence can "read" other people and presumably can take a situational approach to interactions with others. They are able to understand the approach that is necessary (or perhaps the approach that would not be fruitful) in securing the desired actions or outcomes from someone else. In the context of policing, emotional intelligence has been framed as a central element of effective leadership (Drodge and Murphy 2002). Emotionally intelligent leaders are characterized as being able to use their personality, their own emotions, and their relationships with others to achieve goals and preferred outcomes (see Hersey, Blanchard, and Johnson 2008; Hennessy 1992).

Part of being a charismatic person is having an engaging personality. A charismatic leader is often a "great 'people person,' gregarious, friendly, a good listener" (lieutenant large municipal agency). They are the type of people who has a lot of friends and contacts at work, in the community, in their neighborhood, and various other networks. Even during tough times, challenging days, and dire situations, charismatic leaders "possess a generally good attitude and demeanor no matter what the situation (lieutenant small municipal agency). This does not mean the leader is telling jokes or singing songs at appropriate times. Rather, it implies the leader does not become bogged down when budgets are being cut or other aspects of organizational life have lowered the mood of the workforce. The leader remains positive and focused on the accomplishments and potential that exists within the workplace. As a leader, they set the tone. By not allowing tough times to win, they formally and informally encourage others to focus on opportunities and not merely challenges, to consider the positive and not the negative, to focus on what can be controlled over than which cannot. This type of behavior serves to "actively motivate and inspire others" (lieutenant large special jurisdiction agency) and to "generate a positive attitude in his men [sic]" (lieutenant medium municipal agency). In this way charisma is not simply about the leader's individual personality traits, it is also about his or her outlook and demeanor within and toward the workplace.

To date it has been difficult to empirically validate the outcomes of personality and interpersonal skills on police leadership outcomes. Anecdotal evidence, however, lends credence to the importance of this particular leadership trait. Two brief examples derived during the course of the research for this book are illustrative of this point. First, the author was told a story about a probationary special agent in a major federal agency who was accidently shot during a firearms training exercise. Upon hearing about the accident, the chief executive of that agency immediately went to the hospital, meeting the injured agent within minutes after he arrived to receive care. The agent's injuries were not going to be lethal, but it was immediately evident some time would be spent in the hospital. The executive asked the trainee what could be done to ensure the agent's parents (his immediate family) were able to travel to be with him during the hospital stay. The trainee explained that would not be possible because his parents were the primary employees in their family restaurant and could not afford to close the business for a few days. The executive located several employees in the agency that had a work background in that type of restaurant and dispatched them to relieve the parents so the business could remain open while the parents were with their son. If accurate[2] it might be questioned whether the leader made fair use of public resources by assigning personnel to operate a restaurant. Viewed alternatively, however, the leader placed what was right (the personnel needs of an employee injured in the line of duty) ahead of what was easy (not finding a way to help the family). Though the leader has an uneven reputation within the agency, it was widely expressed that he did what was right for his employees.

As a second example, the author knew of a police chief who was hired from the outside to take command of a major police department in the wake of a modest scandal. From the onset, this chief sought to be highly visible and accessible to employees throughout the agency, despite its size. Upon accepting command, he held a number of meetings at all hours of the day and throughout the agency's multiple facilities in an attempt to explain his vision and answer questions for all employees. This initial practice transitioned into a long-term habit of attending pre-shift line up for at least one patrol shift every few weeks, as well as preparing routine written messages sent to all employees detailing and reinforcing his vision for the agency and the state of police professionalism. Though he did not know all employees by sight, he frequently received positive comments from of-

---

2. The author was never able to validate the story from independent sources, but it was related several times and was clearly part of agency lore.

ficers about his visibility and down-to-earth leadership style. The chief of such a large agency is inevitably issuing commands from "on high," but this particular chief tried to do a strong job minimizing this situation and seeking to explain policy changes, budget reductions, and major staffing decisions in person whenever possible. In an agency that had a history of strained labor-management relations, this chief reports a healthy and respectful relationship with the president of the patrol officers' bargaining unit. The union president, while not applauding all aspects of the chief's approach, commended the chief for doing his best to minimize the effects of budget cuts on the pay, benefits, and working environment of front-line officers. In these examples the chief's efficacy as a leader extended beyond simply having a charismatic and approachable personality (i.e., into the realm of communication skills), however the example illustrates how charisma can play a central role in mediating a leader's other efforts in the workplace.

Balancing People & the Organization

In a classic essay Robert Tannenbaum and Warren Schmidt provided one of the first articulations of the idea that leaders make choices from an array of leadership "patterns" or styles. Their "continuum of leadership behavior" arrayed a leader's approach from being "boss-centered" to "subordinate-centered" (1958, 96). Boss-centered leaders make decisions based on their personal interests, expertise, and beliefs. Subordinate-centered leaders actively seek extensive input from relevant and affected employees in reaching a decision. In between these poles are a range of approaches from less to more input from employees, respectively. [3] In policing contexts, this continuum is often compressed to the two poles and discussions of whether a particular leader made decisions for the betterment of the community/organization or employees. Leaders who tend to make decisions with an emphasis on the interests and needs of the community and/or organization would be more akin to Tannenbaum and Schmidt's boss-centered leader, because that is the approach that will often ensure a chief (who often serves at the pleasure of the city leaders) or sheriff (who is normally elected) retains their position. Leaders who make decisions with an emphasis on the interests of employees (sometimes referred to as "a cop's cop") are closer to a subordinate-centered leader.

Renford Reese (2005) provides an insightful discussion of the contrast between community/organization-centered leaders and officer-centered leaders. Reese's book reviews the leadership demonstrated by Los Angeles Police Department (LAPD) chiefs from the 1950s into the 2000s. He uses the metaphor that leaders walk a tightrope between the interests of the public and the interests of their staff; "[a]t the end of the day, which is more important: one's high approval by the public or one's high approval among staff?" (xiv). Reese contrasts Daryl Gates, who he sees as the prototypical "cop's cop" police chief, with Willie Williams. Gates never wavered in his support of his officers, a stance that periodically placed him in the "hot seat" with the media, city leaders, and members of the public, particularly the minority community and ultimately lead to his dismissal from the agency. After Gates'

---

3. Tannenbaum and Schmidt's essay also did much to advance the idea that leadership is situational. They described how leaders often struggled in deciding where to "fall" on that continuum in a given situation, when making a given decision, or seeking to influence a given employee. Inherent in this perspective is the idea that a leader might not have a fixed style or pattern, but rather that a leader's approach might vary by situation.

departure in the aftermath of the Rodney King beating and subsequent riots, Willie Williams was hired as the outsider who would reform LAPD's image, culture, and approach to policing. Williams is sometimes characterized as making decisions that were wildly unpopular with officers, that were contrary to LAPD's culture and norms, and that did not reflect a strong understanding of the community and its crime problems. Reese frames Williams as making decisions from a basis of trying to restore LAPDs standing within the community. It is often suggested that Williams did garner more support from the community as he sought to enhance the agency's standing and reputation among the citizens of Los Angeles.[4]

Interpersonal relations are not only something that helps leaders influence their workforce, but can also help leaders deal with various external constituents, such as government officials (of equal or greater power standing), community leaders, citizens, social service providers, and others within the criminal justice system. At times there can be real or perceived tension between leaders doing what is right for (or merely popular with) followers and doing what is right for a unit or organization. A leader might be expected or required to make a critical decision that will be viewed as either favoring the community or organization, or favoring officers. For example, a video may capture officers using force in an arrest situation. These types of images often generate controversy within a community, as they frequently are shot from a poor angle, do not capture the entirety of an encounter, lack quality audio, and may fail to convey the entire set of circumstances available to officers as an arrest was being made. To the public, a video might show excessive force and police brutality. To officers, that same video might show a violent, but lawful and appropriate, arrest. Needless to say, the media often amplifies tension or debate surrounding such events.

A leader responsible for officers in such a controversy faces a difficult set of choices. She or he is usually expected to speak to the media, community, and civil leaders about that event, even as the incident is still being investigated. The leader treads a fine line of needing to "say something," while not wanting to violate law or protocol by appearing to have prejudged an officer or seeking to bias or influence an ongoing investigation. The leader also confronts a variety of expectations. Officers generally want to see their leaders stand beside them in such controversies (presuming there is no immediate evidence of actual wrong-doing). Officers want the leader's message to be supportive of the individuals being investigated and their actions. The community and political leaders might expect a very different message. Leaders may find themselves in a proverbial "catch-22" situation where nothing they say will satisfy all concerned parties and neither commentary nor silence will yield the "right" results. The leader must choose a course of action, knowing that all available paths will create problems with one or more groups.

Beyond this example, leaders are routinely confronted with situations that create a degree of tension between the interests and needs of the various constituencies relevant in a given situation. "Effective leaders will always have the welfare of officers & the good of the organization in mind, which can be difficult balance" (captain small municipal agency). Arguments can be made that in most situations what is in the best interests of the agency and/or community actually *is* good for officers. Outcomes that satisfy the community

---

4. In Williams' defense, it must be conceded that as someone hired to reform the LAPD, he had an implicit (if not explicit) mandate to make decisions based on public interests more so than the desires of LAPD officers. Given Gates' very strong support among LAPD personnel, it is likely almost anyone hired to take his place (armed with a charge of reformation and building bridges with the community) would have struggled to gain appreciable standing with officers.

should, in the long-term, ensure the agency and officers have greater community support. Maximizing community support should make it easier for officers to perform routine duties (e.g., officers face less questioning, hostility, and opposition from citizens; they enjoy more cooperation and receive more information; they have an easier time handling calls and clearing cases) and might mean the agency enjoys greater fiscal resources. In the heat of the moment, however, officers may perceive a false dichotomy in many situations where they do not exist. Followers may be of the false and shortsighted belief that if their leaders are not with the officers, they are against the officers.

Effective leaders recognize and find ways to negotiate such situations. They might not always win and there might be some interpersonal "casualties" to the leader's decisions, but the leader is able to find ways to minimize the consequences of these "no win" situations. This does not mean leaders always take the easier internal route by siding with officers. Such a path could help the leader in the short term, but result in the leader being fired. "The great leader must know how to balance the needs of his/her people with the needs of the public/government. Failure to do so would result in either a disgruntled work force, or a dissatisfied customer base" (captain large municipal agency). The leader needs to "make the tough decisions [while] keeping both the agency and staff in mind" (lieutenant medium municipal agency). When a leader knows followers will be upset (at least in the short term) with a decision, they might take more time to discuss and "sell" that choice and its long-term virtues to the affected officers. Will this ensure an easy path forward in all situations? Certainly not, but if the leader has taken "a hard look at difficult situations and developed good policy that includes taking care of his or her people" (lieutenant large state agency) in the longer term more favorable outcomes might be achieved.

Effective leaders demonstrate "care about how their decisions affect the staff while moving the agency forward" (lieutenant large state agency). They seek to treat followers in a fair manner and ensure that decisions respect their rights and interests. Their actions show an ability to "balance the accomplishment of objectives with the welfare of those tasked to accomplish those objectives" (chief investigator mid-size special jurisdiction agency). When subordinates make positive contributions to the organization and its mission, charismatic leaders take the time to recognize that situation. Such recognition serves many purposes, including reinforcing (generally and specifically) desired behavior and performance in the workplace. The recognition also can help validate that hard work is acknowledged and appreciated.

Traits & Habits of Leaders with Interpersonal Competence

Strong interpersonal skills, including charisma and being a "people person" may be one of the most challenging traits for a leader to develop. In the end, interpersonal skills might be very much embedded in an individual's pre-existing personality. They seem to come naturally for some leaders, while others may struggle with interpersonal relationships and connecting with co-workers and potential followers. Some leaders like to be in the spotlight in any social situation, whether at work, out in the community, or socializing with family and friends. Others prefer to be on the fringe, observing others, seeking to understand the "lay of the land" in a social situation. Being the center of attention might make them uncomfortable or apprehensive. There could be a risk in trying to "force" one's personality. Peers and followers may see a leader as trying too hard, being artificial, pandering, or coming across as disingenuous. It is possible the risk of being viewed as a leader with a false personality may be greater than the limitations of not having a highly dynamic and engaging personality. In considering the liabilities that might limit leadership efficacy, being perceived having a disingenuous personality may trump being perceived as having an insufficient personality.

Despite this situation, prevailing literature and responses from the National Academy participants suggest there are ways leaders can enhance their interpersonal skills. There are traits and habits to which a leader might attend in an effort to improve interpersonal competence. These measures offer promise to aspiring leaders who recognize that interpersonal skills might be one of their weaknesses. The measures might also be of help for more charismatic leaders who are simply seeking to further enhance their efficacy. The traits and habits discussed in this chapter reinforce the notion that the traits and habits described in this book are often reinforcing and overlapping. This chapter reinforces ways in which leaders can seek to be open, approachable, empowering, and trustworthy individuals in the hope that potential followers will move in the desired direction. Attentive leaders should consider which might work with their personality and organizational context.

Leaders Show Care in How They Treat Others

Leadership efficacy is not just the traits and habits displayed by the leader, but also a function of how the leader treats others. Leaders with interpersonal competence "have earned the respect of their supervisors, peers and subordinates" (captain medium municipal agency). This respect is not solely provided in order to influence subordinates. Respect is shown so subordinates will reciprocate by respecting the leader. Having a reciprocation of respect, fairness, and trust can be an important element of leader efficacy (see Chapter Seven). By treating other people with respect and in a manner that demonstrates professionalism (both those within and outside the organization) leaders earns the respect of their superiors, peers, and followers. Their behavior over time ensures these leaders "have the respect of the peers, [in part because they are] willing to hold people accountable" for their conduct (commander mid-size county agency).

Personality and charisma should not be confused with being patronizing, sycophantic, or "kissing up" to followers. A leader's actions and intentions ought to be genuine. A leader does not avoid doing what is right simply because it will be unpopular among followers. Wanting respect and cooperation also does not preclude a leader from asserting their authority. Being a transformational leader does not rule out having to use transactional approaches. Transformational leaders will still use discipline and rewards, but they will not use them as the basis for their power and authority. When followers are not living up the trust they have been granted or when they take advantage of the leader's good will, problems may arise. Even in social terms, leaders have to make sure that followers understand there are boundaries and that "you don't cross the line with them. You have to separate your work relationship from being buddies" (lieutenant large state agency). But a leader might use care to not "dress down" a follower in a public manner or might be deliberate to respond to an irate, screaming citizen with calmness and tact.

Officers are expected to seek mutually agreeable ways to resolve conflict situations and to negotiate orderly outcomes for chaotic circumstances. The author was once affiliated with a municipal agency located in a college community. The police chief had a standing mantra that officers should be "firm, but friendly" when dealing with the public, particularly the major "business" of that agency—regulating alcohol-related behavior for young adults (i.e., underage drinking, loud parties, public intoxication, possession of a false identification, etc.). This chief wanted his officers to use discretion while helping youth learn the parameters of acceptable conduct; however, a youth who took advantage of that leniency was likely to receive a harsher outcome. For example, if an officer ordered a resident to shut down a house party where presumably a number of guests were drinking under the legal age, that situation might not initially result in any legal sanctions. If the officer was called back to that same problem, however, enforcement actions were a far more likely outcome. But professionalism and an even temper were still expected at all times.

A leader who is attentive to the feelings and perceptions of followers may operate under a similar premise (Hennessy 1992). Followers are treated with respect and are presumed to be deserving of trust and respect until circumstances and experience prove otherwise. Violating the leader's trust does not necessarily result in positive interpersonal techniques being set aside. Leaders might give followers a chance, but they also know when and how to assert their authority when followers do not live up to their end of an arrangement. Beyond how leaders handle individuals, they need to be attentive to how they themselves behave. The leader "speaks well of other [and] does not pit employees against each other or create factions within the department" (lieutenant large municipal agency). The leader does not indiscreetly gossip, spread rumors, or otherwise spread discontent, ill will, or tension in the organization. Though such traits and habits seem simple and obvious, it can be incredibly difficult for leaders to embrace and live up to these standards. Most leaders likely believe they are fair and treat others with respect (at least when it is earned). The key may be focusing not on how the leader perceives their actions, but on understanding how his/her actions are perceived by others.[5]

Care & Compassion

More humanistic perspectives on leadership and organizational dynamics emphasize the need to understand and strengthen the human element of a group (Conger 1999; Hennessy 1992; Murphy and Drodge 2004). For aspiring leaders seeking to maximize interpersonal relations, this means demonstrating legitimate concern, compassion, and care for employees. Because policing is a "people business" much of a patrol officer's success on the streets and in the station house is a function of her or his ability to engage with a variety of people in situationally appropriate ways. Officers and investigators need to be able to demonstrate empathy and engagement to diffuse volatile situations and secure the trust and cooperation of victims and witnesses. Front-line and mid-level supervisors must have the ability to develop and sustain the trust and cooperation of the officers working under their command. Executives and chief executives must be able to motivate and inspire personnel, some of whom they may rarely see and with whom they might not directly interact. Though

---

5. Veteran police chief and long-time friend Chief Richard Myers reminded the author that one way to mitigate this risk is through the use of trust advisors. Leaders should not surround themselves only with those who either share their worldview or will only say what they think the leader wants to hear ("yes men"). To do so is the raise the risk of "groupthink" (Janis 1972), the gravitational pull toward group consensus without critical questioning and the tendency to suppress contrary thinking. Groupthink is a concept of relevance not only to group decisions but actions of the leader, as well. Wise leaders will empower trusted advisors to point out when the leaders have perception gaps that are causing them to miss danger in the "blind spots" of their decision making process. These trusted advisors should help the leader understand how decisions and actions are or will be perceived by followers and others of relevance.

accomplishing these outcomes is a multifaceted task, National Academy participants repeatedly reinforced that it was very important that leaders demonstrate care and concern for those inside and outside the police organization.[6]

This means that leaders "care for their people (personally [and] professionally)" (lieutenant medium municipal agency). This extends the idea of leaders being engaging and personable. It suggests leaders must be conscious of interpersonal relationships, must understand that employees are humans with lives outside of the workplace, and must think about what this means for leader-follower relations and interactions.[7] Leaders demonstrating care and compassion show they "care about the officer and his family" (lieutenant small county agency), as well. Leaders who excel on this front may know when an employee has a birthday, when a child has been accepted to college, or when a parent has to be placed in hospice. The leader is able to see employees as humans with outside lives that bring many fortunes, both good and bad. In addition to granting requests for relevant forms of leave, this may mean the leader takes time to ask a follower how a personal situation is going, to congratulate the follower on an important life event, or to ask what can be done to help accommodate a situation arising in the follower's family life.

In expressing this relatively simple situation the National Academy participants repeatedly used terms such as "concern," "care," and "compassion."

- "Care about others, not just themselves . . . caring for their subordinates" (assistant chief large municipal agency).
- "They actually care about people- not just themselves" (captain medium special jurisdiction agency).
- ". . . care about the people that make up the organization" (lieutenant large municipal agency).
- "Caring & supportive" (lieutenant mid-size municipal agency).
- "Concerned for others, rather than focusing on personal advancement" (lieutenant major municipal agency).
- "They are not a [sic] 'all about me' type person" (lieutenant medium county agency).
- They show "concern for the welfare of subordinates" (lieutenant medium municipal agency).
- "Above all, however, an effective leader *MUST* have compassion for those who follow. True leaders never forget the people who worked for them to accomplish the goals" (captain mid-size municipal agency).
- "The leader looks often and is concerned with the welfare of the people he leads" (executive officer major state agency).
- "Ability to make a personal connection with subordinates; ability to show compassion and caring for personnel, while at the same time, ensuring that the mission of the

---

6. Leaders cannot ask or expect officers to demonstrate care and concern as public servants if leaders do not first demonstrate that orientation in the workplace. Ideas of legitimacy and procedural justice are just as relevant to considering leader-follower relations as they are to the study of police-community relations (see Tyler and Huo 2002).

7. Murphy and Drodge (2004) write about a story related to them by a Canadian police manager. When that manager's supervisor needed command personnel to work late covering an evening function on short notice, he would call the manager and suggest he take his wife to lunch since he would not see her until late in the evening. The mangers appreciated their boss recognized the importance of spending time with a spouse and that the boss was willing to afford the manager some time during the day to account for asking the manager to commit extra work hours in the evening.

organization is met. The great leader must know how to balance the needs of his/her people with the needs of the public/government. Failure to do so would result in either a disgruntled work force, or a dissatisfied customer base" (captain large municipal agency).

Demonstrating care, concern, and compassion cannot be false efforts—they need to be genuine. Over time, personnel will distinguish between a leader who truly demonstrates these attributes and one who is merely being manipulative. Leaders seeking to leverage interpersonal relations cannot sustain those efforts over time if they are putting on a false face. A bright smile, forced levity, and false laughter will eventually be detected and may be more lethal to leadership efficacy than leaders who are true to themselves and do not force or fabricate interpersonal skills they lack. False care will likely be seen as manipulation rather than as true compassion.

The author was discussing this idea with the chief mentioned earlier in the chapter. As an executive hired from outside the agency, he had worked hard to cultivate a reputation as a leader who cared about his people. One morning the chief and his wife were at the city's airport preparing to leave on a trip. Sitting in the terminal awaiting to board the flight, the chief thought he recognized someone else waiting for the same flight. He engaged this man in a short conversation and found out it was an officer from his traffic division. The officer complemented the chief for how he had handled an off-duty fatality involving another officer from the traffic division. In particular, the officer spoke highly of how the chief had mourned alongside officers in the agency, though he had not personally known the officer who lost his life. The officer complemented the chief for working hard to maintain relatively close interpersonal relations and showing himself as a leader who cared, a daunting task in a large organization where a chief can quite easily be insulated from those on the front line.

Was the chief a perfect leader? Certainly not and he would humbly attest to that fact himself. But central to his approach upon taking command of such a large agency was to lead (in part) by showing his officers he was human. He did not want to be viewed as a detached executive, ruling with authority and an iron hand. He wanted his officers to view him as someone who understood them and as someone who was engaged in the agency. As he implemented tough policies and led the agency through a deep fiscal recession, he sought to make the road easier by garnering the respect of officers and other employees, many of whom he could never personally know. Though it is always difficult to assess success in such efforts, by all accounts, the chief made his very difficult job a bit easier by taking the path of compassion and caring. He did not have perfect success in all situations. All officers did not love him. But his efforts were intended to motivate officers to follow him because they viewed him as a human being, rather than as a detached authority figure. There were other elements to his leadership style and he had to avoid being "fake" in cultivating interpersonal relations, but demonstrating care and compassion in the workplace was one of the core ways he sought to lead across multiple commands in his career.

Caring and compassionate leaders have "the ability to reach out to people & touch them on an emotional basis" (captain major municipal agency). They are able to empathize with others by "being able to 'put yourself' into a situation and see how it is perceived by others" (chief small municipal agency). This does not necessarily mean the leader makes the same decision those others might make in the same situation. By understanding these alternative perspectives, however, the leader can modify their approach. For example, knowing the specific reasons a policy or proposal might be unpopular with followers, the leader can take steps to address and alleviate specific concerns. These steps might include spending more time explaining the reason for the decision, allowing affected personnel to "vent" their frustration and displeasure, and being more patient than normal in waiting for behavior to shift in accordance with that change. This does not mean leaders refuse to make tough or unpopular choices. Doing what is right must always trump doing what is popular. Leaders can, however, be simultaneously "empathetic, yet firm" (lieutenant major municipal agency).

Communication

Communication is certainly a process by which leaders show their interpersonal skills. The earlier discussion of listening and communication showed there are various methods, modes, and moments when leaders convey they are worthy of being followed. Leaders ultimately will find ways to overcome agency size and distance (physical and/or temporal) in a way that uses communication as effectively as possible. Clearly this demonstrates how leadership is situational. The executive of a small agency can communicate with all employees directly and with relative ease. The only likely barrier to that process is negotiating the fact employees work different shifts and days-off rotations. As agencies become large, executives and even mid-level leaders might have a more difficult time personally knowing and connecting with all employees. Alternative approaches will be needed to communicate to and connect with employees. The same method might not be used in a 200 employee municipal agency operating out of a single facility versus a 200 officer county or special-jurisdiction agency spread across multiple facilities.

Yet in all but the very largest of agencies, it is possible for top leaders to have functional and largely direct interpersonal connections with employees. Additionally, mid-level and front-line leaders in such agencies might be able to serve as a proxy for the top executive (i.e., a chief executive might not be able to routinely be present in multiple districts of a state police agency, but district commanders can provide that interpersonal connection). Jack Enter (2006) suggests that leaders schedule short meetings with a few people from throughout the agency each week. Even in a very large agency, this practice would allow a leader to establish communication and "touch base" with at least someone from every major employee group (i.e., patrol, records, communications; civilian and sworn) with regularity. This practice shows that the leader is approachable, listens, and cares what people have to say, provided the leader takes things seriously and is genuinely trying to connect with workers.

Even though a single employee might only have direct contact with a top leader every few years, the practice helps take away some of the mystery surrounding a leader who is removed by space and time from those they hope to influence. Followers might not always agree with the leader's decisions, but routine contact between the leader and employees throughout the agency helps to take away some of the vilification that can occur if that leader is seen as distant and detached. Communication and interaction humanize the leader to followers and the followers to the leader. As emphasized earlier, the method cannot be symbolic on the part of the leader. Yet when there is a genuine desire to understand and connect with followers, the results might be quite favorable.

Servant Leadership

Chapter Two laid out several leadership theories of relevance to situational perspectives on policing and police organizations. It is worth revisiting the idea of servant leadership and what it might mean in the context of considering interpersonal relationships in policing. Servant leadership is an important perspective on the nature of power dynamics and relations between leaders and followers. At first this perspective may seem an odd issue to consider in relation to discussions of charisma and personality; however, in reality the intersection is quite profound. Servant leadership is based on the belief that leaders are most efficient and effective when they focus not on controlling and directing others, but rather on serving others, especially followers, subordinates, and constituents. The servant leader views his or her ultimate goal as fulfilling the needs of subordinates; she or he place "service to others over self-interest" (Douglas 2003, 9). This requires leaders to develop and sustain trusting relationships, to treat followers as a valued resource, to share power and control, and to not see admitting mistakes or asking for help as a weakness. At the core, servant leaders see themselves as stewards who seek to help followers achieve the realization of their own potential.

Understood in this way, favorable interpersonal relations are a necessary condition for successful servant leadership. Servant leaders need to have the trust, respect, and cooperation of those they seek to assist and enable. That requires strong interpersonal relations and the right personality to accomplish those objectives. Rather than coming across as phony, patronizing, or condescending, a servant leader should be perceived as genuine, honest, caring, and someone who can be trusted. The leader's personality, charisma, and concern for others will, over time, prove to be a legitimate concern rather than a tool adopted to achieve the leader's own interests, ambitions, and aspirations. Servant leadership is not something that can be faked in the long-term.

The servant leader approach enhances leader efficacy because it attracts followers to the leader and motivates those followers to work diligently to be effective employees. Most people would likely prefer to work for someone who respects them, shows reasonable consideration for them as a person, and wants to support their development and growth as an employee. Most followers will remain dedicated, hard working, and devoted employees. It would be expected that followers would also come to accept many aspects of the leader's vision and goals. This approach does not imply that leaders can only be effective if they are directly interacting with and serving each employee. Rather, it might be enough to demonstrate the leader is there to help employees achieve their personal goals and objectives, while attempting to buffer the employee from organizational politics, pressures, and other "nonsense" (see Trojanowicz 1980).

This approach is not without potential liability for the leader. It is easy to do what is comfortable, convenient, and will ensure a leader retains his or her job or stays on her or his career trajectory. Doing what is right can be difficult and will periodically generate consequences. This does not imply that leaders needlessly engage in mutiny against their own leaders. But a leader who stands up for her or his officers may suffer career consequences. Many police chiefs have found themselves outside the pleasure of those they serve because they have attempted to buffer personnel from "nonsense" imposed by those outside the organization. Those in this group often find themselves looking for a new employing agency. To be sure, "what is right" is subjective; undoubtedly Chief Daryl Gates believed he was standing up for the men and women of the LAPD (Reese 2005). The court of public opinion, the Webster Commission, and various actual state and federal courts would seem to counter the assertion Chief Gates was in the right. Regardless of what one thinks about his actual beliefs and policies, Chief Gates is an example of a form of servant leadership and of a leader who demonstrated unwavering support for the interests, rights, and concerns of his followers. He is also an example of the risks associated with that approach, as it ultimately cost him his job.

Humor

When considering interpersonal relations and leadership personality it is salient to briefly consider the role of humor in the workplace. That policing is dangerous, particularly to the emotional and psychological well being of employees, is a fact clearly established in research and professional literature (Barker 1997; Muir 1979; Rubinstein 1973). Also documented is the use of humor among patrol personnel as a means to diffuse tension, stress, and emotional toxicity (Garner 1997; Hunt 1985; Pogrebin and Poole 1988). Much of the stress and emotional strain officers experience is produced by the organizational environment (Barker 1997; Lambert 2007). This would suggest that leaders might secure more followership and help employees handle some of the occupational stress through the strategic and appropriate use of humor, among other stress diffusion practices.

In any organization it can become easy for employees to become too absorbed with organizational politics and pathologies. Being able to laugh about the perceived absurdity of a decision made by a top executive can help alleviate stress and reinforces that all employees ought not to take themselves or the job too seriously. This is not to say that everything is a laughing matter or that humor is appropriate in all places and times. Hoffman (2007) found that leaders who made use of humor and were transformational in their approach were more likely to avoid conflict. Leaders in her study reported using humor to diffuse some of the tension created by taking on conflict situations within the workplace. Humor was a tool to manage the problems associated with taking on the tough issues in the organization. An effective leader might do well to develop a sense of humor about the organization, its work, and, most importantly, themselves. The leader must always be conscious of when, where, and how that humor is displayed to others, but situationally appropriate demonstrations of that trait can be helpful for the leader and their followers.[8]

Do Charisma and Interpersonal Relations Always Matter?

It is legitimate to question the true importance of personality and relationships in the totality of a leader's style and efficacy. Accepting that leadership is situational could also suggest that interpersonal aspects of the leader and her/his relationship with followers are of varying significance as influences upon efficacy. Boas Shamir and Jane Howell (1999) offered an insightful consideration of this question. They noted that leader charisma seems more important during times of crisis. When nations fall into chaos and disarray,

---

8. Leaders should use care when employing humor. Though it can diffuse tension in the moment and can help bond leaders and followers, there are potential liabilities. A leader should avoid making fun of anyone but him or herself unless confident those observing the remark will not see the leader as being mean, abusive, bullying, or arrogant. Though joking comments about city and civic leaders might be tempting and can help followers understand the leader is "just one of us," how will that comment be perceived and explained by the leader if it gets back to the target? Does the leader care if that happens? Should the leader care if that happens?

the emergent leader often has a "larger than life" personality. By extension, Shamir and Howell see charismatic leadership styles as more important when an organization is "psychologically weak" or in need of appreciable change. Do these circumstances and conditions accurately describe the New York City and Los Angeles Police Departments at the respective times when William Bratton assumed their command? If so, what does that suggest about the generalizability of Bratton's successful approaches in other places and times?

Though Shamir and Howell are focusing on general business environs, support can be seen for the idea that charisma will be more likely to emerge and succeed when an organization is early or late in its lifecycle, such as the creation of a new police department or a major organizational restructuring. Personality and charisma might also be more important when the leader is taking the organization or unit into a new domain of tasks requiring initiative, innovation, creativity, and group effort. Radical innovation might be easier to achieve (but never easy) when the leader has a stronger personality and greater interpersonal skills. At the onset, charisma may also matter more when a leader is not established and/or is new to the agency. Such leaders have less legitimacy embedded in their track record. Shamir and Howell also suggest that in larger agencies charisma and interpersonal relations might actually be less important for top leaders. In effect, they suggest that employees expect a weaker interpersonal relationship with top officials as the organization or unit increases in size.

Conclusions

The interpersonal relations a leader establishes with followers create a connection. The absence of such relations can yield opposite effect, a sense of detachment, ambivalence, or perhaps hostility on the part of the follower. This connection does not mean the leader and followers are best friends, agree on all matters, have routine personal interactions, or even know each other particularly well (if at all). Certainly as a unit or agency becomes smaller, the latter element should be increasingly evident, but it may not be mandatory in medium and larger agencies as a leader assumes responsibility for larger numbers of officers and support personnel. By leveraging this situation to his or her advantage, interpersonal relationships can help engender loyalty toward the leader (Hennessy 1992; Zigarmi, Blanchard, O'Connor, and Edeburn 2005). This loyalty will not be absolute, limitless, or boundless. It can be destroyed or lost quite quickly. It is fragile and fleeting.

What loyalty allows, however, is a motivational basis. It provides followers with a reason to want to trust and follow a leader, even if they may rarely have personal interactions with that leader. Loyalty garnered through personal relationships will not likely be enough to ensure effective outcomes for a leader. As an element of a more holistic approach, however, loyalty serves as one pillar supporting a foundation of effective leadership. As with other traits, habits, and attributes, interpersonal skills by themselves are likely insufficient as a foundation for sustained leadership success and excellence. Though the absence of interpersonal skills might not preclude efficacy, leaders would be well served to make a concerted effort to connect with those they seek to influence.

This does not suggest using interpersonal skills will be easy, even for a leader who is a "people person." It can be challenging to develop a capacity to "relate to numerous personalities and make the subordinates [sic] feel like he/she has the leader's undivided attention & even empathy" (deputy commander small state agency). Over time, good leaders may find themselves making decisions that are unpopular, even though the leaders know they are the right choices. "Effective leaders will always have the welfare of officers & the good of the organization in mind, which can be difficult balance, however they figure it out" (captain small municipal agency). American political lore contains numerous quotes by elected officials speaking to the inability of a leader to universally please more than a handful of people. Yet effective leaders seek interpersonal relationships that minimize the consequences of unpopular choices and work to ensure that, even when followers do not agree, they are still generally supportive of, and loyal to, the leader.

Chapter 7

Trust & Fairness

The nature of policing leans toward cynical views of the human condition, motivation, and behavior (Niederhoff 1969). It has often been noted that officers develop a high degree of cynicism (Langworthy 1987; Regoli 1976; Regoli and Poole 1979), and it makes sense that front-line personnel might turn that cynical eye inside toward the organization. The Theory X presumptions (McGregor 1960) embedded in traditional police management models are predicated on the belief employees cannot be trusted and must be controlled. This situation manifests itself both implicitly and explicitly in assorted aspects of police organizational structures, supervisory systems, policy demands, and reporting requirements. Supervisors are drawn from a pool of personnel who have been trained, socialized, and conditioned to distrust, control, manipulate, and coerce (Crank 1998). These behaviors might be viewed as helpful for an officer dealing with the uncertainties of street-level policing, however they are problematic when they are also directed toward those inside the police organization.

It is ironic that on the one hand the police want the public to trust them and view them as fair, yet officers often struggle to fully trust both the public and their own supervisors and executives.[1] Police leaders are also in the untenable situation of never being able to fully satisfy all concerned parties in making decisions. Perhaps it is inevitable that a long-time leader will periodically be viewed as having acted in an arbitrary, capricious, or unfair manner given the subjectivity of interpreting decisions and their rationales. It makes sense that supervisors might express cynical perspectives, having difficulties both trusting subordinates and being trusted by subordinates (Hays, Regoli, and Hewitt 2007; Reuss-Ianni 1983). Though policing, as a major component in the criminal justice system, is situated in an operational environment in which trust and fairness are central to effective and equitable outcomes, police organizational environments are fraught with distrust and unfair practices (or at least practices perceived as unfair).

Police executive, author, and trainer Jack Enter (2006) noted that in working with supervisor development programs he routinely asked participants how many of their supervisors or managers are "true leaders." Enter writes that based on this anecdotal process, participants on average indicated that five to ten percent of those in positions of leadership demonstrated "true leadership" in performing their duties. This is reinforced by the National Academy survey data. Less than half of the participants reported that they regularly observed effective leadership in their employing organization. It should be noted in that project participants were only asked how often they observed effective leadership, not

---

1. Clearly this is a very broad generalization. While most officers likely have supervisors they trust, they probably do not trust all of their supervisors. Nor are they likely to believe even a trusted supervisor will watch out for their interests in all situations. Union leaders in large agencies often advise new officers to never discuss disciplinary matters, complaints, or major incidents (such as officer-involved shootings) without the presence of a union representative. Whether this represents paranoia, is justified, or is simply protecting one's interests in imperfect organizational judicial systems is open to debate.

how many of their leaders were effective. Followers have good reason to be skeptical about their supervisors when experience repeatedly shows that, as a group, supervisors routinely fail to be effective leaders when given the opportunity. They have been let down repeatedly by their leaders and have experienced various forms of ineffective, bad, and evil leadership. They have observed decisions made based on incomplete information or to advance the career interests of the decision maker instead of the professional interests of employees. Consequently, it makes sense that officers will be distrustful and cynical toward the motivations, actions, and initiatives of their supervisors.

This process is not unique to policing (Cyert and March 1963). In organizations of all sizes and types it is generally true that one's position shapes perceptions, priorities, and perspectives. The beliefs and judgments of those carrying out the core tasks of the organization will differ from organizational executives. The two groups exist in similar, but distinct environments, have different perspectives, and are influenced by different pressures. Consider the deployment of wearable video recording devices by police personnel. Chief executives might like the idea of such systems, assuming they can be afforded. Having video documentation in police-citizen encounters can provide important evidence in situations where officers have taken enforcement action. A chief might speculate such a system, while expensive to establish, might pay for itself over time if it reduces the number of cases that go to trial (i.e., savings realized through reduced overtime payments to officers subpoenaed to testify). A chief might also believe the system will be important in processing complaints against officers. There might also be pressure for city leaders to address officer conduct through the use of better supervision and oversight. Officers, however, are less likely to be fans of such systems. They might believe their words and actions will be twisted against them in court or complaint proceedings. They might be concerned those who do not understand the harsh realities of the environments and circumstances officers police will second-guess or even vilify their tactics, words, and techniques.[2] The chief and her officers exist in different worlds and can reach very different conclusions about the same approach, technology, tactic, or policy decision.

Being an effective leader requires that followers trust their leaders. When situations are fluid, when change is being imposed, when the status quo is being replaced by a "new normal," in all of these situations leaders need the trust of their followers (Shamir and Howell 1999). To be effective, leaders need those around them to have faith that they are being led to a preferable set of conditions. In times when change is being imposed by the external environment, followers need to be able to trust their leader will guide them into the best possible outcome under the circumstances. Followers need to have faith that leaders will make good choices, will take needed action, are motivated by the right goals (i.e., the good of the organization and its personnel, not the career advancement of the leader), and will treat employees in a fair and equitable manner. Closely related with trust is demonstrating fairness. Leaders who are equitable and consistent in how they treat others and make decisions are likely to enjoy greater support from followers. Being perceived

---

2. The author has periodically discussed in-car video recording systems with officers. Many officers have related that in the early years they and their peers liked having video, but not audio, documentation. Video protected officers (in most situations) from complaints of excessive force. But words could be used to paint an officer in the wrong light or be twisted to suggest an officer had violated a citizen's rights. One officer related how he and his peers "accidentally" kept experiencing problems with the microphones they wore. Consequently the system worked as the officers wanted. Video was captured, but audio was not.

as fair helps earn and maintain trust (Hennessy 1992; Murphy and Drodge 2004), which can facilitate an easier and more successful administration for a police leader. The leader may reap what he or she sows.

As is the case in broader society and social interactions, in order to be trusted, a leader must first trust. Theory X and transactional approaches to management are less likely to result in a supervisor being deemed trustworthy by followers. Those managing from controlling and directive orientations focus on command and control, the use of punishment, and the need to regulate and monitor subordinates. Those tactics are unlikely to engender a feeling of trust among subordinates. Rather, subordinates would be expected to experience a divide between managers and those they seek to manage (Reuss-Ianni 1983; Trojanowicz 1980; Van Maanen 1983). The result may be a group of officers who provide symbolic compliance, but who secretly subvert the supervisor's intentions. Officers working the nightshift in a quiet community might meet several times a shift to discuss work related matters or simply to gossip. A new supervisor, being ambitious and oriented toward transactional styles, might start to monitor the radio to find when officers are making plans to meet and "check up" at those locations to make sure the officers do not visit for too long. As a result, the officers might create a system in which calling to meet at location A actually means meet at location B. When the supervisor checks location A, no one is there and it is assumed to officers had a short conversation before returning to patrol. Just to spite the supervisor, the officers might even make it a point to visit longer than normal before returning to patrol, safe in the knowledge they have subverted efforts to monitor how they spend their time.

Theory Y and transformational approaches are predicated on the belief employees can be trusted to do good work when empowered and delegated the necessary rights and authorities. Underlying the idea of transformational leadership is that followers have to trust leaders. Followers have to trust the leader is competent, capable, and working toward appropriate goals and objectives. Followers have to trust that leaders generally have the right interest in mind as they make decisions. Followers have to trust that leaders are not assigning impossible tasks or shedding unwanted work when they delegate responsibilities. Leaders must have demonstrated they can be trusted to treat all employees in a just, fair, and equitable manner. Absent these elements, the leader will struggle to earn the genuine commitment, passion, and efforts of their followers. When employees realize they are being trusted it is far more likely they will reciprocate. A leader will fare much better when seeking to guide people and processes in a new and innovative direction if that leader has the trust and respect of her or his followers.

At the core of delegation and empowering approaches is a level of tacit trust on the part of leaders. They must demonstrate that they truly believe the best outcomes will be achieved when workers are given the freedom to use their training, education, experience, and intellect to solve problems and design new and better ways to perform the core tasks of the organization. This does not mean there is never oversight, accountability, policies, reporting requirements, or standards within the workplace. But where rules and regulations exist, they will be focused on matters of vital importance (ethics, use of force, civil rights) rather than issues that are largely trivial (defining standards for facial hair or setting dates when uniformed officers must switch from wearing long-sleeved to short-sleeved uniform shirts). If it is accepted that the leader-follower relationship is an interpersonal dynamic based not strictly on authority and fear (a transactional relationship), then fairness and trust become important elements of these interactions. Implicit, if not explicit, in this process is that the leader trusts the follower to effectively use authority, discretion, and judgment to accomplish desired outcomes. Consideration of fairness and trust invert these dynamics. Does the follower perceive the leader to be fair and someone who can be trusted?

Thinking About the Role of Trust

Trust in its idealized form is a two-way street. The effective leader is both "trusting and trustworthy" (captain large municipal agency). The leader trusts followers will perform their duties professionally, ethically, legally, and within departmental and community standards. Followers trust the leader will make appropriate decisions with the best interests of the organization and its employees in mind. Because the leader shows trust and confidence in followers, the followers will presumably be more dedicated, diligent, and committed to their jobs. Followers can focus on doing the core work of the organization rather than trying to manage, mitigate, subvert, or sabotage a leader who is perceived to be out of touch, overbearing, or "out to get" employees. Consequently it would be anticipated that followers would generate work of greater quality and caliber. The leader has reinforced that followers can be trusted in the performance of their duties. The flow of trust will ideally become a reinforcing loop between leader and follower, with both sides experiencing enhanced performance as a result. Though such a characterization may strike some readers as overly optimistic, the allure of the prospect of such a healthy leader-follower relationship should be clear.

Beyond simply extending trust (in the form of delegation, empowerment, or a similar mechanism), leaders earn the trust of their followers. By demonstrating the traits discussed in other parts of this book, as well as other behaviors, the leader establishes that they "can be trusted to do the right thing" (major mid-size state agency). They demonstrate they are "trustworthy and have good morals, character, people skills and [are] credible" (lieutenant medium municipal agency). A lieutenant from a major county agency noted effective leaders "inspire trust . . . [through] common sense . . . [and] the ability to make mistakes and admit them." On the whole, the leader's action "creates an atmosphere of trust and confidence within the agency" (sergeant small municipal agency). Followers are expected to find comfort in being led by someone who is in-touch with front-line personnel, is willing to take responsibility for their own mistakes, and conveys they understand the job, its objective, and how officers will realistically need to go about realizing those objectives. Followers want more than a leader who simply makes judgment calls from behind a desk.

Trust is closely related to integrity and honesty, though it is also broader and distinct. Earning and maintain the trust of followers requires that a leader engage in an honest and honorable manner. Leaders who are fair and worthy of trust keep their word and "they are honest [and] therefore trustworthy" (lieutenant medium special jurisdiction agency). While honesty is an element of this dynamic, trust is not simply limited to being a person of integrity. Being trustworthy and trusting in others encompasses a sense of confidence that the leader will do the right thing. That is not always an issue of conventional ethics. It might mean an effective leader will approve an investigator to work overtime on a rapidly-developing investigation or that officers trust the leader will think carefully about a policy decision sitting on their desk. Fairness and trust are engendered when effective leaders "care for his people (officers) leading to mutual respect" (director major international federal agency). Trust is something akin to a plant. A leader must earn and cultivate trust, just as a gardener would seed and care for a plant. Its rewards cannot be reaped immediately and, once damaged, it takes time to heal (and may bear the scars from past violations). Nurturing trusting relationships with followers, constituents, and peers is central to leadership efficacy (Douglas 2003).

Through their actions and behaviors effective leaders ensure that "their subordinates respect them" (lieutenant mid-size municipal agency). This respect is not only based on actions, but also on how others perceive a leader's actions. This can certainly result in different assessments of fairness and trust between leaders and followers and/or between groups of followers. Leaders may believe their actions are just and appropriate, but all or some followers may derive alternative perceptions. Effective leaders are able to minimize such divergent assessments. They maximize the likelihood of being perceived as fair and trustworthy in how they exercise their leadership. "These acts earn respect" (lieutenant medium special jurisdiction agency) from followers. This might be done through communication, participatory decision making, and transparency in leadership approaches, among other strategies. As with other aspects of leadership, being perceived as a fair and trustworthy leader might be a situational consideration. It is not as important how a leader achieves that perception; what matters is the leader is aware of, and attentive to, the importance and outcomes of employee perceptions.

Fairness and trust are a function of leaders keeping their word and honoring their commitments. An effective leader is credible and "does what he says he will do" (captain major international regional agency). Though this statement seems obvious and a given, if readers reflect upon their experiences over time, it is likely they can think of numerous examples where their supervisors or leaders failed to keep promises. Certainly our nation's popular lore would suggest elected officials routinely, and perhaps intentionally, fall short of living up to this objective. To be fair, many circumstances the leader cannot control might result in a situation shifting in such a way that promises cannot be kept. Yet how often do leaders of all types make promises they know they will not or cannot keep? How often do leaders make an arbitrary choice, and then try to defend it as having been calculated, well formulated, and the right thing to do? How often do leaders provide two very different explanations or responses to two groups, telling both what they want to hear, while never being honest? How often do leaders admit when they have made a mistake?

The following sections elaborate on the role trust plays, how it can be developed, and how it can be lost. Leaders who display and hold others to a high ethical standard are more likely to be deemed trustworthy. Likewise, trust is likely to follow leaders who display a calm demeanor, do not make rash judgments, and show the courage to make difficult choices and take unpopular actions if they are the right things to do. When trust is lost or damaged, effective leaders work to repair that situation and do not let pride, ego, or arrogance stand in the way of rehabilitating that harm.[3]

Honesty & Integrity

At the cornerstone of trust are honesty and integrity. Leaders may have a difficult time securing trust if they are not true to their words, maliciously manipulate and use people,

---

3. The author worked several levels below an organizational leader who, in the wake of a highly charged time of employee-management strife, publically stated they were going to work diligently to help those in the workplace heal, rebuild trust, and move forward. In reality, nothing substantive was ever done to bring about such healing in employee-management relations. Making a statement and then not fulfilling the promise was worse than saying nothing. An executive already viewed as being untrustworthy solidified that reputation.

hold others to a higher standard than they can honor in their own conduct, or engage in serious morale lapses, even in their personal life. Trustworthiness and a willingness to trust must be demonstrated through action. Trust is fleeting and can be unforgiving if a leader is not conscious of the importance of this commodity. Like money in a bank, leaders must be aware of the balance of their trust "account" and should be judicious in the use of this commodity. A leader who commits a serious breach of their followers' trust may appreciably or completely eliminate cooperation, compliance, and support, at least for a period of time. A single minor indiscretion or ill-advised comment can reap significant damage to the trust relationship. All too often, trust is damaged due to indifference and inattention, not because the leader knowingly acted in a manner that would reduce their balance.

For a transactional leader, operating from a base of power and punishment, such matters are perhaps of less concern (though the harmful outcome might still be profound). Trust is less important when the motivation and interpersonal systems are focused on the use of rewards and punishments, versus intrinsic influences. For a transformational leader, seeking to lead by securing the trust and followership of others, greater care is likely to be devoted to avoiding such problems and outcomes. Transactional leaders are far less likely to demonstrate trust in their workforce in comparison to transformational leaders. This appreciably influences the nature of work commitment, job satisfaction, loyalty, and work productivity within the workforce. The latter would, of course, be expected to vary based on the degree to which the workforce wants to be empowered, enjoys discretion, and expects to exercise free judgment to better the workplace and its outputs. Though it is likely modern and educated personnel will want to work in a transformational environment that is likely not universally the case.

Leaders can develop and earn a reputation as being people who are trustworthy through conducting themselves with integrity. This includes seeking help when it is needed and being willing to admit (and accept blame for) mistakes (Douglas 2003). This point is echoed in Edwin Delattre's volume on ethical policing; "those who aspire to strength of character hold themselves answerable for their faults . . . they become worthy of trust by being genuinely accountable to themselves" (1996, 224). Stated another way, followers need to trust that their leaders will "do the right thing" not only as police officers, but also as supervisors and individuals. New leaders and those new to a group of workers or constituents will often have to work to prove they are worthy of trust, respect, and cooperation. Even leaders who have held the trust of followers in prior commands must recognize that in different contexts and environments trust must be earned anew. This will be particularly relevant in medium and large agencies where a supervisor accepting a new command has less history with those they are charged to supervise.

Calm Demeanor

One reason a leader may be deemed trustworthy is because of the way they handle themselves in the face of chaos, crisis, conflict, and adversity. Such a leader is "calm under pressure" (major large municipal agency). This might be demonstrated during a major event or critical incident. While others are panicked, uncertain, and emotional, effective leaders may be able to "have a calmness about them because they are at ease with their experiences" (assistant chief medium municipal agency). At the very least an effective leader might not convey their own misgivings and uncertainties to others. By demonstrating calm, focus, and confidence, the leader sets an example for others. Followers see that panic, anger, fear, passion, and irrationality should not govern actions or decisions, especially in difficult moments. This calm can engender trust and confidence on the part of subordinates. "Effective leaders must be relied upon during tense, rapidly evolving events. Knowledge and experience combined with trust and confidence from your officers are key traits. You must lead by example and always from the front" (lieutenant mid-size county agency). Just as officers need to demonstrate control and behave in a levelheaded fashion when dealing with uncertainty on the streets, a leader must do the same in all operational environments. If others see leaders who are panicking, agitated, or failing to control their emotions, they may follow suit (for once, a situation in which we might not want to see good followership).[4]

In small-scale interpersonal clashes, effective leaders "avoid moody emotional outbursts and personal conflicts" (sergeant medium municipal agency) that might later be regretted. Leaders are only human, however, they contain their base impulses and emotions. This can include addressing conflicts in private venues rather than in public. A leader "speaks well of others, [and] does not pit employees against each other or create factions within the department of us vs. them" (lieutenant large municipal agency). It is likely that leaders often do not even realize when their actions contribute to internal disputes, petty disagreements, or long-standing personality wars within the workplace. A leader might believe he is being friendly with subordinates, not realizing that sharing some extraneous information (i.e., gossiping) contributes to tension, jealousy, or stress in the workplace.

The effective leader is calm and even-tempered. Listening far more than one speaks is likely a good step to advance this trait. They seek to solve long-standing feuds in the workplace or at least find ways to manage those conflicts, rather than ignoring their presence. A leader is "someone who exhibits an inner calm even in difficult situations. Can detach emotions & think logically through highly emotionally charged situations" (sergeant large special jurisdiction agency). Trust is not just about what a leader does, but the processes and methods they use to do so. Unilateral choices made in a manner deemed erratic and unpredictable will not be likely to generate and sustain followership, even if the decisions are often correct. Decisions that are perceived to be rash, unpredictable, contradictory, or driven by ego or emotion will do little to inspire others to trust and have confidence in the leader.

Making the Right Decisions

Trust is predicated on the belief that leaders will act in a judicious and appropriate manner. A leader can be deemed trustworthy because followers know "that he will make the right decision time after time" (captain large county agency). This does not necessarily mean the leader will be perfect or infallible.[5] Making mistakes may be less influential in shaping leadership efficacy than how the leader responds to such events. Admitting errors demonstrates leaders are human. Stubborn denial of error can result in the impression of ego, arrogance,

---

4. This does not suggest the leader is not panicking or upset . . . merely that the leader controls those emotions. Jacob M. Braude is often given credit for the colloquial instruction that one should "always behave like a duck- keep calm and unruffled on the surface but paddle like the devil underneath."

5. This might imply that effective leaders not only admit mistakes, but also admit when they do not have immediate answers to questions or ready solutions to problems. It is likely better for the leader to admit uncertainty, take the time to find/make the correct decision, and move onward. Making a quick choice for the sake of appearing to be knowledgeable or in control can not only result in mistakes, it might also work against the leader's status and standing among followers. Leaders are human and should not fear being seen as such by followers.

and false bravado. Even worse outcomes can arise when leaders seeks to push blame for their mistakes onto others. A leader who admits mistakes might actually enhance their power relative to a leader who refuses to concede that a choice was incorrect. Police leaders ask officers to make the best decision possible with limited information in an imperfect world and with a willingness to stand up for those choices, even when the outcomes are not ideal. If officers are expected to do so when making split-second life and death decisions on the street, the least a leader can do is behave the same way when dealing with what are often far less consequential decisions within the workplace.

Making the right decision (in most instances) and taking action is of appreciable importance for a leader seeking to be effective. This can encompass being able "to consider all sides to a situation & problem to make proper decisions" (major large municipal agency). Followers need to have faith that leaders will act when action is needed. Though this seems common sense, the National Academy survey responses suggest inaction is far too common (see Chapter Eight). The survey respondents repeatedly expressed that too many leaders wound up being ineffective in part because they were unwilling to take on tough situations by accepting risk and making difficult decisions. They did not want to make unpopular choices, take on the task of slaughtering sacred cows, or make decisions that might derail their career ambitions.

Effective leaders, while perhaps not perfect on this front, have the courage to be open and honest in confronting the tough situations in the workplace and challenging popular (but ineffective) practices. Police officers working the street are comfortable making tough decisions with limited information and accepting the consequences of their choices. Officers do not always have to be right, but they do need to be reasonable. Good police work is predicated on an ability to be comfortable operating in an imperfect environment with incomplete data to support decisions. Comfort with that situation too often fades away among supervisors. They do what is right, rather than what is easy. Using "facts and common sense . . . the decisions that leaders make are usually the right one for all involved, even if it is the most difficult to institute" (lieutenant small municipal agency). Importantly, leaders are willing to act in situations where inaction might be an easier path. Effective leaders are willing to make difficult decisions under imperfect situations, rather than stalling or leaving problems for someone else to resolve. In performing their duties, leaders "do the right thing. They never worry about themselves only about the people they lead" (lieutenant major state agency). Their motivation is not their personal self-interests. They are motivated by what is best for their organization and/or personnel.

It is through the choices and actions leaders take that they demonstrate, cultivate, and nurture the sense in followers that they are fair and trustworthy. Their choices inspire confidence and earn respect. Though a leader might preach such principles and espouse that they embody these behaviors, the proof will ultimately be found in how followers perceive and assess the leader's actions. This situation introduces a degree of complexity and ambiguity. The "right" decision in response to a choice is frequently a subjective interpretation.

When Trust is Lost

Morgan McCall and Michael Lombardo (1983) studied corporate executives who rose to the top of their professions and organizations and contrasted them with executives who had once been tracking toward success but "derailed" along the way. Their study revealed that both successful and failed executives started out looking very similar in terms of education, experience, and aptitude. Both groups demonstrated strengths and weaknesses. Successful executives were not perfect and did not always achieve desired outcomes. In considering where the two groups split on their professional trajectory, McCall and Lombardo noted failed executives exhibited one or more "fatal flaws." Of particular relevance to considering the role of trust in leadership, failed executives tended to be: insensitive, abrasive, intimidating, and bullying in their interactions; perceived as cold, aloof, and arrogant; perceived as untrustworthy; perceived as overly ambitious, focusing more on securing their next promotion rather than performing well in their current position; and, managers who could not effectively delegate or build teams.

When others view a leader as focused more on themselves and their career aspirations than on the good of the organization or unit, their followers, and their assigned tasks, it becomes difficult to trust that leader. Followers may believe they are "expendable" if it is expedient for the leader's professional interests. Followers may find the leader's actions to be unfair, showing favoritism, poor judgment, or shortsightedness. The leader may be viewed as making decisions that provide short-term gain at a high long-term cost and this situation is often most apparent to those working closest to that leader. For example, an executive might make a policy or funding decision that will generate immediate positive attention, knowing there are long-term negative consequences. The executive in this case is likely banking on being transferred or promoted by the time those negative effects are fully recognized. Doing what is right is sacrificed in the interest of doing what is right for the executive and his/her career advancement.

When a leader is viewed as lacking the proper personality and interpersonal skills to develop reasonable relationships with followers, problems are likely to follow. A leader who does not pay enough attention to the psychological needs and emotional health of employees would be expected to experience strained leader-follower relations. Even more toxic, a leader who cavalierly ignores the motivation, needs, and well being of employees, or seeks to rule through fear, intimidation, or coercion, is not likely to sustain a team of dedicated, loyal, and hard-working employees. Though images of successful, but tough athletic coaches and military commanders may come to mind when considering leaders in this mold, harsh tactics are very rarely the path to successful outcomes. There is a tendency to romanticize tough, rugged and hard leaders, or to presume that success with that strategy is universal across all contexts and sets of followers (Mastrofski 2002; Meindl, Ehrlich, and Dukerich 1985). Though some notable leaders have achieved athletic or military success using harsh styles, experience has tended to show that approach is far less likely to yield success in general police operations.[6] Tough approaches only work when followers are willing to respond with greater effort and motivation, as opposed to responding with resistance, hostility, animosity, or withdrawal.

Officers will not trust supervisors who: go back on their word; ask others to hold themselves to a higher standard than the supervisors live up to themselves; do not admit fault; do not support personnel who have acted in good faith; push blame for mistakes onto others; or, avoid making needed (but difficult and painful) decisions because it might harm their career. Trustworthy leaders are honest. They are honest with followers, with constituents, with peers, with their superiors, and, perhaps most importantly, with themselves. This is actually incredibly difficult to achieve. It is easier for leaders to tell themselves

---

6. This may have particular relevance with certain sub-groups of employees. In general, newer and/or more educated employees might be less likely to respond favorably to a harsh or directive leadership style.

they are wonderful, that they are doing a great job, that they are treating people with dignity and respect, and that they are worthy of trust. It is also difficult to say that honesty is always the best policy for those in leadership positions. Whenever possible, however, leaders need to avoid engaging in behavior that will cause others to question whether they can be trusted and whether they are persons of integrity.

To some, such matters might seem ill-suited for policing context. Police officers and leaders deal with violent situations, work in toxic environments, face life-and-death decisions, and do so year after year without burn out, emotional fatigue, or negative consequences. Or at least this is the image the profession seeks to portray. Servant-leadership may initially seem ill-suited for policing, but readers should also recall earlier discussions of situational leadership styles. Servant-leadership is ill-suited for many aspects of policing where leaders must issue commands and trust that followers will skillfully act on those commands to bring a safe resolution to a high-risk situation. But in many other policing circumstances and activities, choices and outcomes are not "life and death" and decisions can be made in more than a split second. Servant-leadership, transformational methods, and other forms of humanistic leadership are not "soft" and do not mean the "inmates run the asylum." The leader is still in charge and holds authority over followers.

Fairness

One of the ways leaders establish and nurture trust is through demonstrating fairness. Privileged treatment for friends and supporters, even if it can be justified based on merit and achievement, will be viewed as favoritism. How many chiefs and sheriffs have hired (and later promoted) their own sons or nephews? Whether that second-generation officer was qualified or not, they are put in difficult situations with their peers because there will always be questions about whether hiring and promotions were made in a fair and appropriate manner. Like trust, fairness has a prominent subjective element and leaders might not be able to convince everyone they are operating in a fair manner. In the aggregate, however, leaders who are conscious and attentive are more likely to be perceived as fair by more people, more of the time. Leaders who are fair are more likely to be considered effective by others, which will result in that leader being "respected by their peers & work[ing] very well with little supervision" (lieutenant major municipal agency).

Ultimately, fairness and respect may emerge when leaders follow an approximation of the Golden Rule. As expressed by a captain from a large county agency, being an effective leader means that you

> Don't ask or expect of others to do something
> - You haven't done
> - Something your [sic] not willing to do
> - Something your [sic] not capable of doing
> Simple rule: treat others in a fashion you would want to be treated.

A leader is able to cultivate and sustain respect, trust, and followership when they are viewed as working in a way that is consistent with these types of principles (Hennessy 1992). The leader will presumably be viewed as fair and trustworthy because they treat others in a similar fashion. The leader is fair to followers and treats them in a way that generally demonstrates the leader trusts them and their judgment. Once again, the irony can be noted in the fact that police officers are expected to operate in a manner that will ensure the public will view them as fair and just in how they make decisions. Yet all too often, police supervisors seem to have difficulty cultivating the same perception of their decisions within the workplace. It is far too common to hear about biased, unfair behavior by supervisors that demonstrates favoritism, arbitrariness, or poor judgment.

Leaders are able to generate and leverage the perception they are fair and trustworthy when they display: "promptness, loyalty, honesty, and dedication to duty . . . [and when they show] effective knowledge of the organization" (division head major international federal agency). Leaders are less likely to be viewed as fair if they are making impactful decisions about aspects of the agency they do not understand. The effective leader "should be well versed in all aspects of law enforcement policy and procedure and capable of adjusting to various situations" (lieutenant mid-size municipal agency). Some agencies actively promote leaders who are broadly versed in police operations and administration. The Lakewood (CO) Police Department routinely moves supervisors to new assignments throughout the organization to promote the expansion of their competence in all aspects of the organization.[7] Diversity of knowledge and competence should elevate not just the perception the leader is capable of making good choices—it should actually result in improved decision making.

In many ways, fairness is a proxy for predictability. Policing is a chaotic profession. Officers deal with dynamic, confusing, and dangerous situations on a routine basis. They make life-and-death decisions based on very limited information and have to live with the consequences of their actions. The streets confront them with unpredictability and uncertainty as they are tasked with bringing some semblance of order to chaotic and disorderly circumstances. Officers are asked to confront the most psychologically damaging aspects of the human experience (violence, neglect, abuse, poverty, hopelessness, etc.). They routinely experience situations where the legal system, social services, and society as a whole fail to protect the innocent, represent the rights of victims, and make both victims and society whole again. Offenders and other individuals who are in the wrong are too-often not held sufficiently accountable for their actions and choices. Front-line policing is dangerous, unpredictable, and (all too often) unfair.

Because of this, the organization becomes a necessary psychological safe-haven for officers; the organization offers constancy and order.[8] Street level policing will never have predictability, so officers seek stability and predictability (fairness) in how the organization operates. Studies demonstrate that officers want a workplace environment that is fair and supportive (Noblet, Rodwell, and Allisey 2009). More broadly, when people perceive the government to operate in a fair fashion, they perceive it as more legitimate (Tyler 2010). By extension, we would expect that when officers perceive leaders are behaving fairly, they are more likely to accept leadership decisions. An officer might not like being passed over for promotion or special assignment, but if they perceive the selection process

---

7. Retired Lakewood Police Department Division Chief Al Youngs has repeatedly told the author that his former agency has produced more police chiefs per capita (sworn officers) than any other department in the country. Though the author has never seen hard data on this particular issue, Lakewood likely has a rate that is far higher than the national average and the claim is likely accurate. The rotation program the agency has used for decades undoubtedly contributes to that success because it produces leaders who are well versed when interviewing to take command of agencies.

8. My thanks to Chief Richard W. Myers for pointing out this perspective on why police officers resist change and seek stability within the department.

was fair and the selected candidate was suitably qualified they are more likely to accept that choice, albeit with an air of understandable disappointment. Research also shows that when officers trust and support their leaders, they are more likely to support change initiatives in the workplace (Ford 2007; Ford, Weissbein, and Plammondon 2003). Thus, when supervisors and executives are perceived to be fair in how they function and make decisions, followers would be expected to be more likely to follow. If organizational decision making is perceived to be an unpredictable and unstable process, it is more likely to generate stress, confusion, unease, and animosity among personnel. Those emotions and experiences distract personnel from the task at hand, confuse their understanding of organizational processes, and diminish the likelihood they will actively comply with new ideas, directives, and changes. Officers want stability in the police department to serve as a buffer to the chaos of street-level operations. It is incumbent on leaders to do their best to provide such an environment.

Equal Treatment

Fairness and trust imply a degree of consistency in decision making. This is easily seen in the context of discipline and rewards. Effective leaders avoid the appearance of making capricious, arbitrary, or preferential choices in hiring, assigning, promoting, and sanctioning employees. They avoid the perception that they are giving preferential treatment to friends, family, or specific groups; they avoid the appearance of punitive treatment targeting enemies, adversaries, or specific groups. Followers want to know a proverbial level playing field exists upon which all personnel are judged. This consistency helps followers understand what motivates the leader and anticipate future decisions s/he might make. Ensuring that actions and decisions are perceived in a proper light highlights the importance of communication. Leaders might need to explain choices that are likely to be misunderstood or misinterpreted. This is not, of course, possible under all situations and circumstances. In disciplinary matters, for example, the rights of the accused officer may preclude a leader from discussing or explaining why punishment was or was not issued in a given situation. And certainly, though leaders can seek to convey their rational for making certain decisions, they cannot force others to believe such explanations.

What does it meant to say "effective leaders treat people fairly" (lieutenant, medium county agency)? Effective leaders provide trust and fairness in how they impose standards and make disciplinary decisions. They demonstrate "equal and consistent treatment of subordinates, peer and bosses" (captain, mid-size municipal agency). This includes holding "all people accountable to the same set of rules" (commander, mid-size municipal agency). They have "the desire and/or ability to handle discipline and problems in a fair manner . . . [and] are consistent in their decision making" (captain, medium municipal agency). As a result "they are respected because they are fair and consistent" (major, large municipal agency).

This equality and consistency is important. Equality of treatment demonstrates that everyone in the organization is held to the same set of standards and expectations. Police organizations are similar to any other organization, where favoritism and nepotism can have toxic effects on employee morale and corrosive effects on leader legitimacy. Policing history is replete with a long and unfortunate history of making hiring, assignment, promotion, and disciplinary choices for reasons other than merit, performance, and evidence (Manning 1997; Walker 1977; Wilson 1968). Though the introduction of civil service standards, employee rights, and labor associations has helped quell this situation, agencies may still experience inequitable treatment, or the perception thereof. How often do agencies big and small provide at least the perception that hiring and promotion decisions are made based upon family ties, favoritism, and informal connections? While this is far from a universal problem, the author has seen and heard of innumerable examples in agencies of all size across the country. A sheriff hires his son, who very quickly begins promoting up the ranks ahead of more senior and (in some views) more qualified candidates. A new chief begins promoting personnel with whom she went to the academy years earlier. Such nepotism and favoritism is in no way unique to policing and there can be some rationale for leaders wishing to surround themselves with a staff they can trust and with whom they have an established relationship.[9] Care must be taken so that leaders avoid the appearance of these types of questionable decisions. Even if a friend or family member is the most qualified person for a job or is the focus of a disciplinary decision, effective leaders will use care to handle such situations fairly, honestly, and consistently. This might include delegating critical personnel choices to a neutral party to avoid the appearance of impropriety.

Equal treatment can also been seen extending beyond personnel matters within the workplace. An important form of equal treatment that can enhance the view of a particular leader being fair and trustworthy relates with that leader's consistency in making decisions. A leader who is consistent in her of his vision, message, decisions, and actions becomes an easier person for followers to follow. Consistency instills confidence that the leader has a well-designed and well-thought-out vision for the unit or organization. A leader who repeatedly shifts in the articulated goals and accepted methods of attaining those objectives is less likely to instill confidence among followers and will struggle to generate a strong level of supportive behavior. Inconsistency makes the leader's vision seem capricious and arbitrary; followers are likely to quickly realize the message and mission are continually changing. It is difficult to generate support for change (especially change that is a more radical departure from current conditions and circumstances) if the definitions of the endpoint or the accepted route to that endpoint are continually changing. That is not to say effective leaders never shift their strategy upon recognizing the current goal or method is not optimally effective or otherwise problematic. However, such shifts should be sparing and their rationale might need to be explained so they do not generate the impression the leader lacks confidence or certitude in his or her own plan.[10]

Consistency in mission and message allows followers to figure out how to work in a manner that is in sync with such principles. Whether the follower truly believes in the direction a leader wants to move or if the follower is simply trying to be a "team player," she or he needs a degree of predictability. The follower cannot do things in furtherance of the objectives defined by the organization or leader if there is not a clear understanding of what those objectives are and in what acceptable ways they can be achieved. Consider

---

9. In defense of leaders, there can be a variety of situations, circumstances, and rationales that justify personnel decisions and other choices made by the leader. Even actions that are made in an unbiased fashion will not always be viewed as just or appropriate by followers. Ultimately leaders cannot control how their actions and choices are perceived, but through awareness and conscious action they might be able to minimize the likelihood of being viewed as biased, unfair, or inequitable. Sometimes the sheriff's son is a good candidate for promotion, but the sheriff needs to recognize how that action will be viewed. It would be similarly unjust to deny a promotion chance to the son simply because his father is the sheriff.

10. In the absence of trust and a believable explanation, followers will jump to conclusions about motive and rationale for management decisions, whether those conclusions are right or wrong. When decisions are not explained personnel in any organization will tend to assume the worst.

a drum major leading a marching band. The band members might not like every song, but can still perform the movements and play the requisite music notes at the proper time if they know the song and routine. If there is consistency in what is being played and how it is to be performed, the band should be able to execute a given performance and the band's members should be able to set aside their personal views, behave professionally, and perform in the agreed upon and prescribed manner. If the drum major keeps modifying the routine or changes the song selection altogether, confusion, anger, and indifference may all arise. Even those who wish to perform as directed and intended may struggle to do so in the face of repeated changes, big or small.

Consistency is also important in the way a leader approaches more mundane and routine aspects of their command, such as tasks that are more administrative or managerial in nature. Followers like a degree of consistency and predictability. They want to know how a leader is likely to respond to a certain type of request. They want to know their vacation request will be handled in a manner that is uniform with how other requests are received and judged. This goes beyond the problem of a supervisor treating some followers with favoritism or separate sets of rules or standards. What becomes important is that supervisors handle situations and personnel in a routine manner and avoid behaviors and actions that might generate the perception (false or not) that the supervisor is inequitable. Though a leader's decision making patterns may change with time, there should not be radical variations from incident to incident or week to week. This lends the appearance that a leader cannot be trusted because he or she lacks confidence, dependability, and competence. Whether the leader has those traits or not, the perception they are lacking can yield significant problems within the workplace.

Conclusions

Trust and fairness are important components of how leaders operate. Being trustworthy and fair demonstrates a leader is truly a person of honor and integrity. Followers can develop greater confidence in a leader who exhibits a calm demeanor, makes good choices, and is fair toward all employees. That confidence is of critical importance when a leader needs followers to have faith and acceptance as the organization moves into new directions. One way for leaders to generate and sustain trust and fairness is to be conscious of the leader-follower relationship and interactions. This might require considering how actions, decisions, and processes will be viewed by those the leader seeks to influence. The answers to such questions might not cause a leader to make a different decision, but could suggest alternative ways to communicate, implement ideas, and attend to interpersonal relationships. Perception can become reality in its consequences; whether or not a supervisor is *actually* trustworthy and fair is far less relevant than whether personnel perceive the supervisor as such.

Leaders need to earn and maintain the trust of others. They need to be authentic, honest, and people of integrity (see Murphy and Drodge 2004). Interpersonal skills matter not because leaders need to have winning smiles, but because they need to have emotional intelligence (Drodge and Murphy 2002; Hennessy 1992). Transactional leadership approaches can be an appreciable asset in advancing trust and fairness in the workplace. Involving workers in defining objectives, goals, methods, and decisions can greatly advance the likelihood the leader will be trusted and viewed as fair. In the end, the trajectory is relatively simply, vitally important, and often difficult to maintain. Supervisors need to be honest in how they approach their duties and how they treat others. They need to work to nurture and maintain the trust of those around them. They need to operate in a manner that is reasonably transparent and predictable whenever possible. Doing this maximizes the likelihood that followers will accept the leader's decisions, embrace the leader's vision, and support the leader's initiatives. In this way, leaders actually make their jobs easier in the long run.

Chapter 8

Taking Action

> The single most important trait that makes an effective leader is the ability and willingness to accept responsibility and to act on it, while not being intimidated into inaction through fear. Too many weak leaders avoid responsibility and avoid issues that they know they should address, but are too timid to do so.
> —Captain, medium municipal agency

At first it may seem unusual to suggest that a police supervisor could be someone who struggles to take action. Popular social and media images of policing suggest that "action" is at the center of what front-line officers do on a daily basis. Documentaries, "reality" programs, and fictive accounts of street-level policing imbue an image of police officers that are in constant motion, continually dealing with chaotic, unusual, and sometimes dangerous situations. Taking action seems a requisite element of functioning as a front-line patrol officer. By extension, it would be expected that supervisors (by virtue of starting their careers as police officers) should also be oriented toward action—identifying problems, enacting solutions, fixing what is broken, and taking control of situations. Despite this perspective on police officers and supervisors, National Academy respondents indicated that true leaders were those who took action and that many holding supervisory positions failed to act when needed. Leadership is ultimately about action. It is not words, promises, hyperbole, or platitudes. It is truly accomplishing something, not just motivational or inspirational thinking.

All too often, ineffective leaders were characterized as supervisors who failed to act. They ignored clear problems because taking action was difficult or messy. They avoided taking actions that might derail their career paths because they were risky or unpopular. They emphasized the management of routine administrative, supervisory, and reporting tasks because they preferred to focus on control rather than achieving true leadership. The absence of action is not always a willful and intentional situation. Some supervisors did not address lingering issues within the unit or organization because they did not understand how to go about fixing deeply entrenched problems in the context of the resources and restrictions that defined their operational environment. Avoidance of action became their preferred supervisory tool, either by design or by default. Perhaps some lacked a true understanding of the distinctions between leadership and management, believing they were leading, while reality was quite different.

It is curious to note the emergence of a tendency toward inaction among some working in police supervision given the presumption that street level policing is an action-oriented profession with a supporting culture geared toward decisiveness, bringing order to chaos, and fixing problems. For example, in writing about her studies of New York City PD officers, Elizabeth Reuss-Ianni (1983) articulated rules embraced by "street cops." A number of these rules demonstrate the primacy officers placed on "taking care of business" in their assigned beat. These rules include the idea that street cops needed to take responsibility for their assigned area during their shift; other officers should not regularly have to come into their assigned area to handle routine calls. Likewise, efficient officers did not leave work for the next shift to complete. These rules reinforced the vision of front-line officers as being focused on the importance of the efficient provision of policing services (Skolnick 1994). Once again we are confronted with circumstances where the behavior of front-line personnel seems to be "switched off" among far too many supervisors.

This chapter considers the role of action and inaction in shaping leadership outcomes. It begins with a discussion of prior policing literature that informs our understanding of why the tendency toward inaction might emerge. Next, it examines the nature of action in organizations. This includes discussion of when and how change is initiated, including consideration of the fact leaders seek to make good choices and accept the consequences of that situation. The chapter concludes with an analysis of the role self-interests and career advancement play in shaping leadership inaction.

The Emergence of Inaction

Regrettably a review of policing literature provides numerous examples and insights contributing to an understanding of how leadership inaction can emerge. Despite the dominance of action as a theme in policing (Crank 1998) its counterpoint is not in short supply. William Muir's classic work on street level policing included a typology of officer working styles (1977). Based on his observations in a single urban police department, Muir noted variation in the extent to which officers were effective and trustworthy. He associated this variation in part to how officers viewed the human condition, morality, and social order. The ways in which officers responded to these factors shaped how they performed their duties and their orientation toward policing as a profession. Muir labeled one of his typologies "avoiders," characterizing these officers as those who struggled to resolve moral ambiguities and lacked a degree of passion for their job.

Avoiders hoped to evade contentious decisions, sidestep situations that required independent judgment, and elude being expected to take initiative on the job. In effect, despite working on the front line of the policing profession and despite the need to frequently take control of chaotic situations, avoiders sought to minimize the frequency with which they were in situations requiring that they take action. Other policing scholars have noted similar patterns in their observations of front-line personnel (Broderick 1987; Worden 1995). For example, Michael Brown's (1988) policing typology included a category he labeled "service style" officers who were characterized as engaging in little proactive work and having a strong predisposition to handle dispatched calls in a cursory and informal manner. In his observations, these officers were either focused on other responsibilities (a second job or school), were "burned out," or were "coasting" toward retirement. Though researchers have tended to categorize officers into groupings that are suggestive of a more active working style, most typologies include a category for those who are less active and vigorous in their approach to the job.

Dorthy Guyot (1979) issued a stark and germane critique of rank structures in American police organizations. She noted the heavy emphasis on strict adherence to chains of command allows personnel to pass undesirable questions and tasks off on their supervisors. This does not imply officers always follow the chain of command, but rather that the chain of command gives them a natural "out" when they wish to avoid certain situations. Bureaucracy generates inaction because it can grind decision making to a halt. At the same time, bureaucratic systems provide natural excuses and buffers allowing inaction when a worker does not actually wish to pursue a particular form of action. Worse, it creates a very easy way for a vengeful worker to deny citizens the services and responses they request of their government (Brown 1988; Lipsky 1980; Reiss 1971; Wilson 2000).

Likewise, police agencies of all shapes and sizes tend to utilize salary structures that allow personnel to quickly reach the peak of their possible pay scale (Guyot 1979). Patrol officers nearing retirement may earn roughly the same (before pay adjustments based on shift, education, and overtime) as officers with five years of service. High performers and avoiders are organizationally and economically analogous. The resulting system creates disincentives for remaining a patrol officer. In many organizational structures the only way to visibly increase one's power, money, and status is through rising in the ranks. Dominant pay structures in policing mean that officers reach a point relatively early in their careers when promotion is the only way to advance to higher standing in the agency. An officer with less than ten years on the job may never realize an appreciable salary increase (except for cost of living increases) if they stay on the front line. If the organization tends to punish risk and error, supervisory inaction becomes further reinforced. Personnel can only achieve greater formal power, money, and official status by obtaining a promotion. The way to continue securing promotions (and greater formal power, money, and official status) is to avoid actions that generate risk and controversy. When change is pursued it is often for its own sake. Initiatives are generally safe and in response to clearly recognized needs (or demands) to change. It can be all too rare to see leaders engaging in proactive efforts to fix persistent problems, overlooked concerns, controversial matters, and unrecognized needs.

It might be supposed that officers with a predilection toward inaction and avoidance would be less likely to receive favorable consideration when it is time for an agency to make promotions. Avoiders would not be expected to fare well in testing and assessment procedures used to inform promotional decisions. It would be expected that those with less inclination to act would suffer from disruptions to their career advancement because this failure would be recognized by the organization, which would hope to avoid this attribute among supervisory personnel. There are two potential faults couched within this presumption. First, an officer might drift into inaction once they have already achieved a supervisory position in their agency. Inaction might become a learned supervisory behavior that is reinforced by agency culture and tradition (i.e., avoiding "career killer" moves to continue up the organizational hierarchy). Continued advancement might be predicated on avoiding matters that are controversial, challenging, unpopular, or that have a perceived probability of creating political, professional, or legal consequences.[1]

Second, several aspects of police organizational behavior might support viewing a "cautious" (read: inactive) officer or supervisor as an ideal candidate for further promotion. Action and decisiveness often involve risk, whether an officer is on the street or in the station house. Personnel who repeatedly take risks will eventually make mistakes. In many organizations that is expected, accepted, and tolerated; perhaps it is even encouraged. It is recognized that perfection is impossible. Far too many police agencies do not have such a tolerance for errors made in good faith. Taking a risk resulting in injuries, property loss, or damage to an agency's reputation can have dire consequences for an officer's career prospects. The agency might not consciously make choices or create structures to repress risk taking. Unspoken traditions and values can have a repressive influence discouraging risk takers, innovative thinkers, creative thinkers, and those who ask the tough questions.

---

1. Recall the quote on pages 22–23 from the senior executive in the large state police agency. It is also possible that selection and socialization patterns in far too many agencies push out unconventional thinkers early in the career cycle and encourage and reinforce conformity over time.

Personnel displaying these attributes might not be placed in positions of formal authority where they would have the opportunity to exercise their tendencies.

The Nature of Action

The recognition, wisdom, strength, and courage to take action represent important distinctions between effective and ineffective leaders. This is particularly true as the action becomes more involved and complex. Though minor changes are continually needed in any organization and though that process requires a level of leadership, a much higher level is necessary to take on the large, daunting, controversial changes to core aspects of an agency's traditions and operations. In characterizing the need for action, the National Academy participants were more focused on discussing effective leaders as those who had the resolution, foresight, and willingness to take on the latter issues. Real leadership was not defining new ways to order printer paper, approve pending vacation requests, or conducted pre-shift briefings. Though these may be matters of some consequence, they are management and administrative tasks.

Effective leaders take action above and beyond basic administrative tasks. They do not hide from making the tough decisions that might aggravate some followers, generate hostile public reactions, and create the possibility of liability, among other consequences. They do what they believe is the right thing, though it may alienate them (at least temporarily) from some peers, constituents, supporters, or followers.[2] Leaders do not shy away from difficult discussions and decisions, even if it might represent a "speed bump" on their career trajectory. For chief executives this can mean a willingness to be fired, voted out of office, or asked to resign. They do not place their personal interests and objectives ahead of doing what is best for the organization or their followers, or what is right, just, and moral. There is certainly a degree of partiality in labeling a particular choice or action "the right thing," which further complicates how a given situation is interpreted. Whether a choice is right or not is, of course, highly subjective and dependent on the position of the person evaluating that decision.

The following discussion explores the nature of leadership action, as conveyed by the comments of the National Academy participants. These comments can be grouped into five main themes. First, true leaders are able to identify problems and then seek to confront and correct that situation. Second, leaders articulate their vision to others in order to generate support and "buy in" for subsequent actions. Third, leaders seek to make choices that are grounded on broad expert input. Fourth, leaders do not allow tradition to stand in the way of needed change; "that's how we've always done it" is not an acceptable answer to questions of policy, protocol, and procedure. Finally, leaders accept responsibility for their actions, sharing praise and shouldering blame.

Identifying & Confronting Problems

All too often organizations and units have problems with personnel, practices, and protocols that work against efficient, effective, and equitable operations. Long-time em-

---

2. For the purposes of this discussion, readers should presume leaders are doing the "right thing" when seeking to take action about issues they deems necessary and which a neutral observer might agree is the case.

ployees, including supervisors, learn the speed bumps and procedural traps that hamper those processes. Those problems often persist because they are daunting or difficult to correct. Fixing them requires taking on tradition, dominant personalities, egos, and/or complex paths toward resolution. Many in positions of authority may opt to live with such situations, believing they cannot be resolved or simply lacking the will or energy to take on the matters.

For mid-level leaders it can be easy to rationalize that "the systems" or "the bosses" will not allow the implementation of needed solutions. Resources will not be made available, policies will not be changed, and authority will not be granted, so asking for permission or pursuing action can be dismissed as pointless. In some situations mid-level leaders might be correct in this assessment and the barriers to successfully solving persistent problems might be (nearly) insurmountable. Unfortunately, it can also become far too easy to accept these rationalizations and use them as excuses to not pursue needed improvements or actions when a leader is lazy, preparing to transfer or retire, or simply does not want to take on the headaches of difficult processes.

Effective leaders defy this convention. "They bring to light problems that need to be addressed" (commander large county agency). These leaders bring a critical eye to assessing the organization and its operations. Rather than generally believing that most matters are being handled well already, they are continually looking for ways to make improvements. These are not simply change for the sake of change, nor are they changes intended to allow a supervisor to "write their name" on aspects of the operation (which is often based in the belief that supervisors need to make their mark and accomplish something substantial to help secure their next promotion). Leaders operating with this orientation are continually seeking ways to make improvements in the efficiency, efficacy, and equity of operations, even if it is accomplished through the "relentless pursuit of incremental improvements" (first line supervisor major federal agency). Even that which is "good" in the agency and its operations might be made "great" with the right change.

They are "not afraid to address problems . . . [and they do] not avoid confrontations" (captain small municipal agency). Effective leaders take action by not allowing inertia, easy paths, or personal ambitions stand in the way of doing what is right. They do not simply resign themselves to having to work around existing flaws in the agency or unit. They seek ways to fix the flaw, even when it is difficult or unpopular. As with "doing the right thing" there is a degree of subjectivity in making these observations. Effective leaders seek ways to solve entrenched problems, but this does not mean they needlessly "tilt at windmills." There are times and situations where specific forms of action would be ill-advised or where patience is the most prudent course of action. What this means is effective leaders have "a willingness to get involved in the task" of leadership (lieutenant large municipal agency).[3] Doing what is popular cannot be allowed to trump doing what is right. "Effective police officers (leaders) are the ones who are not afraid to speak up if it is not working or they notice that something is not right" (lieutenant large municipal agency).

---

3. This is, of course, a generalization. There can be reasons why a leader does not take on a given issue at certain points in time. Some issues are more volatile than problematic; deriving and enacting their solutions can create new and greater issues. A new leader may wait to address entrenched problems while they are learning the landscape of their unit or agency and building a foundation of support. The point here is that a leader does not avoid action simply because doing so will be uncomfortable, hard, or unpleasant. When the "right thing" to do is to act, the leader does so, even if it will be difficult and unpopular.

Articulating a Vision

Charles Lindblom (1959) argued that incremental approaches to public policy might actually yield better long-term results. In his famous essays on the matter he articulated why he believed a policy process of change predicated on "disjointed incrementalism" might make empirical and practical sense (Lindblom 1959, 1979). When change is particularly large, complex, and revolutionary, it can be difficult for a leader or leadership team to fully see and understand the whole in order to craft a full policy at the initial stage of implementation. Rather, Lindblom suggested that even though the decision making process would take more time and perhaps more resources, it was rational to break major change efforts into stages. At each stage, analysis and consideration would suggest the next step in the process.

There is, however, a risk of a leader operating based solely on the relentless pursuit of incremental improvements. These endeavors only work if the leader has articulated a clear vision. Underlying Lindblom's arguments is the notion that leaders have developed and communicated a clear vision of the end-state they are pursuing. When followers understand and embrace such a vision, disjointed incrementalism can be a powerful tool. For example, in tight economic times an incremental approach to major change would lead an agency to question how it can best position itself to make substantial progress when resources are available in the future. Until that time, the agency can plan and pursue low- or no-cost efforts toward the desired goal. In the absence of a clear vision there is a risk the leader will simply be asking followers to "wander in the desert" without a clear sense of direction. The latter approach is more akin to Herbert Simon's (1956) concept of "satisficing" in which the decision that is reached is simply acceptable, rather than optimal.

In order to optimize the effects of taking action, leaders must be able to consider the future and be "willing to look outside the 'box' to find solutions. An effective leader must be willing to take chances to change an organization for the better" (lieutenant medium municipal agency). Leaders are not constrained by tradition and culture in thinking about possible solutions to problems, though tradition and culture should be accounted for in the planning and implementation processes. Leaders must also be "guided by what they believe is right" (assistant chief medium municipal agency). Importantly, others around the leader must understand these guiding principles and visions. It is necessary that leaders have a set of core beliefs and objectives that govern decision making, planning, and the use of discretion. To be effective, it is also necessary that those around the leader have an understanding of those values and visions, as well. In the absence of such an understanding followers will have an exceedingly difficult time working to support the leader's plans, goals, objectives, and actions.

Making Well-Founded Choices

Taking needed action requires that leaders have self-assurance in their own judgment. As decisions involve increasingly complex tasks, have more unpredictable outcomes, and involve issues with which a leader is less familiar, this might be more difficult for leaders, who must have "confidence in themselves and their abilities" (deputy chief small municipal agency). Such a circumstance may initially seem a given, but in reality leaders often find themselves with responsibilities for new units and tasks they do not fully understand. Or leaders might find themselves confronting situations where the consequences of their actions are significant, including the risk of injury, death, and property damage. A supervisor with new responsibility for a tactical unit might have to decide aspects of how to handle a hostage situation or barricaded subject. If the supervisor has little or no personal experience with tactical operations, he or she might be reluctant to issue the order to conduct a forced entry, fearing what may happen to the offender, hostages, or officers. This is why seeking input from others can be so important for leaders.[4]

In and of itself, taking action and making changes in an organization or its operations is not necessarily a good thing. Respondents were not expressing that leaders were effective because they simply made change. They were not advocating change for the sake of change. Rather, they were focused on leaders making needed changes by bringing about necessary reform, correction, and innovation within the workplace based on sound information and reflecting appropriate judgment. There is a distinction between a leader bringing about change in pursuit of personal career advancement or ego (sometimes referred to as "careerism") and a leader bringing about change because it is the right thing to do and/or is in the best interests of the organization.

Unfortunately there are abundant examples of careerism in policing and many other professions. Leaders seeking to continue on a promotional track may be motivated by what they can do to earn their next advancement, rather than doing the best job they can in their current position. In some situations, this may result in change for the sake of change, as leaders seek to "make their mark" in their current position in order to ensure they will advance to the next rank. Large-scale change may occur not because it is needed, but because it will presumably demonstrate the leader's skills and aptitude. For example, a leader assigned to direct a larger agency's training academy might pursue an expansion in the duration of the pre-service academy completed by new officers.[5] This change might not be motivated by any rational basis (i.e., a change in state mandate or a conscious discussion that additional training in certain subjects will yield more successful and qualified officers). Rather, the director of the academy might be seeking to make a "signature"

---

4. Research into the psychology of power and behavior suggests there can be dangers when supervisors are not confident in their abilities. Clinical experiments have found the "power paired with self-perceived incompetence leads to aggression, and . . . this aggressive response is driven by feelings of ego defensiveness" (Fast and Chen 2009, 1406). Those in positions of power do not always perceive they are powerful and do not always have confidence in their abilities. In other words, having formal power does not appear to buffer individuals from psychological threats. Supervisors who have power and self-confidence in their competence to make good decisions and do their job correctly have no need to be aggressive (Fast and Chen conceptualized aggression as doing things that might induce discomfort or be emotionally bothersome to others). Individuals who are granted power but feel their base is weak because of self-perceived incompetence may become hostile, aggressive, territorial, or defensive.

5. This example is loosely based on an actual situation related to the author in the course of this research project. An upwardly mobile executive was rotated into an agency's training facility. By all accounts, the executive was not particularly interested in training. The executive's time at the academy served to "punch" the executive's ticket for a future promotion. As director of the academy, the executive wanted to prove that more training could be delivered with existing personnel and funding. Staff in the agency's academy felt quality would decline without additional resources. They taught more students in a less personalized manner. When the executive advanced to another position in the agency, the academy reverted to the old way of operating. Output was increased not because it was needed, but because it served the career interests of a single executive. It might be argued whether careerism is really leadership behavior or simply serves to demonstrate management and administrative skills, as well as the ability of the supervisor/executive to force change and impose will.

accomplishment with which might demonstrate her or his success and suitability for further career advances. Effective leaders avoid such situations, making changes that are needed and based on well-founded input and information. Their actions are well-reasoned and well-informed, at least to the extent that time and circumstances will allow (i.e., in tactical matters a leader may have very little time to solicit input and evaluate information before choosing a course of action). "They make well founded decisions and do the right thing" (chief small municipal agency). They avoid making knee-jerk decisions, instead finding ways to make reasonable choices based on available evidence, resources, and time.

"Effective leadership is someone who makes decisions (right or wrong), based on facts and common sense. The decisions that this individual makes is [sic] usually the right one for all involved, even if it is the most difficult to institute" (lieutenant small municipal agency). Effective leaders are notable because of "their ability to weigh both sides of an issue and to decisively make the difficult decision, their ability to look to the future" (sergeant small municipal agency). Taking action can necessitate a degree of foresight on the part of the leader, who must anticipate how the agency must change today to be adaptive and responsive to the circumstances of tomorrow. In this way, leaders are futures thinkers. They do not limit themselves to only taking action when its need is clear and apparent. Rather, leaders seek to also anticipate what actions need to be taken today to place the agency in a better position for the realities of tomorrow (Schafer, Buerger, Myers, Jensen, and Levin 2012).

As noted throughout this volume, effective leaders are not always in positions of formal authority or office. At times the most effective leaders in an organization might be frontline personnel. Though the actions taken by these personnel are likely exclusively tactical, as opposed to strategic, the ramifications of (in)action from the front line are no less profound. Tactical actions taken by uniformed patrol officers can result in, or reduce the likelihood of, injuries, fatalities, property damage, eroded police community relations, and civil liability, among other consequences. In describing informal leaders in police organizations, a lieutenant (major state agency) noted "effective leaders possess the ability to make sound decisions in the absence of detailed instruction." Though tactical decisions might seem less significant from an organizational perspective, poor tactical actions or the lack of tactical actions can be as profoundly transformative as any strategic decision made by agency executives.

Unfortunately, the impact of tactical actions is most evident when those actions produce undesirable outcomes. The importance and value of good tactical choices and actions are less evident, because they preclude the loss of life, serious injury, major property damage, damaged police-community relations, and civil liability. Success is often nearly invisible because it attracts less attention and fewer long-term consequences (i.e., it is less likely a successful resolution of a hostage matter will generate civil lawsuits). Much like the prevention of crime, measuring successful tactical outcomes is difficult; it is hard to quantify an event that did not occur. Though less visible and readily apparent, the tactical actions of front-line personnel (whether formal or informal leaders) can still demonstrate their efficacy as leaders. These personnel "make decisive and good decisions. They know what they are talking about. They have experience to back up what they say. They have the respect of others and are trusted. They have proven themselves many times over" (sheriff small county agency). Organizations need to seek out ways to identify those individuals and encourage them to pursue promotional opportunities to ensure and expand their continued positive influence in the organization.

Action in the Face of Tradition

Taking action at times requires a leader to make unpopular choices in order to do what is right to ensure effective, efficient, and equitable agency operations. This requires the leader to demonstrate courage and integrity over self-interests and self-preservation. Police organizations tend to support the emergence of cultures that resist change in favor of status quo, custom, ritual, habit, and folklore (Crank 1998). Certain practices and traditions become entrenched within organizational practices, taking on the role of "sacred cows" that are not to be questioned or challenged, no matter how clearly unfair, illogical, or inappropriate they might be. Often these circumstances revolve around internal practices and operations. They may have persisted, in part, because they are nearly invisible to the public and pose no obvious liability risk. To an outsider the change might seem logical and it could be surprising that anyone would oppose the modification, yet some inside the organization may fight vigorously to avert the intended action.

Elements of an agency's uniforms serve are illustrative of such situations. State police agencies, for example, often issue "campaign" style hats to uniformed personnel, frequently mandating that these hats be worn while in public. Campaign hats often have a three to four inch flat brim that runs around the circumference of the wearer's head. They hearken back to the early days of many state police agencies in the 1910s and 1920s; campaign hats were common elements of military uniforms during and after World War I. These hats have persisted for decades and have taken on strong symbolism in many state agencies because they have become emblematic and iconic of these types of agencies.

In some perspectives, campaign hats lack functionality and could represent an officer safety concern. The large flat surface area of the brim can capture wind and the draft from passing vehicles. Recall these are worn by state police officers who often conduct traffic stops on the side of state and federal highways while being passed by semi-tractor trailers and other large vehicles. Officers may have to frequently place one hand on their hat in order to keep it from blowing off their heads and onto the roadway. An officer holding a ticket book, a citation, and a driver's documents (license, registration, proof of insurance, etc.) in one hand and holding on her/his uniform hat with the other has no free hands to respond to a threat from a motorist or to operate a portable radio. Though campaign hats offer form, they certainly lack functionality, which might explain why military personnel are no longer seen wearing them or other more decorative or formal headgear in operational situations. It is curious and telling that police agencies of all types routinely defy that practice, requiring officers to wear a variety of hats that lend a visual appeal, but have no operational function (though this practice has likely declined appreciably in recent decades).

Consider, as well, holsters for duty firearms carried by patrol officers. In the early decades of the 1900s many agencies issues their officers "crossdraw" holsters for their duty revolvers. A crossdraw holster positions an officer's weapon on the front of their "weak side" hip with the grip angled toward the strong side. For a right-handed officer, the firearm would be worn at the front of their left hip. The weapon would be situated so it was in between being perpendicular and parallel to the officer's belt. The original logic for this design was that it allowed an officer to access his/her firearm in a wide range of circumstances, including while sitting in an automobile. In the mid-20th century many agencies moved away from this style of holster in favor of the "strong side" holsters that dominate contemporary police uniforms (i.e., right handed officers wear their firearm squarely on their right hip, with the weapon positioned barrel-down). It was believed this way of carrying the weapon maximized speed of accessibility, weapon security, and weapon retention for officers. Yet some agencies persisted in requiring officers to wear crossdraw holsters, in some cases mandating officers wear "full flap" versions in which the weapon was completely covered by a large flap of leather. The latter version required a more complicated (and time consuming) process for drawing the weapon, though it was still argued that in certain duties, such as traffic enforcement, this positioning was optimal. The Iowa State Patrol persisted in this weapon configuration until 2003.

On the surface uniform hats and firearm holsters may seem far removed from serious consideration of effective police leadership. Both issues, however, illustrate the power of symbolism, tradition, and custom within organizations. From many professional perspectives, campaign hats and crossdraw holsters were outdated. They appealed to a customary image of the police profession but also represented potential risks to officer safety in routine patrol operations. Yet their use in some agencies persisted long after this operational dysfunction and danger were clearly apparent to those outside the organizations. The hats were tradition, custom, and a hallmark of these agencies. They symbolized the history and heritage imbued in agency uniforms. Likewise, crossdraw holsters (and shoulder straps for Sam Browne duty belts) represent an agency's early legacy and the officers who have come before, serving their jurisdiction with the same equipment and look.

Consider a leader in a fictive agency issuing campaign hats or crossdraw holsters. Though some officers might support a change, others are likely to have strong affinity for those conventional elements of the agency's duty attire. Though these elements may no longer serve a rational purpose in modern society, may have been "phased out" by most other peer agencies, and may hold little visual symbolism for the general public, they become tradition and custom. Continuity in their use/application is driven by history and inertia from the past. Even though change might make sense, the power of that custom can continue to propel an irrational or outdated practice into the future.[6] Though hats and holsters might seem trivial aspects of agency operations, most organizations of all types have a set of customs and practices that are outdated, outmoded, and illogical, yet they persist because they are dear to the hearts of employees and executives. Initiating change is considered complicated, difficult, or simply beyond the realm of comprehension. Though action might be needed to make the agency more efficient, effective, or equitable, the pursuit of change becomes very difficult because so much passion, tradition, and inertia are driving matters toward continuity and status quo.[7]

---

6. The author has been told every FBI agent has completed his or her initial firearms qualification on the same range. The FBI Academy, located on a Marine base in Quantico, Virginia, opened in 1972. Prior to that time, however, the Bureau conducted firearms training on a small tract of land provided by the Marine Corp. When the Academy was built, it was positioned adjacent to these existing shooting ranges. Perhaps a few exceptions exist to this blanket statement and likely some early FBI agents (as well as agents from its precursors, the Bureau of Investigation and Division of Investigation) were trained elsewhere. Nonetheless, consider the symbolic power conveyed when a new agent is told that everyone who came before her or him learned to shoot on the same firearms range. Setting aside fiscal concerns, what would it take to convince special agents and Bureau executives to ever consider constructing a new facility at another location? At what additional expense would the existing facility be modified to maintain this tradition, even if building a new facility elsewhere might make more sense?

7. These observations and critiques are certainly not unique to policing. The author has observed similar passions ignited by suggested changes to aspects of higher education operations, such as extremely modest modifications to requirements to receive various academic degrees, proposed changes in graduation ceremonies, and even the suggestion that an academic department change the timing of routine meetings. A common refrain among faculty and administrators on college campuses is that "the fighting is so fierce because the stakes are so low."

Taking Responsibility for Actions

Due to careerism and other cultural forces, police organizations can breed a degree of risk aversion within personnel and organizations. In advocating for community policing in the 1980s many practitioners and scholars observed that policing would need to develop a tolerance for failure that had not traditionally been a part of American police organizations and culture (Trojanowicz, Kappeler, and Gaines 2002). Kelling and Bratton (1993) aptly noted that the police and other public sector organizations have difficulty tolerating failures, even those made in good faith. This is due in part to the fact that "rewards for success are rare but penalties for failure are potentially severe" in most public sector agencies (10). These observations remain lucid decades later and can function as a drag factor against innovative and necessary (but difficult) change in policing.

The reality of intentional change efforts and actions is that not every initiative will produce the desired outcomes. In a classic essay on planned change, sociologist Robert Merton (1936) noted that unanticipated outcomes could arise even when action has been carefully planned and implemented. These unforeseen outcomes have the potential to be both favorable or unfavorable. At times, leaders will act with having the benefit of sufficient time or information to support an educated decision. In other circumstances, even when they have adequate time and evidence, leaders will make a decision that ultimately proves to be incorrect or less than ideal. Being able to take action, tackle tough situations, and fight for what is right requires a leader "have a strong sense of themselves. [Leaders are] self-confident people who are willing to risk failure to be successful" (chief medium municipal agency).

Leadership requires a willingness to take responsibility for failure and to share the credit for success. If leaders are performing their duties properly they will recognize the majority of the "good" they accomplish is done in concert with others. The leader should be soliciting expertise and input from workers. The leader might be making difficult choices, but others often act upon those commands. Credit and glory are rarely individual commodities, particularly as one rises in the ranks of an organization. Somewhat counter-intuitively, leaders must be willing to accept the majority of the blame when decisions were incorrect. Blaming others or "passing the buck" when situations go awry will not help a leader cultivate and maintain the trust of others. True leaders "are not afraid to make a decision but can also admit when they are wrong" (lieutenant large county agency).

Summary

As with many other issues described in this book, the leader walks a fine line between demonstrating too little and too much of a given attribute. A leader wishing to demonstrate decisiveness should not fall into the trap of going into situations with (literal or figurative) guns blazing. Action for the sake of action can be as dangerous and destructive as inaction. Effective leaders recognize the limitations of their personal experience and knowledge and are not afraid to ask for input from those with greater knowledge of the situation and circumstances at hand. As such, leaders are willing to listen to others in order to secure the knowledge and insight that will guide them in making good decisions and choosing the right action. The new commander of the tactical unit or investigations division, armed with no real personal experiences in working with such matters, will hopefully show restraint in seeking to prove they can make tough decisions. This may include not letting ego (a reluctance to show ignorance by asking pointed questions of trust advisers) stand in the way of pursuing right and just outcomes.

In the end, the leader realizes that within and throughout the organization "effectiveness is accomplished by a leader's actions" (deputy chief medium municipal agency). Being an effective communicator and a person of integrity only goes so far. A leader must ultimately lead, which necessitates action. Sometimes those actions are difficult and unpleasant, such as telling employees their work performance is not up the standards of the agency and/or leader. A leader must "not be afraid to make a decision and also question a decision" (chief small municipal agency) made by others, whether that other was their predecessor, peer, friend, or even their own supervisor. Despite the fact police officers routinely engage in action and behave decisively, at times we see far too little of this same behavior reflected in the work routines of supervisory personnel. One dimension separating the supervisor from the leader is having the vision, courage, and fortitude to take action, particularly when that action involves the tough conversations, sensitive topics, and challenging issues found in every organization. Passivity is often the path of least resistance and can help preserve a supervisor's popularity and career trajectory. A person of integrity, however, will not allow these latter concerns to stand in the way of doing what is just and right.

Courage and Integrity over Self-Interests

What much of this chapter's discussion implies is that effective leaders demonstrate courage and integrity. They do what is right, even if it is unpopular. Leaders are willing to do "the right thing for the right reason, whether popular or not" (sergeant small municipal agency). They do what is right, even when doing what would be easy might be in the best interests of advancing their career. This may seem simple, common sense, and something any leader would embrace. In reality, doing the right thing is often very difficult. As the old saying goes, "if it was easy, everyone would do it." If action and change were easy, there would not be long-standing, unattended, and lingering (even festering) problems in organizations and social groups. Yet such conditions exist far too often in groups of all sizes and purposes. And "good" leaders avoid such situations and circumstances, applying a variety of rationalization techniques to justify inaction.

This is not to say that action is *always* a good thing or that a leader who fails to take certain actions is always "bad" or "ineffective." There can be situations and circumstances that justify delaying action in response to situations or waiting to correct a long-standing problem. Sometimes money may not allow for needed change to be pursued. In other situations, a leader may lack the needed support and buy-in to launch an initiative, though it would be hoped the leader will be quietly seeking to generate needed support so it is in place when the time is right. In other situations, a leader may lack sufficient authority to initiate action. Or the opposition from higher ranking officials, labor associations, or other constituents may be such that action would be ill-advised at a given point in time because it may work to ensure the failure of the reform effort or other action.

These circumstances do induce a degree of subjectivity that will preclude universal agreement on when the time is ripe for change and when a leader is failing to show courage and integrity by initiating action. Ultimately the leader must interpret the circumstances and constraints, deciding whether the timing is suitable to maximize the likelihood of success. What is important in this mix is that leaders do not deny the need for change that followers, peers, or external constituents believe is required. Effective leaders will listen to that call to action, secure needed input, and carefully consider whether these external voices are correct. If the leader deems that action is still not necessary, she or he will be careful to communicate that fact and its justification back to her or his constituents. If action is required, the leader will not use excuses to avoid doing something that will be unpopular or difficult.

Effective leaders are open and honest with themselves and their workforce. They do not pretend an organization or unit is operating in a perfect fashion or is doing "the best it can" with the resources at hand. Effective leaders reinforce the mindset that there is always room for improvement. Units and agencies can operate in a more efficient manner, employees can grow and develop into better employees, and the leader can find ways to achieve greater efficacy. Inherent in this mindset is that a workforce needs to periodically ask itself tough questions. Is a police department doing its best to effectively, efficiently, and equitably serve its public? Are internal processes operating in a manner that is efficient, effective, and equitable to all employees? What changes to structure, policy, culture, mission, or operations would enhance internal and external outcomes? What changes might individual employees (including the leader) make to improve the quality of their performance?

True leaders demonstrate commitment to this type of orientation by asking difficult questions specific to their own behavior and situation. They lead by example, showing others the importance of pursuing continual improvement. Even in fiscally tight times, when resources are limited, constraints seem insurmountable, and major change seems impossible, effective leaders will push all employees to embrace the relentless pursuit of incremental improvement. Sometimes action requires that leaders and others make difficult choices. It requires that leaders, followers, and organizations are honest about limitations, short-comings, mistakes, weaknesses, and historical failures. None of these situations provide a blanket justification for not exploring the need for change and pursuing modifications when they are deemed to be necessary.

Effective leaders do not avoid the uncomfortable and distressing process of being honest with employees and organizations about sub-par aspects of performance and operations. They are:

- "fair, honest, and willing to confront difficult situations, instead of ignoring them" (lieutenant major municipal agency).
- willing "to make difficult decisions that might even impact them negatively" (captain large state agency).
- people who possess the "courage to make tuff [sic] decisions" (captain mid-size county agency).
- "not afraid to make timely decisions" (lieutenant medium county agency).
- "willing to make tough decisions and stand by them, even when unpleasant or unpopular" (supervisor major federal agency).
- "not afraid to take a position even if that position is not a popular one" (chief mid-size municipal agency).

Fulfilling these responsibilities requires courage, honesty, and self-awareness. Unfortunately, it would seem far more leaders believe they excel in this regard than is actually the case. Though leaders might believe they exemplify this attribute, those around them might not see that as the case.

Conclusions

> Followers want comfort, stability, and solutions from their leaders. But that's babysitting. Real leaders ask hard questions and knock people out of their comfort zones. Then they manage the resulting distress (Heifetz and Laurie 2001, 131).

It is easy to discuss action as if it is simple and virtuous. In reality it is often very difficult to pursue the changes and actions that are most needed in an organization. Leaders do not have the privilege of only leading the changes they desire and personally embrace. The recession that arrived in 2008 has shown examples of leaders having to initiate major change in austere times (Police Executive Research Forum 2010) and calls for more cost effective approaches to policing (Gascon and Foglesong 2010). Across the country government and corporate sector leaders have had to confront harsh fiscal realities. They have had to pursue change that may be counter to their personal beliefs about the core services their organization should provide. Some agencies have stopped immediate response to less serious criminal events that historically have a low likelihood of being solved (Police Executive Research Forum 2010). Union leaders in some agencies have had to guide front-line personnel through the process of deciding whether to restructure labor agreements or accept large numbers of officers must be laid off. Austere times force leaders to confront questions many never dreamed they would have to ask. This reality can be frustrating and unsettling for leaders and followers alike.

Setting aside such dire economic circumstances, in many ways American policing of the 2010s is little different than American policing of the 1950s and 1960s. The tools have evolved, but the core tasks and techniques have remained stable. How many agencies entertain discussions of the alternative ways in which fundamental tactics and strategies might be pursued? How many leaders openly invite discussion of the core values and assumptions that guide their organization? This situation is in no way unique to policing. Writing about leadership in education, Heifetz and Linsky observed that "[m]ost of us, most of the time, pass up these daily opportunities to exercise leadership. We stay within our area of expertise and opt to affirm our primary loyalties. Doing otherwise would be personally difficult and professionally dangerous" (2004, 33). It may seem a given that a leader would be willing to take action and make choices. In reality, however, action brings about a degree of risk and error for the leader. Taking action means a leader runs the risk of selecting the wrong action. Even if that takes place "in good faith" there might be organizational repercussions for the leader.

True effective leadership requires action and tough choices. It requires courage. It means not sweeping things under the carpet, tolerating things because confronting a problem is uncomfortable, giving up because resistance is encountered, or leaving a known problem for one's successor to resolve.[8] Being a leader means confronting organizational pathologies and individual shortcomings. It means being willing to do something about a problem rather than learning to live with and seek to manage that deficiency. Perhaps most importantly, a true leader focuses on creating a unit or organization in which continuous

---

8. Recall that one element of Elizabeth Reuss-Ianni's "street cops" code was that officers did not leave work for the next shift. Perhaps a true leader takes the same attitude, attempting to not leave major tasks for the next person holding that position. Readers who are police leaders might ask themselves how much of their time and energy is devoted to dealing with issues their predecessor (or their predecessor's predecessor) should have fixed?

growth, development, and change is valued. The late Clarence Kelley (who followed J. Edgar Hoover as Director of the FBI and also served as Chief of the Kansas City Police Department) addressed this principle at the 1973 meetings of the International Association of Chiefs of Police. Director Kelley remarked that "the specific changes effected are often not nearly as important as *efforts to build an organization capable of continuing change*" (Kelley 1973, 33, emphasis in the original). The most important thing a leader might do is not pursue any specific initiative; rather leaders ought to instill a culture of continual change, evolution, and improvement within their sphere of influence.

Leadership scholar Ronald Heifetz has frequently addressed this challenge in his writings with various collaborators, elaborating on leading change. "Leadership often involves challenging people to live up to their words, to close the gap between their espoused values and their actual behavior. It may mean pointing out the elephant sitting on the table at a meeting—the unspoken issue that everyone sees but no one wants to mention" (Heifetz and Linsky 2004, 33). The gap leaders must seek to close is not just between the words and actions of employees. Perhaps the greatest challenge is for leaders to find the courage and methods to close the gap in their own words and actions.

Chapter 9

Innovation & Growth

Though police organizations and cultures may resist many forms of change initiated either internally or externally, in reality agencies do shift and evolve. Valid questions might be raised as to whether the pace of that change is sufficient, but agencies of all sizes are routinely confronted with various pressures, demands, mandates, and constraints that require reformulation of at least small aspects of their operations, if only symbolically. Laws are passed and court rulings are issued, both of which change administrative and procedural aspects of how officers perform their duties. Personnel and key constituents (i.e., mayors, city managers, municipal and county governing bodies) transition, bringing about new external pressures. Crime ebbs and flows, resulting in new public demands. Budgets rise and fall, creating new opportunities and challenges. Police organizations exist in dynamic and open environments that require innovation and change (Cordner 1978). Unfortunately, too many supervisors are promoted for their technical competency with existing systems and processes. Agencies often promote those who were good front-line patrol officers. The attributes that define a successful and effective patrol officer are not necessarily consistent with being a successful and effective supervisor or leader. Among other traits, effective leaders must be able to innovate, grow, and develop (Krimmel and Lindenmuth 2001).

When considering the nature of change in policing, a distinction should be made between change that is voluntarily initiated by an organization and change that is an adaptive response to the demands of the open environment in which the agency is situated. Experience, anecdote, and history have shown that police supervisors and organizations tend to pursue innovation and growth when it is forced upon them; proactive and elective change is less typical (Greene, Bergman and McLaughlin 1994; Pagon 2003). Unfortunately it is all too uncommon to see the pursuit of purposive, intentional, planned change in policing. Far too few supervisors and agencies seek to anticipate the need for change and pursue that process in a proactive manner (Schafer, Buerger, Myers, Jensen, Levin 2012). National Academy participants identified the need for effective leaders to bring about innovation and growth within their agency and domain of responsibility. Their comments were generally not focused on externally mandated changes brought about through changes in the agency's open system. Rather, the participants focused their comments on elective, purposive, and anticipatory changes leaders opted to bring about to ensure growth and innovation in their followers, in their organization, and in themselves.

The National Academy responses were emphasizing proactive modifications leaders pursued because they are "open to change, [and they] innovative, challenge others and challenges himself, [and] always strives to better himself" (chief small municipal agency). By pursuing this type of growth and improvement the leader was demonstrating an "ability to embrace change and accept new ideas and stay open minded" about policing, leadership, personnel development, and public safety innovations (lieutenant medium county agency). Effective leaders realized the need to "stay up with the times . . . [because] police work is always changing . . . .[so past practices] cant [sic] be hung onto forever" (captain small municipal agency). These leaders did not see policing as a static profession. They were cognizant of the dynamic aspects of the field and saw it was their duty to make sure there was appropriate currency in skillsets, approaches, and methodologies for their followers, their organization, and themselves. Change was not viewed as something to be feared and avoided; rather, it presented opportunities for growth, development, and innovation for followers, organizations, and even within the leaders.

This willingness to pursue innovation and growth did not mean leaders pursued change for arbitrary or capricious reasons. "They aren't afraid to try new things but they do not jump into fads or have knee-jerk decisions" (sergeant mid-size county agency). Rather, they "look for input from others to gather the best information to help them make informed decisions" (lieutenant large municipal agency). This might suggest effective leaders are paying attention to new ideas, innovations, and advances being discussed in professional and academic literature, as well as those practices being advanced in training and at the meetings of professional organizations (Burruss, Giblin, and Schafer 2010). Staying connected to the trends and advances in the broader policing profession ensures the leader is seeking the proper growth and development for the organization and its personnel. Effective leaders seek to "guide their people in the direction to accomplish their vision and goals" (lieutenant large municipal agency), but those visions and goals are grounded in prevailing trends within the profession. As addressed in earlier chapters, the change and action leaders pursue are not motivated by self-interests or careerism. Instead, they are motivated by the leader's desire to enhance practice in appropriate directions based articulable needs and rationales.

Why do leaders take these steps? Because they "care about the future of the department and the future of the employees" (sergeant mid-size county agency). They pursue growth and innovation not simply for the purpose of self-improvement, but to improve themselves so they might better serve the organization and their followers. Leaders seek to ensure their agencies are on the cutting edge of the policing profession and contemporary policing practices and innovations. They seek to help employees grow and develop as individuals by exposing them to new ideas, training, education, and practices. "The leaders encourage & promote outside thinking and plan ahead by mentoring new employees" (sergeant mid-size county agency). These leaders are "able to change with the constant ebb and flow" of the profession (lieutenant small municipal agency). That which is good can potentially be made great. The procedures and techniques used today might not be viable tomorrow. The pursuit of innovation and opportunity are key attributes of leaders when the efforts are tempered by the realistic assessment of which initiatives have relevance and feasibility within the leader's agency and context. True leaders do not subscribe to the "paradigm of the month club," forever chasing the latest trendy fad in policing or leadership.

This chapter is organized into three major sections. First, it considers how leaders pursue, nurture, and support innovation and growth among their followers. Leaders want their employees to develop new skills and expertise; they support that goal rather than viewing it as a threat to their own status and standing. Next, the chapter examines how leaders seek to do the same within their unit or the organization as a whole. Leaders are continually seeking to improve the efficacy, efficiency, and equity of operations. Finally, the chapter concludes with a discussion of how leaders challenge themselves to pursue new innovations and grow as individuals, officers, and leaders. A leader cannot encourage and expect growth and development from and within others if they do not hold themselves to that same standard. In the end, the innovation and growth described by the National Academy participants was more than just the "normal" types of changes a leader might pursue (i.e., budget, law, training requirements, equipment, technology, etc.). What was being conveyed was that effective leaders sought to make deeper changes because they recognized better outcomes could be achieved, including within themselves.

Followers' Growth & Innovation

Because leaders are not self-focused, they consider not only themselves, but also their followers. This extends into consideration of how to help followers develop to become more competent officers and leaders, among other roles. Many National Academy respondents indicated these two elements (development and growth of both self and others) were often co-occurring traits. Effective leaders "always seek to learn and improve while raising those around them up a notch. They actually care about people- not just themselves" (captain medium special jurisdiction agency). They "strive to improve [themselves] and help others improve and attain professional goals" (lieutenant small special jurisdiction agency). This co-occurrence is not just a form of modeling and leadership by example (though it is also an instance of that trait). Effective leaders are not afraid to allow a critical examination of the mistakes and missteps they have made during their careers to serve as an example to others. They may use their own mistakes as lessons to help followers avoid the same circumstances. "They have done the job, made mistakes and are *not* afraid to use their experiences (good & bad) to educate personnel" (deputy chief large county agency, emphasis in the original).

Early in an officer's career the leader may focus on developing a follower into a competent entry-level patrol officer. This would entail "mentoring them to take pride in theirselves [sic], their profession and the organization they represent" (lieutenant mid-size special jurisdiction agency). As officers advance in their careers, this process of development would likely shift to involve developing new skill sets (i.e. higher levels of mastery and proficiency as a patrol officer, such as accident reconstruction, becoming a field training officer, certification as an armorer, etc.). At other times or for other officers, this might extend into developing skills and experiences that will make a follower more qualified for special assignment or promotion to supervisory positions (Anderson, Gisborne, and Holliday 2006). The very objective of growth and innovation manifests itself in evolving ways across a follower's career. Supporting a follower to attend the National Academy program is a prime example. Development can be manifested in a variety of methods, including training, education, mentoring, and providing followers with new and diverse experiences.

There are many ways in which a leader can support the growth and development of employees. This might entail prioritizing, encouraging, and supporting followers in the pursuit of education and training. Even if an agency and/or leader cannot compensate an officer for taking college courses, it might be possible to ensure a duty assignment that will support that officer attending class and completing homework. Leaders can encourage follower development by promoting and prioritizing training within the workplace. To be sure, this can be challenging in tight economic times when top leaders often must choose between retaining personnel and all other fiscal priorities, including training. The latter might be changing with improvements in the quality of online, asynchronous training programs. In very simple terms, leaders can support and encourage followers by creating "suggested reading" lists drawn from academic and professional publications on policing, leadership, technology, politics, society, and world events. Leaders can also delegate and empower so employees can develop new skill sets with a degree of independence (Anderson, Gisborne, and Holliday 2006). Perhaps the most important way in which leaders encourage the development of followers is to create an environment in which continued growth, learning, experimentation, and opportunities becomes so normal and routine that employees take it for granted.

It is not enough to develop followers by just providing them exposure to new and diverse ideas and experiences. An effective leader can seek to help followers learn by providing constructive feedback on the follower's performance. In this way the leader can seek ways to "help officers do their job" (lieutenant mid-size county agency) through patience, communication, understanding, and mentoring. Leaders working in this fashion might be wise to be "quick to praise for good work & [to] teach when the work is sub par" (commander large municipal agency). A leader might seek to offer growth and development opportunities to their followers. At times this could extend to opportunities followers do not seek, but the leader believes will be instructive and beneficial. In some contexts this might mean "allowing subordinate personnel to try & fail in a safe environment" (lieutenant small municipal agency). A follower questioning why an agency uses a specific process or approach might be asked to develop an alternative strategy for the leader. An officer demonstrating potential might be given the authority and latitude to take the lead on a certain case, incident, or event to develop more experiences and understanding. "There is nothing an effective leader will ask of you that is above your ability. They see your potential far sooner than you, and the effective leader will guide you in the exploration of your own potential through mentoring and side by side assistances" (lieutenant large state agency). Effective leaders have the ability "to identify the strengths and weaknesses of the subordinates and direct them towards their strengths while building on their weaknesses" (captain large state agency).

The development of followers is important for a variety of reasons. Certainly development keeps employees engaged and empowered within the workplace. It presents workers with new challenges and opportunities (which many will value, though some will resent and resist). It opens doors for promotion and special assignments. It shows that police organizations need to be "learning organizations" (Brown and Brudney 2003; Geller 1997; Levitt and March 1988) that are continually seeking ways to improve their efficiency, efficacy, and equity. It demonstrates that innovation is a continual goal for organizations and operations, just as growth should be a life-long goal of all employees. Developing followers can help keep them engaged in, and committed to, the organization, which can reduce turn over, apathy, burnout, and cynicism. Exposing officers to new ideas and opportunities keeps them from becoming stuck in a "rut" of routine. Indirectly, development can save agencies money by reducing the need to hire and train new officers, reducing absenteeism, and reducing liability. It emphasizes that the relentless pursuit of incremental improvement is not just a goal for organizations, but should also be a priority for all works in the agency.

Supporting employee innovation and growth can be used to accomplish two additional critical tasks. First, it provides employees with the knowledge and skills needed to perform their jobs. Employee development is necessary, particularly when a leader is pursuing change and innovation within their domain of responsibility and authority. Change and innovation often mean that personnel are asked to assume new responsibilities and/or perform old tasks in a revised manner (Lurigio and Skogan 1994). Development efforts ensure followers "have the tools to do the job" (lieutenant large municipal agency) and the "knowledge to do it correctly" (captain mid-size municipal agency) as it is being envisioned by the leader. Followers "must be trained to perform what is expected of them" (lieutenant small municipal agency). While successful change requires more than simply training, effective leaders recognize that if they are pursuing substantial modifications they need to provide all employees with the skills required to achieve success (Schafer 2001). Whether employees utilize those skills in the pursuit of the desired success is another matter.

Second, employee development ensures there are people who can perform the leader's jobs when the leader is absent, moves to another assignment, or retires. Many supervisors and managers have an aversion to training others to perform their tasks or allowing employees too much discretion, latitude, or freedom. They fear that others will see the follower performing their duties (or the leader's duties) in an innovative and effective manner, which might compromise the leaders' positions, stability, or career trajectories. Ego, arrogance, and self-interest may encourage supervisors and managers to avoid allowing followers to "shine too brightly" lest the supervisors find they are replaced, leap-frogged, or simply upstaged. Fear that the "student will become the master" stifles the organization and precludes a supervisor from ascending to be a real leader in their organization. Unfortunately, there may be times when supervisors do not realize they are falling into this particular leadership trap. The supervisor's protection of their own interests and career ambitions might be masked by labeling the follower as "reckless," "ideological," or someone who has not "earned the right" to have more influence in the organization.

Effective leaders are able to avoid falling into this pit of self-interest. More benevolent and agency-centered perspectives on how leaders should approach this matter contend that leaders need to train followers to "perform their tasks in his absence . . . to maintain high standards in their work" (lieutenant large municipal agency). Followers might also be trained so they can perform the leader's duties when he or she is absent. Ultimately, this might extend to preparing one or more follower to perform the leader's tasks so the leader "can be effectively replaced at a future date" (commander large county agency). Doing so requires that a leader have the ability to identify "those who have the potential to lead the organization in the future and give them the training needed to become future leaders" (assistant chief medium municipal agency). Succession planning (Ahlstrom 2006) and knowledge transfer (Konkler 2010) remain largely overlooked and undervalued in many public sector contexts, including policing. This is to the detriment of police organizations and their personnel. Retirements and transfers often trigger a cascading loss (at least temporarily) of knowledge, skills, and procedures. Though situations eventually return to an acceptable state, those stepping in to fill the void left by the departure of a supervisor expend needless time and energy learning what they should have already been taught. That lost time might better be spent developing and leading the organization.[1]

The process of developing employees also involves allowing followers to innovate. In some situations these innovations might be quite modest because they are primarily centered on exposing followers to increasing levels of independence, autonomy, and responsibility. As followers grow and advance in their careers, the innovation may become more substantial and involved. Leaders recognize the only way to encourage innovation and growth within their area of responsibility (in terms of the unit/agency and personnel over

---

1. To be fair to those in supervisory positions, decisions made by their superiors or organizational processes for identifying and filling vacant positions can force this situation into the workplace. For example, the common bureaucratic approach to not making a promotion decision until a position is actually vacant forces supervisors to move on before their replacement is appointed, making it nearly impossible to transfer core knowledge. The interests of preserving the bureaucratic process work to the detriment of improved organizational outcomes.

whom they have formal authority and informal influence) is to cultivate the development of followers. It is not enough for the leader to be the champion of innovation; to do so ensures the innovation will cease when the leader promotes, transfers, or retires. Leaders empower others and help them learn to value innovation and growth in themselves and within the workplace. They seek to create a culture and environment in which development, growth, and innovation are valued aspects of "business as usual." In that way, the habits perpetuate even after the leader has left that assignment.

In the end, developing followers to pursue innovation and growth is a teaching process. To accomplish this objective, leaders must have an ability to communicate a vision and objectives to followers, while also convincing the followers that change is the necessary and "right" path to take. It requires trust between the leader and follower. It requires the leaders take needed action. Leaders must set followers on the right path, provide them the right tools, and have the courage and wisdom to let the followers find their own ways.[2] It requires that leaders provide followers with critical and constructive feedback to help improve the application of those processes in the future. To do otherwise will ensure innovation and growth will be fleeting. These principles were clearly articulated by a major from a large municipal agency. In characterizing how leaders develop innovation and growth among followers, this National Academy respondent wrote that:

> Effective leadership involves getting goals accomplished with the resources you have in an efficient manner and in a way that everyone involved has ownership and accountability for the issues and also share in the success of the mission. Effective leaders encourage participation and risk taking and are willing to let subordinates make mistakes. Effective leaders are also teachers and must be good, clear communicators and must give feedback.

Organizational Growth & Innovation

Respondents consistently indicated that effective leaders were concerned with innovation and growth not only for their followers, but also within the organization.[3] Police organizations are often characterized as being highly stagnant and entrenched. Achieving growth and innovation in policing structures, culture, and operations has been likened to "bending granite" (Guyot 1979; King 2003). Despite such assertions, police departments are similar to most other organization. Change is necessary and does occur, though it might be debated whether the volume, pace, and ease of change is appropriate given the contextual realities of policing. Effective leaders pursue innovation and growth in their organization and their domain of responsibility. They recognize and pursue opportunities to enhance agency operations and practices. In some cases the leaders might even be recognized as exerting a broader influence on the police profession as a whole, though such an outcome might not be an overt objective (e.g., see Haberfeld 2006; Reese 2005).

---

2. The Theodore Roosevelt quote at the beginning of Chapter Five is again instructive in this discussion. Leaders have the wisdom and courage to stay out of the way and allow good employees to do good work.

3. The capacity of a leader to influence organizational growth and innovation with vary based on position and context. Informal leaders and those in lower ranks may find it more difficult to have an influence on organizational matters relative to formal leaders of greater rank and formal influence.

Though former New York and Los Angeles Police Chief William Bratton has been the subject of a range of criticisms from various quarters, he excelled in this area of leadership. He not only brought about transformation in two of the most vaunted and watched departments in the country (New York and Los Angeles),[4] the Compstat model he helped develop and advance changed the rhetoric, if not the practice, of police-initiated crime-reduction strategies and accountability methods (Willis, Mastrofski, and Weisburd 2003; c.f. Eterno and Silverman 2012; Henry 2002). Though his particular leadership approaches might be questioned, Bratton demonstrated a clear ability to exert a transformative influence over two departments well-known for being highly resistant to change in culture, operations, orientation, and structure (Reuss-Ianni 1983; Reese 2005). Whether his model of police operations was responsible for crime declines in those two cities might be subject to question and debate. What seems far more evident, however, is that his vision and leadership style exerted a rapid influence on the culture and internal practices of two agencies known for being very entrenched and resistant to reform efforts. For all the faults that might be associated with Bratton's approach to leadership, he was able to advance rapid growth and innovation in two agencies where such outcomes were rare.

Effective leaders are connected with advances in the policing profession and the broader public safety community. They are scanning for trends and drivers that will influence social, economic, political, and cultural circumstances that intersect with their community. They pay attention to new technologies and laws that create challenges and opportunities for their agencies and their operations. They recognize that when change is pursued on purpose, rather than in response to external pressures, success is more likely and outcomes are more desirable. These types of effective leaders are often forward thinking and engage in elements of futures thinking (Schafer, Buerger, Myers, Jensen, and Levin 2012), though they might not always recognize that circumstance. "An effective leader is a person who can lead his/her agency into the future and is always willing to look outside the 'box' to find solution. An effective leader must be willing to take chances to change an organization for the better" (lieutenant medium municipal agency).

These leaders have a "willingness to be involved in positive change for the agency" (sergeant mid-size municipal agency) and are "not afraid to try new things" (sergeant large municipal agency). This requires the recognition that the agency must be fluid, flexible, and innovative to remain viable in a dynamic environment. Static operations are neither acceptable nor desirable. To be sure, the pace of change in far too many American police agencies might accurately be characterized as "glacial." The rate of advancement and evolution in the broader profession has been little better. That is not to say that changes have not occurred, but some critical perspectives argue those advances tend to be more cosmetic than substantive (Bayley 1988; Greene and Mastrofski 1988; Myers, Schafer, and Levin 2010). Though the toys and tools of policing evolve, the core assumptions, models, and methods have progressed only modestly in the past century. Effective leaders are not content to operate within a narrow range of change and innovation. They are seeking to push their agency further toward the leading edge of the profession and do

---

4. Among the other debatable aspects of Bratton's legacy and influence is the true influence of Compstat and allied approaches on crime and policing in NYPD. It is clear that there were changes in New York's crime rate under and after Bratton's command. What specifically changed and whether NYPD efforts were the mechanism of that change is something scholars will likely continue to debate (Blumstein and Wallman 2005). Though Bratton is often given lead credit for the creation, implementation, and diffusion of Compstat, others made important contributions to that trajectory of events.

not automatically fear innovation (nor do they blindly follow popular rhetoric within the profession).

Leaders who demonstrate greater efficacy seek ways to improve not just the surface aspects of their organization, but the core values, beliefs, and behaviors embedded in organizational practices. In many ways this is the classic manifestation of the very idea of leadership. The leader seeks to influence personnel and operations to bring about modifications in people, processes, and outcomes. To accomplish this leaders need to have a "vision of what needs to be done and where an org[anization] needs to go" (captain midsize municipal agency). The leader identifies a preferred state for the organization and/or its processes, and works to transition the agency to that preferred state. Doing so requires a degree of foresight, vision, planning, strategy, and persuasion. This is not done simply to benefit the leader and his/her interests; rather, the leader is seeking to make "change when it's beneficial to the organization" (assistant chief medium municipal agency). The leader is not content to see aspects of the agency being merely "good." Instead they push the organization toward the pursuit of being great.

The tendency for police organizations and personnel to resist change is well documented. As discussed earlier in this text, the nature of police working environments exacerbates this situation. Despite many advances in the ability of supervisors to monitor and surveil the performance and actions of subordinates, the policing profession continues to provide workers with assorted opportunities to defy administrative mandates and edicts. Whether the rapid proliferation of video cameras, wireless communication networks, and enhanced analytical processes will overcome this situation (by subjecting virtually everything an employee does to some level of automated review, with questionable situations "pushed" to the attention of supervisors for further inquiry and assessment) remains to be seen. Though technology might enable such surveillance, it will be a way of bringing about compliance through "brute force" rather than by winning "hearts and minds." Historically the policing profession has valued supervision and control (McGregor's Theory X) over cultivating a workforce that can be trusted and over creating a working environment in which good people can achieve good ends (McGregor's Theory Y) without pointless mandates and interference.

The type of innovation and growth being addressed by the National Academy respondents was decidedly different from technology-enhanced monitoring initiatives, which are fundamentally forms of supervision and not leadership. Innovation and growth pursued by effective leaders are often the types of changes in which "hearts and minds" must be won and influenced (Lurigio and Skogan 1994). Effective leaders are continually seeking ways to improve the efficiency, efficacy, and equity of the operations of their unit, agency, and personnel. They are not simply pursuing change so they can demonstrate their metal as a leader (which often occurs in pursuit of the next promotion or duty assignment). Rather, effective leaders are "looking for changes, have a vision for the future . . . [and an] ability to elicit change" (lieutenant major state agency). These leaders do not arbitrarily and capriciously initiate change processes, but once a need is identified "they are committed and always intend to achieve [the] intended objectives" (inspector major international federal agency). This does not suggest that organizational change, innovation, and growth are easy processes. Despite the many challenges and obstacles, effective leaders persist in pursuing their objectives both individually and for their organization. "Leaders must have visions with purpose and must be able to formulate plans to bring the vision to pass. Effective leadership requires tenacity + determination, as well as the ability to make hard decisions" (captain medium municipal agency).

This commitment to the pursuit of change does not mean leaders remain entrenched and fixed in the approaches they use or even the very nature of the intended change. To be effective in this regard, leaders must recognize that as change progresses, methods and objectives often must be modified to reflect emerging realities and circumstances. Lindblom's notion of disjointed incrementalism (1959, 1979) was influenced by the idea that large-scale change often requires adjustments and modifications. Leaders cannot remain blindly allied to the original plans in all situations. In this way leaders demonstrate "flexibility in methods (not just ideals)" (sergeant small special-jurisdiction agency). Leaders recognize the situational nature of police operations. With the exception of a few core principles, nothing can be sacred and free from critical questions. When change has been initiated, the leader must be aware that the original plan may require additional modifications. A common colloquialism in military operations is that a commander's battle plan only survives until the first shot is fired; after that, situations are too dynamic for effective advance preparation. Similar observations might be made about the nature of change in police organizations. In the pursuit of innovation and growth, situational approaches and flexibility in planning may be paramount in the pursuit of successful outcomes.

On the far horizon of innovation and growth in police organizations is questioning the very nature of how western police agencies have traditionally been structured and operated. The use of command-and-control hierarchies made sense given the circumstances in which they were adopted in the early 20th century (i.e., limited communication technology, limited education and training for personnel, rampant corruption and abuses of authority). It is now being questioned whether this organizational model holds the same utility it did more than a century ago. The U.S. Department of Defense has begun similar inquiry processes by exploring alternative models such as "netcentric warfare."[5] Many questions remain about approaches offered as alternatives to the classic hierarchical approach to policing (Jackson, Myers and Cowper 2010; Myers 2007; Myers and Cowper 2007). The lingering question at the core of net-centric approaches to any organization is whether superior outcomes could be achieved by radically rethinking how personnel and processes function. Though it remains unclear how net-centric systems would work in public sector operations geared toward the provision of public safety services, leadership is found at the heart of considering this issue. Rather than blindly accepting current practice as "good enough" or "as good as we can do," those advocating for alternative models seek to show the courage, reflection, and intellect needed to explore these uncharted territories. The end result may be the continuation of bureaucratic hierarchies as the prevailing organizational approach to policing, but at least the difficult questions will have been asked, even though they take on a sacred element of policing (i.e., the dominance of rank and hierarchy controlling authority and discretion in the workplace).

This discussion should not imply that innovation and growth always have to be time-consuming, involved, costly, or complex. Leaders should never overlook that sometimes it is the simple strategies that are most effective in solving problems. Too often leaders feel the need to demonstrate their worth and value by wrestling with massive changes to confront big problems in the organization. At times that daunting undertaking is necessary to develop and enact a needed solution. However, identifying the right path sometimes requires

---

5. Netcentric approaches reduce hierarchy by creating connected networks of individuals and groups operating with a high degree of awareness and autonomy in pursuit of established objectives. For examples of this idea in application, examine the conferences, publications, training, and research conducted and provided by the Department of Defense Command and Control Research Program.

little more than being willing to seek out and listening to the most relevant input in the organization. A common folklore used in business literature illustrates this principle and is presented here.[6]

A particular company manufactured several consumer products, including toothpaste. The operation was relatively efficient, though occasionally empty boxes of toothpaste were shipped because of a small degree of error in the packaging process. The timing of various machines used in packaging toothpaste into tubes and then tubes into boxes was not perfect with 100% accuracy, as is often the case in production systems. The CEO was concerned the company might suffer a loss of business if consumers became upset about buying a box that proved to be empty. As executives are often inclined to do, the CEO hired an external engineering company to study the manufacturing system and offer a solution to the problem. To correct this small, but persistent, problem surely required outside expertise and appreciable capital investment.

After months of study and the expenditure of appreciable funds on consulting fees, process analysis, and engineering modifications, the CEO believed he had located and implemented an effective solution. High-speed and high-precision scales were integrated into the packaging systems at appreciable cost and effort. When a box was deemed to weigh less than it should, a warning alarm would sound, a flashing light would activate, and the line would stop. A worker would walked to the scale, remove the defective box, reset the system, and restart the packaging line. Some months later the CEO examined the return-on-investment of the process improvements and was very pleased to see no empty boxes were being shipped out, no customer complaints had been received about empty boxes, and their market share was increasing.

Initially the CEO concluded the consultant fees and re-engineering costs were money well spent. But upon looking more closely, he encountered a puzzling statistic. After a few weeks of use, the high precision scales stopped recording any errors. It was as if the production line was no longer producing empty boxes, because none were being detected. This puzzled the CEO, who knew based on past data that about a dozen empty boxes were produced every day. Logic would have suggested the scales should have detected about a dozen errors and workers should have had to reset the production line about a dozen times. The process improvement had been designed to locate those boxes, not to reduce the occurrence of that error, so it was curious to see data suggesting the absence of error in the system. Yet no empty boxes were making it to the point of the high-precision scales within the company's new (and costly) packaging system.

Curious, the CEO travel to the factory so he could examine the system with his own eyes. When he arrived at the point of the packaging process where the scales were installed, he was shocked to see a $20 household box fan had been place just ahead of the high-precision scales on the line. The fan appeared to be blowing empty boxes off the belt and into a garbage bin, while boxes that correctly contained a tube of toothpaste continued unimpeded through the packaging system. He called out to one of the factory workers to ask about the purpose and decision to position the fan on the packaging line. The response shocked him. "One of the guys bought that fan and put it there because we

---

6. Numerous minor variations on this story can be found online and in trade publications. For example, the author located one rendition of this story on the Evolving Excellence blog (http://www.evolvingexcellence.com/blog/2011/12/a-dose-of-common-sense-goes-a-long-way.html) on December 11, 2011.

were all tired of walking over here every time the dang bell started ringing." All of the effort and expense could have been resolved by listening to those who knew the system best. The time and expense of the solution could have been reduced to pocket money. Sometimes simple solutions are the best. And, when executives do not delegate, empower, and listen, sometimes workers will innovate on their own, despite the supervisor's "best" efforts and intentions.

Personal Growth & Innovation

Effective leadership can be defined as having the ability to identify strengths and weaknesses of not only your officers but also yourself.
—chief small municipal agency.

Effective leaders recognize the importance of their own personal growth and development. This is not to say they are only focused on themselves and actions that are in their own best interests (e.g., "careerism" or the tendency for a leader to focus only on what will help them to advance their career interests and objectives). Rather, effective leaders are forward thinking visionaries who are willing to change if it will improve efficacy, efficiency, or equity. This includes a willingness to change their education, training, approaches, styles, and methods. They are looking toward the future of themselves, their followers, and their agency. This does not necessarily mean leaders are ego-centric or only pursuing their own self-interests. Rather, they recognize that change, evolution, and improvement are pivotal to ensuring their continued relevance and efficacy as a leader. Often a leader is only as good as their last success. Continual growth, evolution, and objectives are necessary. Leaders cannot ask others to change if, in the aggregate, they do not demonstrate a willingness to pursue personal growth and innovation.

Leaders seek out opportunities to learn new skills, develop new aptitudes, and explore new elements of the policing profession. They are "always educating themselves through training and education" (sergeant small municipal agency) because they realize that even though they might be effective today, this does not ensure they will remain effective into the future or that they cannot be more effective tomorrow. Leaders have an ability and willingness to look at their own behavior with a critical eye. They recognize that innovation and growth are life-long pursuits for their followers, their agencies, as well as for themselves. Leaders must pursue personal innovation and growth to stay current and make improvements as a member of the organization. Being willing to seek opportunities to improve their own skills and approaches has the secondary benefit of showing others in the organization that personal growth is a necessary and valued pursuit.

An effective leader "shows a willingness to learn" (commander mid-size county agency). They "look at ways for self-improvement, continuing education/training, [and] keeping up with advances in the field" (captain medium county agency). Despite being resistant to change, policing does have some dynamic elements. Changes in laws and technologies influence street-level operations. New philosophies and trends modify general and specific ways of addressing crime and serving communities. In addition, as a leader advances in the organization their domain of responsibility changes and evolves. They may be confronted with new tasks (i.e., budgeting) they have not confronted in the past or they may realize that while they were an accomplished officer or investigator, they know little about leadership, communication, or other skills that become increasingly important to a supervisor advancing through their organization. "They are continually learning about their profession" (lieutenant large county agency) and seeking to improve their own skills as a leader. Although they may no longer work in an operational capacity, they may wish to maintain currency so that they understand the work performed by their followers.

Part of seeking personal growth and self-improvement may reflect that effective leaders are future-oriented agents of change in many organizations. By pursuing self-improvement, they are demonstrating to followers that even good officers can seek ways to become better. They may also be considering what skills are needed to not only be an effective leader today, but also tomorrow. Though there may be a fine line between this trait and careerism, self-improvement is an important trait in a leader. Leaders should be focused on current job responsibilities, but there is nothing wrong with developing the skills that will make them better leaders in the future. Though it is fine if leaders determine they are not interested in seeking further advancement in their organization, they should not be stigmatized for aspiring to continue to be promoted or transferred to new units and opportunities. This is exactly the pattern of behavior often desired among front-line personnel. Officers are encouraged to show tenacity, a strong work ethic, and to pursue self-improvement in order to improve the chance they will be promoted or given a special assignment. Leaders should exemplify this same behavior in their own approach to the job. Even if a leader has no desire to advance into other assignments, self-improvement is important because there are always new and better ways to perform a given task in an organization.

Innovation & Growth: The Role of Futures Thinking

Thinking about the future is of crucial importance in making someone an effective leader, and not simply a manager or supervisor. Effective leaders are "thinking of the future" (captain major municipal agency) of their community, workforce, area of responsibility, and employing agency, as well as the policing profession. Thinking about the future means more than merely a leader who considers how to spend their time during the workweek or contemplates how to work within their budget during the remained of a fiscal cycle. Actual contemplation of the future means the leader is seeking to identify trends and drivers that will be important somewhere "beyond the horizon" of what can currently be safely seen and understood. Future thinkers in some disciplines sometimes seek to understand events that will happen 50–100 years from today (Cornish 2004). A more realistic horizon in policing might be consideration of trends and evolutions that might be expected within the next decade (Schafer, Buerger, Myers, Jensen, and Levin 2012).

Why might thinking about the future in a 5–10 year timeframe help make a leader more effective and help in the development and growth of a unit or organization? Futures thinking encourages the leader (and followers participating in futures thinking processes) to do more than attempt to predict what lies ahead. As every reader knows from experience with weather forecasts, prediction of the future can be very challenging and fraught with probabilities and errors. The promise of futures thinking in policing is not simply to make predictions about future threats and opportunities. Futures thinking allows a leader (and by extension, a unit or agency) to develop more control over that future. Scholars and practitioners working in the area of futures thinking discuss the idea of "preferable futures," which are those outcomes an individual or organization establishes as an ideal outcome. These preferences become goals, objectives, and aspirations. Having identified what we would like an organization to look like in the future, we can begin to identify ways to bring that goal to life. Rather than fumbling around, seeking to extinguish the "brush fires" of today, futures thinking allows a leader to think in a more focused manner (Myers, Schafer, and Levin 2010). One of the ways to deal with brush fires is to manage and address situations before they reach such a volatile state. Futures thinking can enable a leader to identify challenges before they reach a point of crisis, while also recognizing opportunities while there is still time to capitalize on their potential.

The majority of successful formal leaders have engaged in futures thinking, though they might not recognize that fact. In the early years of their careers it is safe to assume most police officers look around their agency and think about their future. New employees in any workplace or professional context likely exhibit similar behavior. An officer identifies opportunities she or he would like to have over the course of their career (e.g., being a detective, working in the canine unit, or being a member of the tactical unit) and accomplishments they would like to achieve (e.g., deciding being a lieutenant is the best mix of authority and responsibility in their agency, thus setting as a goal the attainment of that rank). For some officers, this survey of the "landscape" may lead to the decision to seek work in another agency or profession. The process is a form of defining a preferable future. Rather than passively allowing time and fate to decide where they end up in an organization, the officers define the future they hope to achieve. They did not view their professional life as being a fate they could not control; they took steps to create the future they wanted. Leaders can help create more desirable futures for their units and organizations by applying the same principles that contributed to their individual professional success.

The act of defining that future is not enough by itself. Instead, officers will hopefully also realize they need to take certain steps to achieve the preferable future they have identified. They might decide they need to exhibit certain behavior or actions (e.g., being hardworking, making a lot of arrests, receiving good performance reviews, or showing a willingness to take on less desirable tasks). They might determine they need to "punch their card" by doing assignments they might not enjoy (e.g., the way to a position as a homicide detective is by first showing success and hard work in the burglary squad). They might need to enhance their skill set through the pursuit of educational and training opportunities. None of these steps guarantee achieving the preferred outcome, but many professional goals are not easily achieved and require multiple steps. An officer cannot expect to achieve the rank of lieutenant if he or she is not first a sergeant. It also helps to apply for promotion and go through testing processes. If a graduate degree is a formal or informal requirement in the organization, an officer needs to attend to that situation.

Futures thinking encourages supervisors and other employees to demonstrate real leadership. It helps agencies and personnel to recognize problems before those liabilities grow too large and to realize opportunities before they slip away. It is often an investment of energy and resources today that will pay dividends in the future (just as education and training require commitment today to help an employee realize their preferred tomorrow). The very process of considering the future facilitates asking critical questions, challenging ingrained assumptions, and repeatedly contemplating whether there is a better way to pursue an organization's operations or an individual's objectives. By its very nature, futures thinking works to lead individuals and organizations to new opportunities for innovation and growth to achieve more effective, efficient, and equitable policing outcomes. While not the only tool that can assist a leader advance innovation and growth in the workplace, futures thinking is an important element that can contribute to a leader's repertoire of traits and habits generating successful and effective outcomes.

Conclusions

Police organizations and operations are situated in dynamic social, political, economic, environmental, and technological contexts. Change is a constant challenge and opportunity for both organizations and their individual members. Static thinking about how to serve communities leads to the stagnation and declining efficacy of police organizations. Static thinking about how to exercise effective leadership practices is often a sign of management, not leadership. There is a real risk that the policing profession is reinvigorating management at the expense of demonstrating leadership (Loveday 2008). Leaders have to create systems and opportunities that support the development and growth of personnel and agency operations. Leaders must also continually challenge themselves to new and better levels of performance. In this way, leaders demonstrate the example they want officers to follow and they can work to create an organizational culture that embraces continual improvement and advancement.

The pursuit of innovation and growth with a futures orientation is an important way in which leaders and leadership can be enhanced and expanded within the policing profession. New ideas, practices, and techniques help continually move the discipline toward innovative and enhanced approaches to serve communities and constituents. To achieve this outcome, leaders need to encourage innovation and support the growth of followers, organizational practices, and their personal skillset. Followers need to be encouraged and provided the tools to develop, improve, and enrich their knowledge and practices. This will not only strengthen their abilities to perform their current duties; it will also help followers develop their leadership skills and create a more adaptable workforce. Organizations need to seek out new approaches to tactical and strategic matters. Too often police organizational innovation is "safe" rather than pushing agencies to bolder and non-traditional approaches to operations.[7] As individuals, leaders need to continually challenge their own growth, development, practices, and skills. Leaders must be honest when considering their weaknesses and shortcomings. Leaders cannot be satisfied with their past accomplishments. Leaders must routinely and regularly seek new ways to improve their skills, their approaches, and their traits and habits. Leadership starts with the leader; innovation and growth begin when leaders demonstrate those habits in their own behaviors and routines.

---

7. Two quotes are particularly salient here. R. Buckminster Fuller instructs us: "You never change things by fighting the existing reality. To change something, build a new model that makes the existing model obsolete." Radical and innovative ideas are sometimes needed to solve difficult and entrenched problems. This idea is well understood in engineering and science, but is rarely observed in public sector performance. In a similar vein of thinking, Albert Einstein once remarked: "We can't solve problems by using the same kind of thinking we used when we created them." Too often public sector agencies, legislative bodies, and policy makers fall in the trap of applying the same logic, presumptions, and traditions that created a problem when they seek to solve that situation. This if often followed by amazement that the solution did not work.

Chapter 10

Leading by Example

One of the key ways leaders can be effective is to demonstrate and model the type of behavior desired from followers. General leadership literature and popular vernacular often refers to this as "leadership by example." By demonstrating a strong work ethic, professionalism, and dedication (among other characteristics and attributes) it is hoped the leader will be demonstrating to others the type of orientation and behavior expected of, and valued from, employees. Followers can more clearly understand how they are expected to perform specific duties and/or how to be a good employee by observing the way the leader behaves. Likewise, leaders who hold employees to one set of expectations while themselves living up to a lower standard might have legitimacy problems in the workplace. Ideally, leadership by example involves leaders demonstrating a strong work ethic, both in terms of showing the volume and the process through which work should be completed. Leaders set the pace they expect others to follow, even if they are not involved in the core tasks of the organization. A leader asking for a high volume of productivity from patrol personnel while spending several hours each morning in a local coffee shop or diner might have a difficult time inspiring enthusiastic compliance from officers. In an agency implementing a new policy or strategy, the leader is at the front of that effort, demonstrating and showing the "new normal" for handling the specific task.

For a first-line supervisor, leading by example might mean being active in the field. A patrol sergeant balances her administrative duties with a desire to still handle calls, make traffic stops, initiate field contacts, and engage in enforcement behavior.[1] The sergeant is not engaging in these activities with the overt intention of supervision; rather, she is demonstrating the expectation that others perform their duties with professionalism, skill, and efficiency. By showing that she can handle core policing tasks while still meeting her supervisory responsibilities, the leader is demonstrating that patrol officers should be able to work at a similar pace. An example is set by leading "from the front; don't direct from the rear" (sergeant small municipal agency). Supervisors operating with this approach "are the first through the door" (lieutenant major county agency) in a literal or figurative sense. Even if leaders are not overtly pushing officers to work at a similar pace, it is expected that officers will notice, for example, that their sergeant makes a lot of field stops and that officers will begin to model that behavior in their own work efforts. Even if the latter does not occur in all cases, the idea of leadership by example is that leaders will garner more respect and legitimacy among followers because they are contributing to the work of the organization, not simply issuing orders "from on high."

---

1. This vision of the patrol sergeant is very consistent with Engel's (2002) "active" supervisor. Engel's research findings raise some valid questions about the relative merits of such a supervisory style. She found that active supervisors and their subordinates used force at a higher rate (2001). It is unclear whether this was a function of a more "aggressive" policing style or simply being more active in the field, which might be expected to elevate the frequency with which officers encounter situations where force might be justified.

As supervisors rises through the ranks they might spend less time and energy in direct policing activities, but leading by example in other ways is still important. Thinking about the traits and habits discussed in earlier chapters, leaders should be demonstrating their integrity, communication skills, fairness, trustworthiness, interpersonal skills, and professionalism. Though the tasks and contexts of a large city chief and a patrol officer in the same agency are very different, how they comport themselves and approach those tasks should be consistent. The chief is the one who should be setting the tone others follow. When expressed in an ideal fashion, someone who leads by example is able to "set and keep a high standard and example to their subordinates" (commander large county agency). They "set [an] example via personal discipline . . . a strong work ethic, positive attitude & caring for their subordinates" (assistant chief large municipal agency). More than simply demonstrating the idealized vision of a police officer within her or his agency, the effective leader who sets a strong example does so through tangible actions. Though the chief might not engage in routine street-level enforcement activities, officers might be influenced by seeing that she treats people with dignity and respect, is a good listener, takes a firm line on crime and disorder problems, and exemplifies honor and integrity in serving the community. How those attributes manifest themselves among officers might be slightly different, but the core traits and habits would be expected to translate into all aspects of agency operations.

Even though leaders might not routinely engage in the full range of policing tasks within an agency, followers need a sense the leaders understand the tasks, challenges, and environments in which followers conduct their work. To effectively lead officers, the supervisors must have an understanding of those tasks. Absent direct experience with a given task, leaders need to show they respect and understand the limitations of their direct knowledge. A commander who never worked an investigative assignment should use extreme caution trying to instruct seasoned homicide investigators how to handle a specific aspect of a case. The leader might do better offering suggestions, asking questions to ensure compliance with law and policy, and asking the investigators how the leader can serve their needs and assist their success. Those who lead by example "know what their [sic] talking about inside and out and want to share as much as they can with fellow officers from their own experience" (lieutenant major county agency). Having "knowledge and experience combined with trust and confidence from your officers are key traits" (lieutenant mid-size county agency) that enable the leader's efficacy. This might suggest that a supervisor does not need proficiency in all aspects of agency operations, but at the very least needs to have a reputation as having once been an effective "street cop" (Reuss-Ianni 1983).

Research in a variety of occupational contexts has validated that leading by example is more than an ideal or platitude. Frost, Fiedler, and Anderson (1983) studied the dynamics of leader-follower dynamics in both military combat and firefighting situations. They found leaders who engaged in personal risk taking were judged more effective. This does not imply police leaders need to continually place themselves in harm's way in order to preserve their status and standing in the organization. Presumably these risks were deemed necessary for mission success, rather than being reckless acts. The important idea is that leaders must show they are still willing and able to confront the challenging aspects of being a police officer. Likewise, followers have demonstrated higher levels of creativity and problem solving when their leaders behave with the intention of increasing "self-efficacy" among workers (Redmond, Mumford, and Teach 1993). Followers do notice variation in styles and methods across different leaders. Followers do pay attention to the messages, rights, and restrictions conveyed and provided by their leaders. Whether intended or not, leaders must be aware their actions are observed and internalized by peers, subordinates, and others in and around the organization. In some situations followers might not even be conscious of the ways a leader's actions (be they positive or negative) influence their own behaviors, attitudes, and decision making.

Leadership by example is closely related on many levels to transformational leadership (Burns 1978). Leaders operating from a transformational platform will seek to enhance follower actions and conduct by demonstrating the preferred way to complete a task or even to broadly "do the job" of being a police officer. In contrast to transactional leaders, who operate from a platform of rewards and punishment, transformational leaders will seek to use positive influence, empowerment, increased confidence and competence among followers, and strong leader-follower relations to increase follower commitment to the leader, the organization, and the tasks and missions at hand (Pillai and Williams 2004). These higher levels of positive traits among employees can lead to increased job satisfaction, increased commitment, and improved performance (Ford, Weissbein, and Plammondon 2003; Yukl 2009). While being placed in a formal position of authority can earn a supervisor a degree of public deference, it does not ensure actual compliance among subordinates. Leaders need to understand how their actions may, indeed, speak louder than their words in terms of influencing personnel. Leading by example can be an important way for a supervisor to unify the other traits and habits described in this book. It provides the leader an opportunity to do more than just direct the actions of subordinates. Those who lead by example actually demonstrate the orientation, mindset, and approach they want officers to use in performing their duties.

What Qualifies a Leader to Lead?

Leading by example is a prime way in which an individual with little or no formal rank might in reality play a leadership role in their unit or organization. The influence exerted by an individual can exceed what his or her official position would imply, at least on select matters. Many organizations have front-line personnel who play an important role influencing the mentality and productivity of their peers. Despite holding no formal rank and perhaps having relatively less experience, these officers are the ones to whom others naturally gravitate. At times co-workers might not even realize they are looking to these informal leaders as an example for how to perform aspects of the job or how to respond to new management initiatives. When an aspect of front-line operations undergoes a change, many officers may look toward these informal leaders. If the latter embrace the change with enthusiasm and support, the outcome of that change effort may be very different than if the informal leaders respond with reluctance, skepticism, or open resistance (Schafer 2001, 2002).

At one time the author was affiliated with an agency located in a college community. The college had experienced a number of moderate and large disturbances involving college students and youth who had consumed far too much alcohol. The problems culminated with an event involving several thousand youth that was ultimately labeled a riot. The agency found that it was ill prepared to respond to this incident, as none of the officers had seen such an event in decades in this particular community. Almost none of the officers had worked for the agency long enough to have experienced campus-based unrest during the 1960s. The agency lacked sufficient training, equipment, policies, protocols, and plans to address the first event when it occurred. The available riot equipment had been collecting dust in a corner for several decades. The available gear was outdated or broken; there was not enough functional gear to properly equip and protect all of the officers. The agency was ill prepared to minimize property damage and injuries to both officers and the exuberant youth in the process of restoring order. Change was clearly needed on a number of fronts.

In the aftermath of the first major riot, the agency was able to secure training assistance from the state prison system. One of the trainers sent to the city was a younger correctional officer who had recently served in the Marine Corps. The agency was so impressed with the correctional officer's tactical knowledge and professionalism they were able to lure him away from the state and hired him as a patrol officer. He quickly established himself as the resident expert on tactical matters in both riots and other high-risk operations. Though he was among the least senior of the agency's fifty sworn personnel, this officer was a respected leader, at least on tactical issues. The command staff respected his opinion and insights as they worked to improve the agency's capacity to effectively respond to incidents of large-scale disorder. His skills were respected by members of the agency's tactical unit in helping train for a variety of high-risk events, not just in riot situations. Other officers on his shift, who began to emulate what he taught them about increasing officer safety during routine patrol operations, respected his knowledge and approach to the job. What made this officer an informal leader and respected expert on tactical matters was his knowledge, his temperament, and his professionalism on the streets. When instructing others he was careful not berate, humiliate or embarrass them; instead his approach was to operate from the position of educating peers about ways to do their job in a safer manner. In many respects his approach was quite intelligent. He recognized that while he had strong tactical knowledge he had to be careful how that knowledge was conveyed to experienced co-workers with decades of policing service. Even when he did achieve the rank of sergeant later in his career, this officer's influence in the agency tended to outpace his position on the organizational chart.

What qualified this officer to be a leader? It was his knowledge and approach to his job, as well as the way he interacted with his co-workers. He was modest, hard working, and never boastful or arrogant. In describing the traits that allow some to lead by example, respondents in the National Academy study noted those who exemplify this behavior "know what they are talking about. They have experience to back up what they say. They have the respect of others and are trusted. They have proven themselves many times over" (sheriff small county agency). The responses suggested that to be viewed as legitimate in leading others, the leader must be a "person who is knowledgeable about the job" (lieutenant small municipal agency) and the leader "must have *experience*" (lieutenant major county agency, emphasis in the original comment). They might also have demonstrated a strong work ethic. By making the "most arrests, car stops, search warrants . . . they have the respect of both their peers and command" (lieutenant large municipal agency). In some cases it might be helpful for the aspiring leader to "possess high educational qualifications coupled with vast experience gained through many years of service" (division head mid-size international federal agency).

What is unclear (and perhaps subjective for the individual follower) is to what extent knowledge and experience must be specialized to match the formal leader's duty assignment. Can a supervisor with a background solely in patrol (officer, sergeant, lieutenant) be viewed as a legitimate commander (captain) of an agency's investigations personnel? The answer is likely highly subjective and variable. A leader who recognizes his or her limited direct knowledge of investigations and respects that limitation in carrying out his

or her duties will likely fare better than a leader who seeks to influence case-level operations. It is further likely that individual followers will respond differently to a leader with
that record. Most readers have likely encountered a supervisor who though he or she had
the capacity to legitimately make very detailed decisions about operational issues subordinates felt were far beyond that supervisor's expertise and competence. Likewise, many
readers have probably observed informal leaders who managed to exert an influence far
beyond their formal rank within an organization.

The author had affiliations with another agency in which a given officer had very
quickly ascended the ranks. The officer always studied very hard for promotional exams,
took them as soon as he was eligible, and scored so well that the agency could not easily
justifying passing him over for promotion. This officer also displayed good leadership
skills, was a loyal employee, and was up front that he aspired to some day be the chief of
his agency. Fourteen years after being hired by the agency, he became its chief (his fourth
promotion) despite only being in his mid-thirties. This is a notable accomplishment given
the agency employed over 200 officers and there were other very strong internal and external candidates for the chief of police position. His rise through the ranks was received
and judged in a variable manner by those he commanded. Some felt he did not have the
experience on the streets. Those in this camp felt the new chief had only "book knowledge" but not enough "street experience" to grant him legitimacy. Others respected the chief
for being hard working and shrewd in his professional advancement because he had re-
fused to allow agency tradition to dictate when he sought promotions.[2] Early in his career he identified being the agency's chief as his objective and he pursued that goal with
vigor, never hiding or denying that was his ultimate ambition.

In the end the chief had what was arguably a very successful career. He held the office
of chief for a decade (an admirable tenure given the agency's size), retiring on his own terms
and timeline. While first a sergeant and later a lieutenant in the agency's patrol division,
he had worked hard to maintain visibility on the street. When he was given some supervision of investigative personnel he was respectful of the fact he had never been a detective. He did not pretend to be an expert in all policing matters. He listened to his personnel
when they did have superior experience and subject matter expertise, he exemplified many
of the principles articulated in this book, and he sought to demonstrate the type of work
ethic he wanted from his personnel. He led with an example of professionalism and integrity, worked hard to cultivate interpersonal relationships throughout the community,
and demonstrated mastery of the tasks associated with each position he held in the agency.
Did he have the full support and confidence of every employee in the agency? Certainly
not . . . nor would that be expected of anyone given the agency's size. He did, however,
enjoy many achievements during his ten years as the agency's chief. Though some found
him Machiavellian in his approach, many others respected his drive and dedication not
only to his personal career aspirations, but also to the agency.

National Academy respondents suggested that other aspects of leaders were of importance. Experience itself may not be enough to be viewed with legitimacy. In some ways,
the responses addressing this matter implied that those who lead by example are able to
do so because they adhere to many of the behaviors described in other chapters in this book.

---

2. The initial judgments about this young chief often seemed a function of direct contact. The
agency was large enough that some officers had never worked with or for the chief. Those who knew
him expressed more confidence than those who simply knew of him.

Those who lead by example have an "ability to motivate others to achieve the goals of the department/community" (chief small municipal agency). They demonstrate "honesty, integrity, good morals . . . [and they] are followed by others because of these quality traits" (lieutenant small municipal agency). "They set the example. Everything about them demonstrates their abilities, professionalism" (captain large county agency). "The effective leaders I know are those that led by example . . . [and had] the ability to not forget where they came from, even as they continued to promote higher" in the agency (deputy chief mid-size municipal agency). In the end, effective leadership by example is not just about actions. It is also about words, deeds, and decisions, as well as the things leaders *do not* do that might serve to erode their own trust, legitimacy, professionalism, or standing within the agency, among personnel, and with constituents.

How Do You Lead by Example?

Effective leadership is defined in my opinion by the following: -Leading by example; setting a good example –being a risk taker –modeling the way –standing up for what is right regardless of pressures from internal or external sources. –doing the right thing when no one thinks it is. (major large municipal agency)

An effective leader is one who leads from the front. He/she sets the standard/example of conduct. (lieutenant major state police agency)

Even those not formally holding rank within an agency may be effective leaders, as addressed above. In describing these types of formal leaders, a lieutenant from a large municipal agency noted they are officers "who embrace the core values and missions of our department . . . whose daily patrol activities & behavior is a demonstration of those core values in practices . . . who through their commitment to service have earned the respect of their peers, supervisors, and command officers." Those who lead by example "walk the walk." They behave in a manner that sets the pace and tone for those around them. They are experienced and skilled officers who work hard. They have proven their competence to do the core work of the organization or unit. They have "knowledge of what they are requesting others to do" (lieutenant small municipal agency). In situations where they may lack direct knowledge of those tasks, they are respectful of their own limited experiences. They do not avoid unpleasant tasks or duties and do not shirk work. They demonstrate competence, commitment, loyalty, professionalism, and a dedication to their organization. These conditions are likely not something the leader boasts or brags about. Instead they are unspoken but readily evident to those who work with that officer or supervisor on a routine basis. Those who lead by example tend to be men and women of their word. As eloquently expressed by a captain from a mid-size agency, those who lead by example "are effective because others are comfortable working with them."

In studying police supervisors and their influence on officer conduct, Robin Engel (2001, 2002) identifies "active supervisors" as those who lead by example. In her study active supervisors set the pace they expected others to follow. They did not passively supervisor or lead from a distance. Rather, active supervisors still handled calls for service, made traffic stops, initiated field contacts, and engaged in the provision of front line policing services.[3]

---

3. Supervisors in her studies were limited to sergeants and lieutenants assigned to patrol divisions.

Engel suggested that if an agency were seeking to advance a particular change or transformation, it would be particularly important that supervisors demonstrate adoption of that new approach (see also Trojanowicz 1980). Based on field observations in Indianapolis (IN) and St. Petersburg (FL), Engel's analysis supported that active supervisors were able to influence officers to elevate their own productivity, particularly their level of self-initiated and problem solving activities. This does not imply that supervisor influence is immediate and clearly present in all situations and contexts, but it does reinforce that such an influence does exist and that it can be achieved, in part, through the example that is set.

There are additional dimensions to leading by example that emerged in the National Academy responses. In many ways these dimensions suggest those who lead by example demonstrate the skills we would expect from a professional officer and police leader. Those who lead by example "are very approachable and when asked explain what is needed and why" (deputy chief large state agency). The leaders explain decisions, orders, and directions. They clarify what needs to be done, explain why that objective or priority has been established, and help personnel understand how to achieve the desired outcome; this capacity is, of course, contingent on leaders having an understanding of these elements themselves. In this way, leadership is not simply about taking action or ensuring that followers take action. Efficacy is not achieved by merely issuing commands and ensuring that followers have the respect or fear to ensure they will follow those orders. Favorable outcomes are more likely to be achieved when followers understand why they are being given a certain direction and why that direction is in the best interest of the follower or organization. This is not feasible in every situation (e.g., we might presume a strict command-and-obey relationship is needed in tactical matters where immediate action is required to achieve favorable outcomes). But the majority of tasks to which followers attend in police organizations are not predicated upon immediate action. There is time for the leader to explain to the follower why a command has been issued.

This practice is contrary to the traditional authoritarian command structure found in American policing. Conventionally followers were expected to accept and act upon orders without question or at least provide the appearance of such obedience (Cowper 2000; Reuss-Ianni 1983). Directive approaches to supervision are predicated on the assumption subordinates will be quiet and unassuming in doing what they are told, with little expectation that they will be given an explanation or rationale. Among other outcomes associated with this nation's experiment with the idea of community oriented policing was the emergence of the alternative perspective that leaders need to do more to win over the "hearts and minds" (Lurigio and Skogan 1994; Skogan and Hartnett 1997) of followers. Early case studies with community policing suggested that when leaders took the time to explain a planned change effort to their personnel and help the personnel understand why the requested actions were warranted and desirable, greater success was achieved (Schafer 2002).

Parallels might even be noted in emerging perspectives on how police officers perform their duties. In his autobiography, former NYPD and LAPD Chief William Bratton contended every officer in this nation needed to understand two concepts and integrate them into their patrol operations (1998). Those concepts are "apologize" and "explain." Bratton suggests officers would encounter far less citizen opposition and animosity if they took the time to apologize when they make mistakes and to explain to the public why certain actions were taken. The professional model of American policing downplayed officers believing that they needed to explain their actions to citizen or apologize when errors were made. Bratton saw this mentality as being highly detrimental to the legitimacy of police operations and the health of police-community relations, particularly in urban areas. To be sure, these concepts cannot be employed in the "heat" of every police-citizen encounter, nor did Bratton expect that to be the case. Bratton's point was that too often ego and arrogance get in the way of officers "smoothing over" a tense situation. The result might be a complaint against an officer or adding just a bit more strain to police-community relations in that jurisdiction.

Consider the "common" traffic stop. An officer requests a motorist produce their license and registration. The citizen, nervous about being stopped, makes a sudden move to grab something from under the driver's seat. The officer, detecting a possible danger, harshly commands the citizen to place their hands on the steering wheel. Perhaps coarse language is used . . . perhaps a weapon is drawn. In the end, it turns out the driver was returning home from the gym. He had placed his billfold under the driver's seat while working out. His sudden movement was a nervous attempt at compliance rather than an attempt to reach for a weapon. Once the proverbial dust has settled, how often do police officers apologize to citizens when these types of events occur? How often do officers explain their interpretations of the events and how that resulted in certain actions? Do officers take the time to offer such explanations versus merely issuing a citation and returning to patrol?

Conventional police culture (Crank 1998) would cast apologies and explanations as a sign of weakness. Likewise, traditional authoritarian supervision and management in policing would suggest there is little or no need for a supervisor to explain orders to followers. In recent decades the latter has been called into question in policing. As better educated officers are being hired and as agencies confront recruitment and retention challenges, effective leaders may be required to engage and communicate with followers on an on-going basis. And in so doing, the leaders might serve as an example for their followers by demonstrating how to manage interpersonal relations with respect and communication, rather than through exercise of authority and bravado. How many complaints against officers might be averted if supervising personnel lead by example? Might contemporary officers learn to treat citizens with the same respect and dignity many would like to receive within their workplace? Might the corrosiveness of modern agencies be reduced if respect and communication, rather than authority and discipline characterized supervisor-subordinate relations? Related to this theme, effective leaders lead by example by providing "the right motivation that makes people go above & beyond to perform" their duties (deputy chief large municipal agency).

As addressed in Chapter Five, effective leaders generally allow others to participate in the decision making process. They seek input from those affected by decisions. They listen to those with expertise on the matter at hand. They recognize who has a stake in the outcome of a decision and "make them feel that their ideas were considered" (lieutenant small municipal agency). This consideration cannot be symbolic or superficial. The leader cannot simply provide the appearance of listening, but rather must truly hear the perspectives and opinions of key constituents. This does not mean leaders always side with those individuals and groups, but they must be afforded the chance to provide their input and perspective. This behavior might be particularly important for mid- and upper-level leaders, who are modeling such listening and involvement skills for those who aspire to be more effective and more highly ranked leaders within an organization.

An effective leader may do more than just model how to be a good officer (as that concept is defined in a given organization). Effective leaders might also demonstrate how to be good leaders. Such practice presumably would serve as a model for the leader's followers, helping develop future supervisors and even informal leaders within the workplace. This practice could also influence a leader's peers and possibly her/his superiors. The example leaders set is not only for those positioned below them in the organization's hierarchy; it can also be a process of serving as a role model for others on the same and higher plains. Whether leaders recognize and consciously seek to be an example in the workplace is unclear and likely varies across individuals. Regardless, those who lead by example hold "themselves to a higher caliber and profess positive characteristics out so others can see and want to imitate" that behavior (chief small municipal agency).

In addition to serving as a model for others, those who lead by example "have a belief in the need for what they are doing. Share their enthusiasm for the profession with others" (lieutenant mid-size municipal agency). They are genuine in wanting to be a good employee and wanting to help others achieve the same outcome. It is likely that serving as an example to others is not something that can be faked; others would presumably notice over time that a leader was not "practicing what they preach." A leader espousing ethics might be observed engaging in behavior that did not reflect their own personal integrity. Followers would note that a leader who called on them to behave in a professional and diligent matter periodically used derogatory language, violated policy, or took extended meal breaks. The same leader who preached the importance of participatory decision making in the work place would in time show that while he or she asked for input from others that input rarely seemed to influence the choices they made. "They practice and maintain good work habits. They are fair, respectful, and honest when dealing with the public and their peers. Their peers will feel these habits and follow these individuals" (deputy chief mid-size county agency).

Being regarded as one who leads by example is not something that likely emerges in a short period of time, nor is it necessarily something that persists indefinitely. One who serves as a model for others "leads by both his past performance and his present vision" (lieutenant small county agency). Some may bring experiences into a workplace that allows them to quickly develop a favorable reputation. Those with prior experiences in the military, policing, or other leadership positions might enjoy a faster trajectory to being viewed as a role model by others. There is perhaps greater risk, however, that any leader can damage or destroy their reputation very quickly through exhibiting behavior that is contrary to expectations. Perhaps this is the greatest risk of being one who leads by example. Followers, peers, and superiors come to expect a certain standard from such personnel. Human weaknesses and fallacies might not be forgiven as quickly and easily for those from whom so much more is expected.

What is the Message to Followers?

Leadership by example enhances efficacy because it sends a series of clear messages to followers, constituents, and sovereigns. Someone who leads by example works hard, displays professionalism in working with the public and followers, shows personal and professional integrity, and understands the work performed by their followers (when they have formal supervisory authority). Their behavior sets the tone and demonstrates to followers, peers, those outside the organization, and even their superiors, the character of the leader. These leaders show others the proper way to police in a given community context and the proper way to lead in their particular organization. There will rarely be surprises from one who leads by example because the values, beliefs, and assumptions governing decision making should become evident to all around the leader. Over time these leaders will have made their standards, principles, and objectives clear to others. They have communicated a vision and articulated its rationale.

One who leads by example does not behave as if they are above doing the least desirable tasks in a unit or organization. The leader's behavior demonstrates "a willingness to do the same job that they tell someone to do" (lieutenant small municipal agency). "They are willing to do exactly what they are asking of the group (of have done in the past in some capacity)" and in this way "they command respect" (commander large county agency). In reality, time, technology, and practical considerations dictate that a leader cannot always have done exactly what they ask of followers. An executive in a large agency cannot be expected to take the time to work routine patrol in order to establish she or he is willing to complete a driver information checklist for each traffic stop.[4] Not every leader will have had the chance to work on the front lines of every duty assignment in an agency. Eventually most leaders will have responsibility over tasks that did not exist when they were earlier in their career and they will not have the opportunity to work every special assignment. While having walked in the shoes of followers might be ideal, what is perhaps more important is having the bearing and demeanor that implies the leader would "never ask or tell someone to do something that [they] are not willing to do [themselves]" (captain mid-size county agency).

As addressed earlier, the leader must respect the limits and parameters of their personal background and experiences. Those whose career trajectory resulted in spending very little time working routine patrol must be aware others might question that leader's legitimacy. Those who never worked a specialized unit they now supervise would be advised to not presume they fully understand the front-line realities of that task, at least at the onset of receiving such an assignment. In reality, officers may inflate the importance of certain experiences in making someone an effective leader. Leaders that respect the limits of their direct experiences and knowledge, listening to trusted advisers, can likely be quite effective. Whether those under their command will view them as legitimate is more difficult to control. The challenge for leaders is to seek ways in which to manage that situation, in part by respecting the limits on their direct knowledge.

Those observing someone who effectively leads by example understand the mentality and message of the leader. They see a leader who is the consummate professional and a good employee. "I find it difficult to respect leaders who are only able to give orders" (captain mid-size county agency). Even though the leader may not perform the same tasks as the follower, the latter derives the sense the leader could and would do so, if needed. It is not making others do undesirable, inconvenient, or burdensome tasks that the leader has not, will not, or cannot do. "Don't ask or expect others to do something: You haven't done. Something you're not willing to do. Something you're not capable of doing" (captain

---

4. This does not, of course, suggest the executive of a large agency can never engage in field operations. Leaders in such circumstances might gain considerable standing with core personnel by taking the time to back up officers on stops and calls when their schedule allows. Riding with officers or spending a bit of time on patrol can be important visibility and provides leaders the chance to informally discuss issues with personnel. The executive's actions should not be mere symbolism. Working the streets allows the executive to maintain a proper perspective and understanding of the core duties of the agency, along with associated challenges and contexts. Being visible creates chances for the executive to talk with personnel, learn about them as individuals, and better understand their ideas and concerns. An executive who never leaves a police facility will be known as someone detached from the current realities of the job.

major county agency). Those working for role model leaders should feel positive about that situation if the leader is achieving her or his objective of being an example. "They inspire confidence in you. They are consistent" (lieutenant medium county agency). Because the leader has repeatedly demonstrated sound judgment, has articulated a clear vision, and behaves in a manner that is in accordance with that vision, followers have confidence they understand and can satisfy expectations. The leader is not giving the message to "do as I say, not as I do." The leader does not call upon officers to behave with integrity, while cheating on his or her spouse (an event rarely as secretive as the leader might intend). The leader does not seek to influence others because they hold a given rank or level of authority. Instead, the leader seeks to influence others through the power of her or his personality and behavior. "You have to be the person that others follow for what person and leader you are and not for your rank or position you're holding" (assistant to the chief major international federal agency).

The ability to lead by example is predicated on several important conditions. Perhaps chief among these factors is that leaders must perceive they are competent to complete the task at hand. When supervisors feel their power base is weak because they perceive they lack competence to perform their job, they may become territorial, defensive, and aggressive (Fast and Chen 2009). Supervisors who feel inadequate about their capacity to perform their duties may seek to put others into chaos or disarray, striking out at those the supervisors perceive may have more power (i.e., informal leaders or competent first-line supervisors). Fast and Chen use the term "aggression" not simply to denote acts of physical violence, but actions supervisors might take to create uncomfortable or stressful situations for others. They suggest, "power paired with self-perceived incompetence leads to aggression . . . driven by feelings of ego defensiveness" (2009, 1406). This situation might manifest itself in several ways in police organizations. A new and relatively young supervisor might find herself in command of a unit of veteran officers. Lacking confidence in her leadership skills and absent a list of leadership accomplishments, she might be uncertain how to fulfill her new tasks, choosing to micromanage and administer, rather than truly leading. A supervisor who came through the ranks only working patrol and uniform assignments might be placed in command of the investigations division of his agency. Having never worked as a detective or handled the investigation of more complex criminal cases, the supervisor might be unsure whether followers will perceive him as credible to manage or lead them.

In both examples, what matters most according to Fast and Chen (2009) is how the supervisors perceive themselves. A supervisor who uses control, directive approaches, and aggression in interactions with others is not likely to be viewed favorably, even if subordinates appear compliant. A leader who feels inadequate is likely to ensure followers see him or her as such. Though false confidence and bravado are ill-advised, leaders ought to use care to not direct their self-perceived insecurities in the wrong fashion. The most likely outcome of using control and aggression to compensate for self-perceived limitations is a group of subordinate personnel who do not trust the supervisor as a true leader.

Conclusions

In writing about great management, Rodd Wagner and James Harter identified twelve elements that suggest management excellence. Based on extensive survey data, their list of great management attributes is a series of questions. The answers followers provide to those questions were seen to be suggestive of the presence or absence of management. In reality, though they use the term "management" their list describes the presence of effective leadership. Those who seek to be effective leaders and to lead by example might periodically reflect on the answers their subordinates/followers might provide to these twelve questions. More boldly, a leader might create a mechanism by which followers can periodically provide anonymous responses to one or more of these questions. This would provide important input and feedback to the leader.

A selection of the questions offered by Wagner and Harter (2006) are abridged and recast here in the context of police leadership. As an employee, I . . .

1. Understand what is expected of me within the workplace, including what my duties are and how are they to be completed.
2. Have access to the tools, resources, and skills I need to successfully meet those expectations.
3. Am able to perform the tasks I enjoy and excel at on a daily basis.
4. Routinely receive feedback and recognition from my leaders when I am doing good work on the job.
5. Feel that my leaders are concerned about me as an individual; I am not just a number or a part in the machine.
6. Feel that my leaders support and encourage my growth and development.
7. Have the opportunity to provide input into important decisions; I can tell that my expertise, insights, and opinions matter to my leaders.
8. Believe that the work I do is important and valued by the organization and my leaders.
9. Know my co-workers are dedicated to providing quality policing services to our community.
10. Am encouraged to develop, grow, and learn; my leaders periodically provide me feedback about my performance and are willing to work with me to encourage my growth and development.

Taken as a group, the answers to these and similar questions can provide important input and feedback to leaders. Police organizations routinely evaluate front-line personnel. How many leaders take the initiative, time, and effort to solicit similar feedback from those they wish to influence?

Subordinates and followers will recognize any hypocrisy in a supervisor's actions and choices. Leaders cannot preach the importance of treating the public with respect if they do not extend the same consideration to their personnel. Leaders cannot demand honesty and integrity if they are cheating on their spouse. Leaders cannot push followers to pursue continual self-improvement if they are not willing to look at themselves with a critical eye for growth and development. Wise leaders will presume that someone is always watching, listening, observing, or recording their actions, statements, and decisions. With this in mind, leading by example is really not an option. It is something leaders and aspiring leaders must embrace. Effective leaders are cognizant of the fact that "subordinates learn more from our own example than from what we say" (lieutenant major county agency).

None of this should imply effective leaders are infallible. Quite the contrary, how leaders respond to the inevitable mistakes they make might help shape whether others perceive them as effective. These leaders "admit faults and learn from every mistake" (sergeant small municipal agency). Rather than stubbornly refusing to acknowledge their errors and misjudgments, effective leaders "make mistakes and learn from them" (lieutenant major county agency). William Bratton's mantra of "apologize and explain" is not simply good advice for patrol officers. This perspective is also a good mindset for leaders as they think about how they interact with followers, peers, the public, and the consumers of their agencies' services. Leaders must be willing to admit to their fallibility. Leaders who are unwilling to do so will be viewed as weak, not because they made the initial mistakes, but because they compounded their first error with ego and arrogance.

One of the greatest challenges for leaders is fostering a strong and favorable reputation within the various groups they seek to influence. As is the case with so many other aspects of the social world, it takes considerable effort to develop and maintain positive standing. Paradoxically, it only takes one error or moment of weakness to damage or destroy that situation. Effective leaders will continually evaluate and assess how their decisions and actions might be viewed and interpreted by others. This does not suggest leaders cater to popularity or the whims of others, yet good leaders will avoid situations where they needlessly self-inflict damage on their reputation. They routinely consider how others will view their leadership and evaluate whether they are setting the right examples for those around them. They seek new ways to demonstrate the proper values, beliefs, and behaviors to those around them. They set an example that others in the organization can learn to embrace, respect, and emulate. They lead by example.

Chapter 11

The Ineffective Police Leader

Scholarship and publications considering leadership tend to take the focus this book used in the first ten chapters. There is a dominant tendency to cast leadership as a positive and benevolent process (Bennis and Nanus 1997; Burns 1978; Conger and Benjamin 1999; Kotter 1990; Peters and Waterman 1982). The leader is implicitly or explicitly characterized as someone who achieves success in pursuing lofty or noble goals, or at least advances fiscal interests in corporate settings. Those is positions of authority who abuse their power, engage in corrupt or untoward acts, or otherwise fail to shoulder the mantle of their responsibilities are largely absent from consideration and discussion. Such persons may not be considered to be true leaders because they do not consistently demonstrate the positive traits and behaviors associated with leadership. Though in positions of potential or expected leadership, those who fail to achieve desired outcomes (or who employ undesirable means in pursuit of objectives) are largely ignored in academic and professional consideration. In many cases, the existence of such individuals is not even addressed by authors and researchers.

Whether conscious or not, the general failure to acknowledge the "dark side" of leadership is an ironic omission in leadership literature across contexts and disciplines. In reality, everyone is aware that leaders at times fail. Even the best leader makes occasional mistakes or in time may see their efficacy deteriorate. Anyone who spends any time working in an organization has noted good leaders who occasionally make a poor choice and/or those in positions of leadership who are unable or unwilling to actually express the traits and habits this book has described. It has been suggested the tendency to overlook ineffective leadership in scholarship, training, and education is a key factor contributing to the perceived shortage of leadership noted by so many employees, executives, and others across diverse workplaces (e.g., Burke 2006; Haberfeld 2006; Kellerman 2004a, 2004b). By limiting or omitting the attention given to ineffective leaders or leadership traits, lessons for prospective leaders are artificially constrained.[1] The point of significance for the discussion in this chapter is that effective leaders should not always assume others view them as effective, that they are effective in all contexts, or that they are effective with all groups of followers.

Barbara Kellerman has vigorously and eloquently challenged the idea that "to be a leader is, by definition, to be benevolent" (2004b, 44; see also Clements and Washbush 1999; Einarsen, Aasland, and Skogstad 2007; Gardner 1990; Kellerman 2000, 2004a; Kets de Vries 1993). Kellerman contends the proclivity to focus on skilled and successful leaders is linked

---

1. It could be argued that ineffective and poor leaders are not truly leaders, but rather managers, administrators, or (perhaps worst of all) simply supervisors. Kellerman (2004a) persuasively argues that the distinction is more complicated. She suggests bad leadership can emerge from good leaders, particularly when those leaders are not attentive to their actions, intentions, outcomes, and implicit messages. Kellerman further argues that leadership outcomes are not simply about the leader, but also the followers and the context. As such, a leader can engage in actions that otherwise would be successful, but that are "bad" or yield unwanted outcomes given the situation. At the same time, good leaders sometimes make mistakes or turn to bad habits.

with our society's love for engaging stories with happy endings. Our culture is captivated by stories of leaders who turned around companies or government agencies. Such accounts are compelling reading, validate the human spirit, and serve to motivate other leaders with the belief that meaningful change can be realized. Without denying that such situations might arise, Kellerman (paraphrasing political philosopher Leo Strauss) remarked that "[c]apricious, murderous, high-handed, corrupt, and evil leaders are effective and everywhere—except in the literature of business leadership" (2004b, 43). In reviewing the National Academy data for this book the author prepared a short article discussing ineffective leaders and sent the essay for publication consideration at one of the premier professional journals read by police leaders around the world. The editors of this prominent publication responded the essay was well-written and insightful, but they preferred not to publish materials that had a negative tone or suggested police leaders might not routinely achieve success in well-intentioned efforts. The risk of this perspective, of course, is that the very problems under consideration (ineffective leaders and leadership efforts) might be perpetuated by the failure to acknowledge that even good leaders need to be aware of their personal limitations, short-comings, and habits that contribute to failed or less-than-ideal outcomes.

Restricting the definition of leadership (and, therefore, the focus of most leadership scholarship) to only those who lead properly and effectively ignores the reality that leaders can be bad, ineffective, and failures, either in part or in whole. The "leadership-is-a-positive-action" orientation overlooks the reality that even effective and well-regarded leaders are not perfect. Good leaders have short-comings, make mistakes, pick the wrong path, and sometimes use less-than-ideal means in pursuing desired ends (Bailey 1988). In some instances leaders might still achieve their goals despite choosing poor tactics. Leaders who are generally viewed in a favorable manner can periodically display poor choices and counter-productive behaviors. Those appointed or anointed to leadership positions can fail to live up to the responsibility they are given. This does not make leaders bad people (though some might be viewed that way by followers); it simply means they are not immune to human weaknesses and failures.

Leadership literature has begun to pay more attention to ineffective leadership practices and results. Such situations are often framed as examinations of leadership failures, bad leadership, power failures, derailed leadership, or the dark side of leadership, though to date most of the focus has been set within the context of private sector leaders (Burke 2006; Einarsen et al. 2007; Finkelstein 2003; Kellerman 2004a, 2004b; McCall and Lombardo 1983; McCauley 2004; Schackleton 1995; Swartz and Watkins 2003) and, to a lesser extent, in government executive offices (Barras 1998; Stanton 2003). The ineffective police leader is largely absent from this modestly expanding body of scholarship. In light of the limited direct supervision given to most police employees and the geographically diffuse nature of police work environments, coupled with the centrality of ethics and integrity, it is reasonable to question whether prevailing theories and models derived primarily in corporate venues have applicability for policing. This chapter seeks to build an understanding of the "other side of the coin" laid out in the first ten chapters. What makes a police leader ineffective or less effective; what traits, habits, and behaviors are more likely to yield unfavorable outcomes?

The Emergence of Ineffective Leaders and Leadership

How and why do we see situations in which ineffective (or less effective) leaders emerge within policing contexts? Similar to many other organizations, police departments too often fail to identify those with a strong potential to be effective leaders, which would enable a greater emphasis on leadership development. This advancement process might include developing a greater self-awareness of one's strengths and weaknesses as a leader, presumably a key precursor to minimizing ineffective outcomes. Agencies frequently default to the "safe" approaches in assessing those seeking promotion, rather than tackling the more daunting task of defining and measuring what it would mean to be a good leader in their organizational context. Consequently, promotion decisions tend to focus on assessing a candidate's aptitude in their current position. Informal leaders are not nurtured or encouraged in their growth. Exams and interviews often measure mastery of bureaucratic rules and protocols (i.e., "book smarts" and "bean counting"). Internal politics, personalities, and egos play an interfering role, further complicating the promotional milieu (Hall 1980). The result is the often-observed gap between "street cops" and their supervisors (Manning 1997; Mastrofski 2002; Reuss-Ianni 1983; Van Maanen 1984; Wilson 1968). In other words, ineffective leadership outcomes are a partial product of the leader's personality, behaviors, actions, and choices (Dotlich and Cairo 2003); however, those individual factors are conditioned and constrained by aspects of institutional environments and practices that typify American police organizations.

Also instructive is the popular conception of the "Peter Principle"—that employees rise to their highest level of incompetence (Peter and Hull 1969). This axiom suggests the limits of supervisors' skills and abilities are only discovered once they have been placed in a position that exceeds their capacities. The supervisor's career might stall at that level, but the net effect is the organization has placed a person in a position of authority without the necessary competence to perform the duties required by that assignment.[2] In most civil service environments, that "over-promotion" of the individual cannot be easily corrected, which ensures too many supervisory positions are held by those incompetent to perform the requisite duties. Though the Peter Principle is often used in a joking fashion, the reality of how promotion decisions are made in the public sector lends an unfortunate air of truth to the theory. Promoting good police officers to first-line supervisory ranks because of their aptitude as street officers ensures a certain degree of failure.

McCall and Lombardo (1983; see also Leslie and Van Velsor 1996; Schackleton 1995) studied executives who "derailed" in their careers within the private sector. Their analysis found it was common to see a promising career interrupted when leaders were placed in situations and circumstances ill-suited for their personal skill set and experiences. Though some leaders can adapt and develop to be effective under those conditions, others either refuse to change behavioral patterns or do not know what or how to change. Too often, derailed leaders were unwilling or unable to adapt their styles and techniques to meet the new context. In some cases, the traits and habits that had brought them prior success ultimately became a liability contributing to their downfall (Kets de Vries 1993; Maccoby 2000; Panzarella 2003). Though there is an element of personal responsibility in this situation, organizations also must bear some fault for not only making ill-advised

---

2. The Peter Principle raises numerous questions about the presumed inability of agencies to make effective promotion decisions and an important follow-up question emerges if we accept this situation as a reality. Why do organizations fail to develop personnel to succeed in their assigned position? Why is that development not accomplished *prior* to advancing an employee up the ranks? If skill sets are needed, why are those not imparted on newly promoted or assigned personnel? If deficiencies are observed or perceived, why are those allowed to persist without efforts to correct the situation?

promotional decisions but also for failing to engage in developmental and corrective actions designed to disrupt the leader's path toward "derailment."

Given the situational leadership presumption that guides this book, the position taken in presenting this chapter is that every leader (no matter how effective) is potentially one promotion or reassignment away from derailment. This is not intended to be a daunting or threatening characterization; rather, it is offered to highlight that a given leader's efficacy is largely a function of the extent to which her or his traits, habits, and behaviors mesh with the followers at hand, the present environment, the tasks before the leader, and the attendant challenges and opportunities. Leaders who have long-term relevance and success recognize the need to continually monitor whether their styles and approaches still work within the context of their area of influence. This situation becomes even more critical with new responsibilities, promotion, and transfer to new units/agencies. In addition, an effective leader recognizes their personal growth and development is a key component of success. Effective leaders realize that despite past successes and accomplishments, there is always room for improving their performance. Success and efficacy are not dichotomies; they exist on a continuum, meaning even strong leaders should be aware of their weaknesses and should be striving for improved outcomes. If leaders expect this of their followers, they should expect nothing less of themselves.

Traits and Habits of the Ineffective Police Leader

Some National Academy participants were specifically asked to write descriptions of ineffective leaders with whom they worked. In other situations, respondents provided rich characterizations of the ineffective police leader while describing effective leaders and leadership. A few of the most insightful general descriptions of ineffective leaders are worth presenting at the onset. A captain from a mid-size municipal agency characterized ineffective leaders as exuding "selfishness, unwillingness to make tough decisions, failure to delegate responsibilities, making decisions while angry/upset, failure to trust others. Most of those I am describing failed to use to resources around them, namely the experiences and minds of those around them." Another respondent (captain small municipal agency, emphasis provided in the original response) wrote that ineffective leaders displayed:

> Dishonesty, lack of candor, lack of empathy, selfishness. They fail to inspire, fail to lead by example, and fail to *work hard* to solve long-term problems, and fail to *empower* subordinates to solve the short term problems. Failure to recognize good, hard work.

A captain from a mid-size municipal agency described ineffective leaders as ...

> ... quick temper, judgmental, lazy, inability to follow through, lack of focus, poor communication/interpersonal skills, moody, negative thinkers, lack of ability to delegate, lack of confidence in others, micromanagers. These are all things that make people poor leaders. Most of these, they would like to overcome, but are either unable, or don't know how.

Ineffective leaders were characterized as "self-centered, only interested in making him/herself look good, lack of confidence and trust in subordinates, micro-managing, knee jerk reactions to situations, and over-reacting to simple matters" (commander small state agency). A lieutenant from a large county agency described ineffective leaders as individuals who are "usually inconsistent and do not possess the characteristics or self discipline needed to become an effective leader. Where many fail is by not taking a balanced approach to their role; either too authoritarian or fail to transition into the role and try to remain 'one of the guys.'"

These characterization illustrate a key theme emerging from the experiences and insights offered by National Academy participants. The traits and habits associated with ineffective leaders could be divided into two categories. Acts of commission were actions and behaviors taken by a leader that worked against the leader's objectives or eroded the leader's standing with peers, followers, and external constituents. Acts of omission were actions and behaviors that *should have* been taken by leaders, but were not; in effect, the leaders failed to live up to their labels by not actually leading. The following sections of the chapter detail five acts of commission (focus on self over others, ego/arrogance, closed mindedness, micromanagement, and capriciousness) and five acts of omission (poor work ethic, failure to act, ineffective communication, lack of interpersonal skills, and lack of integrity) that emerged as dominant themes in the survey responses.

Focus on Self over Others

Earlier chapters have described the concept of "careerism," which arises when employees focus on their own professional interests and aspirations above the concerns of others, the organization, and the community. Leaders engaged in careerism will focus on what they believe is good for their individual interests and their future career advancement. What might be in the best interest of followers and the leader's area of responsibility are less influential in shaping the decisions made by such leaders. Those concerned with on-going career advancement and personal ego/status were likely to focus on what was necessary to secure their next promotion, rather than doing what was needed to achieve organizational/unit goals in their present position. "It's all about them and doing whatever is needed to climb the promotional ladder" (sergeant major municipal agency). Rather than doing what is right, the leader does what is right for personal interests. They are less attentive to present responsibilities and obligations, less cognizant of what is in the best interests of the office they currently hold, and less concerned with personal and professional needs and interests of followers and subordinates. "The largest failure occurs when leaders forget their own responsibilities to the position they hold and to the people under them" (investigation supervisor small state agency). As such, they may "look at the position as a job and not a career" (captain major county agency). This could be particularly problematic if the leader's aspirations were outside of the agency (i.e., obtaining employment with an alternative agency or within another industry).

Parallels might be drawn between careerism and the actions of executives caught up in the various corporate scandals that plagued the financial industry in the 1990s and 2000s (McLean and Elkind 2003). The behavior and decisions of scandal-linked CEOs and leaders were aggravated by structural conditions that generated incentives for the executives to be motivated by personal interests. For example, many executives were eligible for performance bonuses that incentivized the pursuit of fast payouts and short-term achievements over consideration of what was best for long-term corporate health and stability (and, by extension, the stability and security of employees and investors). Parallels might be noted in police organizations and leaders who are motivated by pursuing continued career advancement, which might result in the inaction or indecision discussed below.[3]

Doing what is right becomes secondary to doing what is right for the leader. "They fail because they are not concerned about others and more focused on themselves and their progress, instead of the agency being successful and the community being a safer place – self above service" (commander major state agency). This situation might be exacerbated by the low tolerance for failure found in many police organizations. Leaders might be conditioned to avoid actions and judgments likely to invoke negative outcomes. Self-preservation trumps being a true leader (a process that periodically might require doing things that are unpopular). A major from a medium municipal agency encapsulated this idea, noting that "we promote those who do not self-destruct." The risk is that leaders become conditioned to see inaction and self-interests as appropriate behaviors.

Ego & Arrogance

National Academy participants indicated that ineffective leaders frequently expressed a strong ego and a degree of arrogance as they carried out their duties and engaged in professional interactions. This might result in the leader being perceived as someone who expected to be treated with heavy deference. It could also mean the leader gave the impression that he or she felt certain tasks or duties were beneath them. For some leaders it might be acting in a way that suggested she or he did not believe they needed to consult or seek input from others in making key decisions; they were the leader and the expert, so unilateral choices were fine. It is worth noting that ego and arrogance are not always bad traits and for some leaders a bit of self-confident bravado may be well deserved based on that leader's experiences, accomplishment, and background. The higher a supervisor rises in an organization and the larger or more prestigious the organization, the more ego and arrogance become a fine line for the leader to negotiate.

The challenge for leaders is embedded in the fact that at times it might have be advantageous, desirable, and necessary for a leader to have confidence in themselves and their abilities (Lipman-Blumen 2005; Maccoby 2000). Leaders need to convey to others that their objectives and methods are appropriate if they hope to secure followers. Followers need to develop and maintain confidence that a leader is striving to accomplish worthy goals using appropriate means and methods. If taken too far, however, a leader's behavior might have been viewed as "selfish, stubborn, self-righteous, [and] egotistical" (district commander major state agency). When National Academy participants identified ego and arrogance as characteristics of ineffective leaders, presumably the leader had gone beyond the normal realms of confidence and self-assurance that might be healthy and productive. "They have an inflated sense of self-importance and display it" (lieutenant medium municipal agency).

On their own, a degree of ego or arrogance might not generate appreciable problems for a leader. What might become problematic is when ego or arrogance results in a leader

---

3. Some agencies encourage leaders to minimize the approval of overtime as a short-term effort to contain operating costs. While financial limitations are important driving forces that cannot be ignored, there are times and situations in which overtime is needed to advance the organizational mission. In some instances the short-term savings may result in long-term expenses when problems are not resolved in a timely manner.

taking positions or actions that are deleterious or disadvantageous. Ineffective leaders might adopt the attitude that it is "my way or the highway" and demonstrated "unyielding personalities" (commander large municipal agency). "What keeps them from being effective is they cannot see their own faults and accept responsibility for those faults" (lieutenant small municipal agency). This situation introduces a degree of subjectivity into the process of evaluating a given leader's efficacy and behavior; what one person might see as self-confidence and drive, another may perceive as arrogance and a refusal to listen to others. One person's decisive leader is another person's wild maverick. It may be difficult or impossible for the average leader to be judged as appropriately confident and humble by all those around her or him.

Strong beliefs in their own opinions or judgments might result in leaders who do not listen to, or consult with, key constituents and actors. As discussed elsewhere, listening to and engaging with others in the workplace can be of appreciable importance, even if that process does not substantively change the decisions a leader might make. There is strong value in allowing others to express their views, beliefs, and opinions, though these processes cannot be fake or artificial. The message to leaders is that such steps should often be taken, even if leaders' experiences and expertise would lead them to the same conclusions. Certainly the nature of policing means that leaders cannot always consult with others, but the issues that seem to generate the most dissatisfaction for employees are not the street-level tactical decisions made by leaders (which often must be made in a very short period of time). What tends to upset followers are how supervisors make decisions about "big picture" strategic matters, which often do allow for the soliciting of employee input.

Closed Minded

Related with arrogance and ego is the tendency for ineffective leaders to be closed minded to soliciting and/or heeding suggestions and input from supervisors, peers, followers, or other key constituents. There might be many reasons explaining why a leader is unable or unwilling to listen to other perspectives, opinions, and voices. As before, this situation represents a fine line leaders needed to navigate. Leaders need to have self-confidence and demonstrate a capacity to be decisive. Those who would judge or evaluate a leader can consider always asking for input and suggestions as a sign of weakness. At the same time, leaders need to understand the benefit of other voices and, when possible, the need to take time in making decisions to consider alternatives and ramifications. A captain from a large municipal agency described ineffective leaders as individuals who are "inflexible, uncompromising, and don't foster a participatory style of leadership." Though police supervisors bear a tremendous responsibility for the choices they make, management and leadership experimentation has demonstrated there might be ways to enhance organizational effectiveness through the use of models and structures intended to routinize the receipt and processing of input from the workforce, such as participatory models of leader-follower interactions and organizational decision making (Steinheider and Wuestewald 2008).

The National Academy participants portrayed being closed minded as not adapting, innovating, or changing when such actions were needed within the unit or agency. Ineffective leaders "fail to examine issues from all sides. They fail to consider unintended consequences. They don't educate themselves on the big picture, so when circumstances change (as they always do) ineffective leaders fail to adapt" (deputy chief large municipal agency). This stands in contrast to the very concept of leadership, which implies a capacity to move a group to an alternative position. Being closed minded to the need for change could reflect that a leader is out of touch, too stubborn to listen, or fears change might result in failure. Policing has never been a profession that has excelled in cultivating visionary leaders; though exceptions exist, this trait does not abound within even many prominent police leaders. This situation is not altogether surprising given the highly bureaucratic nature of policing and the tendency of the professional culture to value tradition and entrenchment over innovation and change (Mastrofski 1998; Sklansky 2007).

Micromanagement

As noted in Chapter One, leadership scholars, trainers, and consultants have gone to great length to differentiate between leadership and management (Northouse 2009; Yukl 2009). Leadership has generally been conceived as the capacity to move a group and/or organization through a process of change. Management is more concerned with technical proficiency at a finite set of tasks. Leaders embrace and pursue change, while managers tend to value and seek routine and consistency within organizational processes. Effective police supervisors and officers are often both strong leaders and efficient managers (Stamper 1992); they can motivate and develop personnel while attending to the nuances of budgets, law, and contracts. In general, the efficacy of a leader in any context is partially predicated on demonstrating the willingness to delegate responsibilities. Leaders often have responsibility for duties that can only be fulfilled at an optimal level if subordinates are trusted to exercise appropriate discretion and due diligence in fulfilling assigned tasks.

American police agencies have tended to do a poor job developing leadership skills among supervisory personnel (Van Maanen 1984) in support of delegation and employee empowerment. This is a common weakness in a variety of occupational settings beyond the confines of policing. In policing, the problem has arguably been exacerbated by the litigious nature of American society and the expansion of civil liability within the public sector. Numerous avenues exist by which liability for an officer's conduct might be attached to supervisory personnel (e.g., Ross 2000). Understandably, newly promoted personnel might struggle to delegate and demonstrate leadership if they are concerned that doing so might increase personal or organizational liability. It might be considered easier to default to bureaucratic management tactics (Krimmel and Lindenmuth 2001) by focusing on a strict style of supervision in order to mitigate this risk.

The tendency to "micromanage" was commonly associated with ineffective leadership. Micromanagement is the opposite of delegating tasks and empowering personnel. The supervisor focuses her or his attention on monitoring and controlling employee conduct, including minimizing the chances employees have to make independent decisions. Examples of this in policing are as readily evident as the voluminous policy and procedure manuals created by most agencies. Rather than focusing on ensuring employees abide by core principles, too many agencies seek to define and structure as many employee decisions as possible. A sergeant from a small municipal agency noted most ineffective leaders are "far too autocratic and fail to delegate when appropriate." Requiring that subordinates secure excessive permission, approval, and review, particularly for routine choices, slows the pace of organizational action and output, while sending the message to subordinates that their judgment is not trusted. A heavy focus on controlling subordinate and routine organizational actions can prevent the achievement of desired outcomes. Ineffective leaders "fail to delegate authority [to subordinates] that is necessary for the success of desired results" (unit chief, mid-size municipal agency). Some National Academy respondents noted a proclivity toward management may also emerge when supervisors fear subordinates will outshine their own accomplishments. In the case of the latter, ineffective leaders may "lack self-confidence. They make up for it by micro-managing people" (lieutenant, medium municipal agency).

Capricious Choices

Followers presumably understand that leaders make decisions within the context of a given situation and timeframe (Brewer, Wilson, and Beck 1994), thus being influenced by situation and circumstance. An argument could be made that a leader who never waivers or varies might do a disservice to the unit/agency and personnel they command by not realizing there are few absolutes. At the same time, respondents indicated they desired a sense of continuity in how decisions were derived. A follower who has a history with a given leader should generally be able to assess the likely choice that leader will make in a given situation. Ineffective leaders were described as being arbitrary and capricious their actions and decisions. A commander in a large state agency noted such leaders were "inconsistent and [they] don't adhere to a systematic approach." Having a general sense of a leader's likely response to a situation is of importance because peers and followers want to make decisions and take actions in support of the leader's goals and objectives. If they do not understand the base from which the leader operates it becomes difficult for followers to know how to exercise their own discretionary authority. Followers want to function in a manner that supports the leader and her/his objectives, while knowing how to avoid the leader's wrath and criticism. Followers want to understand "what matters" within the agency and to the leader in furthering the standing of the agency and, in some cases, advancing their own career objectives.

Capriciousness also extends into how leaders make personnel decisions. Organizational politics have the potential to become significant sources of stress when leaders demonstrate "[i]nconsistent, arbitrary discipline. Cronyism, nepotism" (sergeant mid-size municipal agency). Ineffective leaders were depicted as putting personal relationships ahead of what was right, just, and consistent with past practices. Although employees might not like every rule within the workplace, they often appreciate knowing that all rules, criteria, and standards are applied equally to all personnel. Friends and relatives of police leaders should not enjoy special privilege. Likewise, officers may sense that leaders are not likely to support them if their actions are appropriate, but generated public outcry (i.e., the use of force or the handling of major cases). Ineffective leaders tend to engender the feeling that "officers often do not know where he stands, they cannot count on him in controversy" (chief small municipal agency). It is well-established that officers prefer to have the sense peers and leaders "have their back" (Manning 1997; Rubenstein 1973) during critical incidents and in their aftermath. An officer lacking confidence in a leader's support could experience distrust, hostility, and strain in the leader-follower relationship (Reuss-Ianni 1983).

Poor Work Ethic

As described and discussed in the prior chapter, leadership by example means a supervisors engages in the type of work ethic and duties they expect from followers. The leader sets the pace and tone for how officers are asked to behave. The leader does not ask officers to work hard and be people of integrity, while operating as a "retired on duty" supervisor who avoids work and violates minor (or major) departmental policies. Descriptions of ineffective leaders provided by the National Academy participants indicated these supervisors often lacked the appropriate work ethic in approaching their own duties and responsibilities. Ineffective leaders were characterized as being lazy, doing the minimal amount of work, and failing to "give 100 percent" to the job and their responsibilities. Ineffective leaders who displayed a poor work ethic were frequently framed as being late in their careers. They were nearing or at the point when they could retire from the job and were described as having lost their enthusiasm and commitment. They demonstrated a work ethic that included "[l]aziness, negativity . . . They fail to have passion for the work" (captain major municipal agency). "They are lazy, don't provide guidance, never jump in and do their fair share, always have excuses," leading to a failure to be productive workers (lieutenant medium state agency).

This situation can be considered yet another fine line for a leader to tread. A leader wishing to avoid being characterized as a micromanager might seek to empower subordinates and delegate responsibility. At the same time, the leader must not hand off too many tasks or responsibilities, lest they be construed as shirking his or her job. Likewise, if a leader shows no interest in putting in more than their required forty hours per week (e.g., never puts in extra hours or days), does that demonstrate the leader is unwilling to "give 110 percent" to the job or suggest that leader has a more healthy and evenhanded approach to balancing their career and personal life? It is likely that most leaders who would be viewed as demonstrating a poor work ethic deserved such a label. They do not empower others or seek to maintain a balance between their work and personal life. By not displaying an honest work ethic and by not demonstrating the proper way to police a given community, ineffective leaders fail to show the dedication and standard of performance they presumably expect from others. Quite simply, they "fail to lead by example" (captain small municipal agency). The inability or refusal to show commitment to the organization and its objectives undermines the leader's credibility and/or implies to followers that a committed, diligent work ethic is neither expected nor valued.

Failure to Act

Leaders are expected to earn and embody that label; they are, quite understandably, expected to lead. Though an effective leader will engage in appropriate contemplation and consultation with relevant parties before making many decisions, being a leader will ultimately require decisiveness and action. Ineffective leaders fail to act in a variety of circumstances and situations. They fail to actually lead. "Leaders must be able to make decisions" (sergeant small municipal agency). A variety of situations might explain why a leader would fail to act. For some leaders, a lack of sufficient self-confidence might cause him to distrust his own judgment. When confronted with a choice, they might have difficulty knowing what to select from the range of options. "Ineffective leaders often refuse to *make a* decision"(captain major county agency; emphasis in original). For other leaders, inaction might be a means to avoid taking critical or unpopular actions, thus preserving popularity and a planned career trajectory. The leader might opt to relegate an issue to the proverbial "back burner," leaving it up to a successor to be the "bad guy" who must make the difficult and unpopular choice. Alternatively, a leader may fear taking action on volatile and high profile matters; if his or her choice is later deemed poor or inappropriate it could harm the leader's career aspirations (e.g., invoking the Peter Principle), generate liability, or, in extreme cases, result in injury, loss of life, or property damage. When they were police officers, most leaders routinely confronted situations where they made decisions and took decisive action. As a supervisor, the leader may struggle to do the same when confronting the reality that a poor choice could result in harm to a subordinate or citizen. More simply, they may be overcome by the "fear of looking bad or not knowing what to do" (sergeant small county agency).

For some ineffective leaders a failure to act can reflect concern over their popularity with subordinate personnel or the aversion to situations that will generate conflict. Inaction arises because the leader is "afraid to be disliked by their subordinates and refuse to discipline them" (sergeant medium municipal agency). Due to a "fear of confrontation, fear of hurting feelings" (sergeant small county agency) a leader might ignore personnel matters that should be addressed. It is unfortunate to consider that a leader might be "more concerned with upsetting their subordinates rather than doing their jobs" (captain mid-size municipal agency). The National Academy participants, however, indicated that for some leaders the "inability or unwillingness . . . to make unpopular decisions that are in the best interest of the organization" (supervisor major county agency) resulted in inaction and ultimately in being deemed ineffective. In considering leaders who fail to lead, it should be acknowledged that in some situations a decision to not act is based on the perception that change might not be actually warranted (at least at a given point in time). A leader who was quite comfortable with the prevailing status quo in a system could disagree with followers who viewed this situation as ripe for change, enhancement, elimination, or modification. In other situations, a leader might agree action is needed, but that the timing is not amenable to achieving desired outcomes.

Ineffective Communication

It is not surprising that respondents portrayed communication as a weakness for many ineffective leaders. This situation was not simply a matter of an individual who struggled with the mechanics of being articulate in written or verbal expression. Ineffective communicators demonstrate a number of fundamental communication omissions, including being unwilling or unable to participate in constructive and meaningful two-way dialog, a refusal to explain key decisions and actions, and a failure to accept input and criticism. Ineffective leaders were described as being unwilling to give a "chance to the team to participate in making the decision" (captain major international federal agency).[4] This circumstance serves to constrain the input and outflow of communication through a leader's office or position. Ineffective leaders exhibiting this trait may feel little need to seek out or listen to the suggestions of others and may see little reason to articulate their rationale for decisions. Subordinates and co-workers find this situation understandably frustrating. Within the National Academy responses it was common to see critiques mentioned in conjunction with comments alluding to a leader being closed-minded or arrogant.

Ineffective leaders are typified by "not [being] willing to explain the reason why a decision needs to be made" (captain medium municipal agency). They "fail to effectively communicate change in an organization or the reason for change or decisions made" (sergeant small municipal agency). Whether this act of omission is due to arrogance (e.g.,

---

4. Trained, educated, and experienced professionals rarely respond well to being treated as children, given only direction and never afforded a voice in the organization.

the belief the leader did not have to rationalize or justify her/his actions) or indifference (e.g., not being concerned that followers might desire more information) varied within the data. Respondents expressed a desire to see leaders who were open to the possibility that there might be ways to improve aspects of an agency or unit's operations. Ineffective leaders are often resistant to this type of constructive input. They do not want to "listen to other ideas or admit there is a better way" (captain mid-size municipal agency).

Lack of Interpersonal Skills

Closely related with ineffective communication was the indication that ineffective leaders lacked appropriate interpersonal skills. This failure included the belief that some leaders were limited by their inability to understand the human needs and motivations of those they sought to influence, including followers and external constituents. This act of omission is distinct from poor communication in that the former relates more with the informal and "human" aspects of the workplace. Interpersonal skills are not simply a matter of communicating and explaining policy changes. They are the processes that enable leaders to develop and maintain positive relations with peers, supervisors, subordinates, and constituents. Of the traits of ineffective leaders, it might be suspected this limitation would be most apparent prior to the point where an officer is promoted to a supervisory position. Other traits and habits only become evident when someone is in a formal position of power or might emerge later in an individual's career. Interpersonal skills, however, might be assumed to be static across duty assignments, rank, and the career cycle. Officers who struggle with their interpersonal skills on the street and in police facilities would be expected to continue to struggle with those skills if they are promoted.

Strong interpersonal skills are often characterized as a hallmark of effective leadership, such as the "charismatic leader" (Conger 1989). While innately easy for some supervisors, ineffective leaders might have to expend considerable and deliberate effort in trying to "know their officers and tend to their welfare" (executive officer major military service). Due to their "lack of basic human personal skills . . . they fail to realize that they are leading people" (investigations supervisor small state agency). In such instances leaders might be viewed as cold, distant, detached, or "robotic" in how they interact with peers and carry themselves in interpersonal interactions. Such interactions may often be viewed by followers as being forced, uncomfortable, and (perhaps fortunately) infrequent. Interpersonal relationships are of appreciable importance because they can engender a sense of trust between a leader and her/his followers. "Sometimes you have to care from the heart, then the mind will follow" (commander large state agency).

Interpersonal relationships matter because they engender a degree of trust and allegiance between leaders and followers. In a sense, the leader-follower dyad might be more effective when the latter has a sense that she or he is in some way personally connected to the former. The failure to "develop some level of relationship with the employees and to gain their respect" (special agent in charge mid-size state agency) can limit a leader's efficacy and impact. Organizational research suggests that bonds, allegiance, and trust frequently condition outcomes, including respect found in leader-follower relationships. All else being equal, people are more inclined to follow a leader they like, trust, and respect. By itself, charisma is likely insufficient to ensure the attainment of desired leadership outcomes. Charisma may, however greatly expedite and invigorate a leader's efficacy in the workplace. Ineffective leaders either do not recognize the importance of relationships or struggle to establish and maintain these connections. Because subordinates and followers see the leader as distant, detached, and disinterested in getting to know them as people, the follower's starting orientation is not likely to be one of trust with a predisposition to enthusiastically perform upon the leader's call to action. This creates an interesting challenge for leaders in larger agencies, where developing that level of impersonality engendered by the organization's size may render connection and interaction difficult or impossible. In such circumstances the role of immediate supervisors is heightened in helping ensure the directives of higher leaders are embraced.

Lack of Integrity

Honesty and integrity have been considered fundamental virtues since the professionalization movement began in American policing in the 1890s. Parallels to this ideology can be noted in the concept of "policing by consent" that has served as one of the anchors of British policing since the Peelian vision was articulated in 1829. Policing by consent is predicated in part on the idea the police are only effective so long as they maintain the public's trust. Actions that abrogate that trust are considered to have a corrosive effect on an agency or officer's capacity to achieve their intended goals and objectives. A similar conception can be applied in understanding the salience of integrity and trust in the relationship between leaders and followers (Villiers 2003). A leader's ability to establish effective relationships with followers is partially conditioned by the leader being viewed by followers as a trustworthy, honest, and ethical person. All else being equal, few people are interested in willingly and earnestly following a leader they believe is immoral, disrespectful, egotistical, and driven by self-interest.

National Academy respondents frequently typified ineffective leaders as lacking the requisite level of integrity to maintain the trustful and sincere following of subordinates and others. Leaders are less likely to achieve efficacy if followers perceive them as being "immoral, unethical" (captain major municipal agency), and having "no core values" (commander large municipal agency). Leaders were portrayed as being less effective when they performed their duties in a manner that lacked professionalism, diligence, and dedication. Such a situation might often have been a subjective determination for individual followers. For example, a leader who allegedly engages in marital infidelity or poor integrity in an off-duty business transaction might be vilified by some followers, while generating indifference among others who see a distinction between one's personal and professional lives. Poor integrity (or the perception thereof) can yield a lingering effect. Ineffective leaders often have "done something in their past to lose the trust and respect of the employees" (commander large state agency). That trust and respect, once lost, can be very difficult to recapture.

Conclusions

It is likely that everyone working in policing realizes there are leaders who could be more effective or who periodically engage in behaviors that erode potential efficacy. It is also likely leaders who fall into these categories do not recognize that fact about themselves. Jack Enter (2006) relates how he once conducted a leadership development program that was attended by supervisors from an agency where he had worked. Several participants were leaders he had worked with whom he considered poor and several of his stories and examples of poor leadership were derived from things these very participants had done.

At the end of the day, Enter was approached by these leaders, all of whom expressed they had loved the training and wished others from the agency could have been there. The poor leaders could not see themselves in Enter's stories. They were blind to their weaknesses and assumed they were doing well as leaders. In this way, self-awareness of leadership skills might be akin to assessing our own driving abilities; we all think we are above the norm.

Ineffective leadership is not simply a product of a leader's actions or inactions. To the extent that efficacy is based on the assessments of those a leader seeks to influence, the leaders traits and habits are interpreted and filtered through the expectations of would-be followers. The relationship between leaders and followers (at times referred to as leader-member exchange) has been the focus of more scholarly inquiry in recent decades (Engle and Lord 1997; Martin, Thomas, Charles, Epitropaki, and McNamara 2005; Shamir, Pillai, Bligh, and Uhl-Bien 2007). Within a discussion of the traits and habits of leaders it is necessary to recognize that followers/members will evaluate leadership through the lens of their individual expectations. Leaders were characterized as ineffective for exhibiting behaviors that undermined and eroded followers' senses of trust, legitimacy, and confidence. Leaders were also characterized as ineffective when they failed to exhibit the key actions that might be associated with actual leadership. These traits and habits represent ways in which leaders worked against their own interests or failed to live up to their labels or positions.

Beyond the action/inaction dichotomy, the ten emerging traits and habits can be loosely grouped into three categories of problematic behaviors: individual problems, occupational problems, and leadership problems. Individual problems were actions, inactions, traits and behaviors that would more generally reflect the character and personality of the ineffective leader, including ego, poor integrity, a poor work ethic, and placing one's self before others. Certainly these characteristics have a strong subjective element; one observer's egomaniac is another's self-confident and decisive leader. In the context of leadership development or enhancement, these individual problems might be the most difficult to overcome. The nature of the problems could suggest leaders would resist seeing a need for personal development or improvement within these or any other behavioral domains. Because they are partially a reflection of the leader's character and personality, it might be difficult for a leader to recognize and acknowledge that he/she is engaging in these behaviors. Even in situations where these traits are recognized it may be difficult for a leader to learn how to overcome and correct such entrenched behaviors.

Occupational problems are, relatively speaking, more susceptible to improvements and enhancements. Issues with communication, micromanagement, and being closed-minded can certainly reflect upon the character and personality of an individual leader, but they also can emerge within bureaucratic and litigious organizations. Given the latter, organizations can take measures to overcome these problems by instituting protocols and practices that, for example, routinize employee input into decision-making loops (see Steinheider and Wuestewald 2008). These problems also represent behaviors more susceptible to correction through leadership development processes. Though a leader might be predisposed to micromanage for a variety of reasons, a common factor might be a lack of familiarity and comfort with alternative methods of leadership and supervision. Absent an awareness of leadership styles emphasizing delegation and empowerment, a leader may understandably default to micromanagement (Krimmel and Lindenmuth 2001). Introducing leaders to alternative styles and approaches would seem to hold strong potential for overcoming occupational problems, particularly when coupled with structures that encourage or even mandate a leader's style.

Finally, leadership problems most centrally relate with the failure of leaders to personify their label and actually lead. The failure to take action can be caused by a variety of organizational, environmental, situation, and personal circumstances. Leaders can fail to act in order to avoid unpopular choices that may halt their professional advancement. Alternatively, leaders can fail to act because they lack confidence in their own judgment. The diverse origins of a failure to actually lead make overcoming this inaction a challenge because it suggests the need for multiple potential corrective measures. The problem is not merely a function of individuals, but is also a reflection of the prevailing culture of police organizations and leadership selection practices. To an extent, ineffective leaders might be products of their own environments. As a profession policing has not placed a high primacy on the development of prospective and current leaders (Anderson, Gisborne, and Holliday 2006; Van Maanen 1984). In the absence of education and mentoring on how to lead in a more effective manner, it is perhaps not surprising that subsequent problems and tensions can be observed in the supervisor-subordinate relationship (Reese 2005; Reuss-Ianni 1983). Those who are or desire to be leaders bear some responsibility for educating themselves on various theories, styles, and perspectives, yet organizations also contribute to this situation. In effect, leadership is lacking in policing because there is a lack of leadership. As a profession, current police leaders have been late in realizing their collective responsibility to develop those who will someday assume leadership roles. Resource constraints, personnel limitations, and lack of suitable training and education opportunities contribute to this divide, but so do ego, culture, tradition, and indifference. In the end the responsibility for advancing the quality of police leadership might lie with the profession itself.

Much of what has been written about leadership failures appears in media sources, rather than academic and professional literatures. The result may be the perpetuation of myths or over-simplifications describing why leaders fail to achieve desired outcomes (Finkelstein 2003). Consideration of these ten acts of commission and omission is not meant to imply that all ineffective leaders display all of these behaviors. It is quite possible that even leaders regarded as effective might demonstrate one or more of these acts periodically or even on a recurring basis. It is not that strong leaders are perfect; rather, strong leaders find ways to avoid repeated and regular personal and professional errors more often than those who surround them. Leaders are periodically called upon to make difficult choices that will displease at least a segment of their followers or constituents. It has been argued that in some instances the most expedient way to accomplish individual or organizational objectives is through manipulative and deceitful actions (Bailey 1988; Kets de Vreis 1993). Those in leadership and supervisory positions are not immune from the allure of "blue lies" and "police placebos" (Klockars 1984). Consequently, "no leader can survive as a leader without deceiving others (followers no less than opponents) and without deliberately doing to others what he would prefer not to have done to himself" (Bailey 1988, ix), at least in rare instances.

The line separating effective and ineffective leaders remains unclear. Framing effective leaders as occasionally using improper, ineffective, destructive or deceitful methods only exacerbates that uncertainty. Subjective individual assessments will mean some leaders are disparaged by many, yet followed by a few. Though it might be unexpected to see an ineffective leader as a highly placed and/or long-standing supervisor, such circumstances do arise. Ineffective leaders might have a long track record of problematic and sub-standard performance, as observed by a commander in a large county agency.

In most cases they were ineffective officers to begin with but somehow get promoted. They do not pay attention to what goes on around them, they do not set
the example, they lack interest, motivation & dedication. They fail to recognize
when something is wrong and correct the problem. They don't lead.

This gives raise to vital questions about how ineffective leaders manage to obtain a supervisory
position. Given the low tolerance for failure in many American law enforcement agencies such undesirable outcomes may be far too common. In addressing this situation, a
major from a small municipal agency remarked that agencies have an unfortunate tendency
to "promote and continue to promote those officers who avoid self-destructing" over the
course of their career.

There is virtually no systematic evidence clearly connecting the prevalence of poor and
ineffective leadership behaviors and with undesirable policing outcomes. Do leaders judged
to display a large number of these traits and habits receive lower evaluations, exert less influence over employees, "derail" in their rise to higher ranks, or receive less favorable assessments from followers? For now, these questions remain unanswered, though anecdote
might provide some readers with a confident and valid opinion based on their personal
experiences. Making such assessments is complicated if, in fact, leaders are accurately
framed as being "warped wood" prone to error or fault. Those working to develop police
leadership and current leaders might incorporate consideration of the "darkside" of leadership into curricula. Those seeking to study policing and police outcomes might be well-
served by considering both effective and ineffective police leaders and leadership. A better
understanding of ineffective leaders and leadership practices might not only enhance
understanding of this problematic circumstance, but might also offer a more realistic and
robust understanding of the type of leadership that is effective and desired in modern
police organizations.

Chapter 12

Suppose We Were Really Serious About Enhancing Police Leadership
Developing More Effective Leaders

> . . . [P]olice leadership decisions, today, tend to preserve the status quo and enshrine the archaic. Somehow, in the police establishment, leadership must be developed that is open, willing to listen, willing to question, willing to experiment, and willing to change even the most revered attitude and practice . . . Many police agencies tend to drift from day to day. They respond excessively to outside pressures; they resort to temporary expedients; they take comfort in technical achievements over substantive accomplishments; their internal procedures become stagnant, cumbersome, and inefficient; and they seem incapable of responding innovatively to new demands and new requirements. But perhaps the greatest cost is the strikingly defensive posture that police leaders, operating under these conditions, commonly assume. (Goldstein 1977, 230–231)

Herman Goldstein's observation has surprising applicability in far too many quarters of contemporary American policing, despite having been made more than thirty-five years ago. Though we know the ideal nature and quality of leadership for the profession, bringing that vision into reality has proven an entrenched and difficult problem. This is perhaps more important today than at any time since London gave rise to the modern policing system in 1829. The demands of homeland security continue to lead police into unclear roles and relationships with the public. Emerging technologies are rapidly changing where, when, and how crimes occur, are detected, are investigated, and are sanctioned. Economic conditions are pushing the privatization and civilianization of policing services, with little coherent discussion of the benefits and consequences of sweeping changes being enacted. Though a clichéd statement in many regards, policing is at a proverbial crossroads. Embracing police *management* will result in the profession continuing to reinvent and refine failed approaches.[1] Embracing police *leadership* will help ensure the viability of police organizations meeting the new demands and constraints imposed by changing forms of criminality, disorder, and deviance committed in the emerging social and cultural landscape.

Contemporary and future American policing will require strong and sustained leadership from all quarters if it is going to be able to adapt to current and future challenges (Schafer, Buerger, Myers, Jensen, and Levin 2012). This leadership will not emerge on its own volition. The profession must build a stronger capacity to develop more effective leaders and leadership. Many supervisors have some level of leadership competency; few will naturally be able to excel in the eyes of all those with whom they work. While a perfect

---

1. Readers are free to insert their preferred cliché about rearranging deck chairs on the Titanic, playing fiddle while Rome is burning, or similar aphorisms. All have equal salience in this context.

success and satisfaction rate is not feasible, the typical formal or aspiring leader has room for improvement. Even good leaders with years of experience can find ways to enhance their efficacy. Accepting that effective leadership has a situational aspect reinforces that leaders should always be seeking ways to improve their performance (Hooijberg, Hunt, and Dodge 1997; Vroom and Jago 2007), just as they challenge those around them to develop and to do the same. Even the best of leaders might only be one reassignment or promotion away from "derailing." The implication is not to fear career advancement, but to seek continual improvements, regardless of past accomplishments, achievements, and even missteps.

Policing is not doing enough to seriously pursue the development of better leaders and leadership (Haberfeld 2006; Rowe 2006). This observation is offered with an understanding that many agencies are struggling to simply provide basic call for service responses (often for a constrained list of offenses) within their jurisdictions (Police Executive Research Forum 2010). It is understandably difficult to prioritize personnel development when agencies struggle to meet basic demands for service. Yet it is precisely in challenging times that leaders and leadership are of greatest value to agencies and the profession.[2] This chapter considers the leadership development process as a tool to enhance effective leadership. It continues with a discussion of some of the unanswered and unresolved questions leaders and scholars seeking to enhance the understanding of leadership processes and influences in police organizations ought to consider. Organizations and individuals must establish systems and practices that ensure the continued development and expansion of leadership. There are ways agencies can develop current and future leaders, even in austere times, provided there is the will and attention toward that objective.

Developing Effective Leaders

Too often leadership is assumed to be a function of nature; it is something people are presumed to either be born with or lack.[3] This is a very narrow view because it treats leadership as a dichotomous attribute that is either present or absent. Subscribing to this perspective renders the notions of development or enhancement largely impossible. It overlooks the possibility that even basic leadership skills can be established in those who lack this characteristic or enhanced in those possessing such faculties. What this perspective further suggests is that those born with some leadership skills always exude those skills in the desired direction and at all times. Warren Bennis addressed this latter point in the preface of one of his recent books, writing:

> As a life-long student of leadership, I've always been fascinated both by those who become leaders and those who don't. Just as intriguing as great leaders, in

---

2. Leaders are sometimes advised to "never waste a good crisis." Never pass over times of chaos and uncertainty when major change can be brought about. Growth comes from adversity and hardship, if one is ready to pursue that challenge.

3. The nature over nurture assumption is, based on available evidence, far more myth than reality. In comparing twins, it has been suggested perhaps thirty percent of variation in leadership role occupancy (rising into organizational positions of formal authority) is accounted for by genetic factors. The remaining variation is a product of "nurture" factors such as education, training, and mentoring, though some underlying complexity has been noted in understanding nature-nurture-leadership relationships (Arvey, Rotundo, Johnson, Zhand, and McGue 2006).

many ways, are those gifted people who somehow get stuck and never manage
to actualize their talents. (Bennis and Thomas 2002, xi)

Leadership development is indispensible throughout all levels of police organizations
(Anderson, Gisbone, and Holliday 2006). New leaders must to be developed. Those with
potential should be provided assistance and opportunities to fulfill that promise. Those
in positions of both formal and informal influence can improve their abilities.

The development of leaders has remained an understudied and underemphasized aspect of police organizations. Much of what agencies do is disjointed, ad hoc, inconsistent, and insufficient to meet the needs of aspiring and existing leaders. Though a true leader
might find some ways to overcome this limitation, there are opportunities outside the
grasp of even the most capable aspirant. Even in situations where leaders can overcome
barriers to their developmental success, it is a poor use of their energies and skills. Leaders should focus on developing their own skills; they should not have to be overly concerned with the mechanics of facilitating that developmental process themselves, though
too often leaders find they must take responsibility for this process because of organizational shortcomings.

A wide range of approaches is used to develop leadership skills. Some are very general, while others are designed for personnel at specific ranks and levels. Some developmental programs seek to speak directly to the context of policing, while others draw more
heavily on military or corporate lessons and language. Programs vary in instructional format, instructor qualifications and background, length, required reading and coursework,
and virtually every other possible dimension of education and training. In short, while development seems a laudable goal, next to nothing is known about which types of developmental efforts produce desired results. Few developmental programs (in policing or
any other industry) have been subject to objective and systematic evaluation (Mastrofski
2006; National Research Council 2004). "Buyer beware" is a well-deserved caution, particularly when books, courses, and other programs claim to produce results that seem too
good to be true.

Research does offer support for the general notion that leadership skills can be developed. A study of chief executives who graduated from a police development program in
Texas suggested they believe their skills as leaders improved (Miller, Watkins, and Webb
2009). Broader studies of transformational leadership support the idea that training programs can develop these skills, as well (Barling, Weber, and Kelloway 1996). Chief executives who have completed major developmental experiences (such as the FBI National
Academy) tend to receive better performance and leadership ratings from their bosses
(city managers) (Krimmel and Lindenmuth 2001). All of these findings should be treated
as tentative support that leadership development can be accomplished, but additional research is needed to derive a stronger understanding of when and how development efforts
achieve desired outcomes. Existing studies are long on the study of perception and short
on an understanding of actual behavior and outcomes.

In some respects, which specific developmental program an agency uses might matter
far less than the fact officers had such an opportunity (Kotter 1990). The difference between graduates of Program A and Program B might be marginal compared to the difference between those who have had developmental experiences and those who have not.
This does not imply "everything works." Comments from the National Academy supervisors suggested, however, that there is a common perception that leaders can be developed through training, education, mentoring, and experience. A number of comments speak

to how respondents perceived leadership development could function effectively in policing contexts.

- Cultivate young officers who exhibit good leadership qualities and those who appear to be natural leaders (lieutenant medium municipal agency).
- Give them the opportunity to work with identified leaders and then allow them the opportunity to take on leadership roles (lieutenant large municipal agency).
- Allow them to engage in activities that might require some decision making. Monitor it but reward/praise all good decisions made. That will bolster their confidence (unit head major state agency).
- Give them small projects for their own to work start to finish. Stay out of way unless assistance is requested. Give an honest critique at [the] end (lieutenant midsize municipal agency).
- By giving them responsibility commensurate with their position and steadily increasing as they improve themselves (sergeant small municipal agency).
- Providing small tasks. Allowing them to flourish. Development is the key to leadership. If you delegate tasks to young officers you are preparing future leaders (lieutenant large county agency).
- Provide examples, slowly add responsibility to each officer, delegate tasks, make them feel that they are an integral part of the organization. Get them to take some ownership in tasks (deputy chief large state agency).
- Expose them to challenging situations, allow them to make mistakes and learn from them, and mentor them (special agent in charge large federal agency).
- Set that positive example first. Then recognize officers accomplishments in public, give them incrementally greater responsibilities. Do not micro manage and do it all yourself. Nothing grows in the shade of your greatness (sergeant medium municipal agency).

Developmental efforts ought to start early and many National Academy participants suggested development should be integrated into the core competencies being established within new employees at the point of entry. In other words, every officer should be considered a leader (Anderson, Gisborne, and Holliday 2006) and developed as such. Waiting until an officer is in a position of formal authority is too late to begin the process.[4] Academy personnel and field training officers must seek ways to strengthen the leadership skills of all employees. "Give them [new officers] opportunities to lead and make decisions during training academy. [Allow them] to think like leaders from the beginning" of their careers (captain, major special jurisdiction agency). First-line supervisors can find early ways to involve new officers in decision making processes and to delegate increasingly important unit responsibilities throughout officers' careers. This does not suggest officers should be "put in sink or swim situations" (sheriff, small county agency). Once armed with basic skills and tools, however, they must be afforded autonomy and independence

---

4. This situation was articulated effectively by a commander from a medium municipal agency, who noted "the average age of the NA graduate is 41 yrs. I am 47 but was a sergeant at 32 and a Lt at 40 and a Captain at 45. Look at the amount of time that was lost." This officer was placed in positions of authority for years before concerted efforts were made to develop her/his skills as a leader. Consequently those in positions of authority may miss opportunities to lead and by the time development efforts are initiated, poor habits might be ingrained and difficult to undo.

to learn, experience, and apply. Officers should develop the mentality that "they need not have stripes to lead" within the workplace (lieutenant, medium special jurisdiction agency).

Beyond formal developmental experiences, prospective and current leaders have to establish strong mentoring and examples in the workplace. It likely does a chief executive little good to train supervisors to have an understanding of leadership skills that are counter to how that executive operates. Encouraging participatory decision making when that is not the operating style of the chief executive might actually be counterproductive and breed discontent. In presenting case studies and examples, developmental efforts ought not emphasize simply the favorable and positive sides of leadership. Participants will be well served to see "both good and bad examples of leadership; this will provide them with a comparison of how the different styles effect [sic] people" (lieutenant, major state agency).

Delegation of tasks, responsibilities, or decisions without assessment or follow-up is a pointless process. Assigning an officer a largely ignored responsibility without taking the time to assess the officer's choices and outcomes does nothing to advance leadership. Those supervising the development process have a duty to ensure the organization and its systems will tolerate good faith mistakes. Those overseeing development efforts cannot "beat them [officers] down for making an error" (commander small municipal agency). Part of learning to be a strong leader is developing an ability to accept criticism, but feedback and critique must be constructive and instructive so the "student" can learn and grow, rather than becoming frustrated or angry. Supervising personnel are obligated "to be honest with officers about their [officers] abilities" (captain large state agency), strengths, and liabilities. If they are going to develop and grow, officers require an awareness of their weaknesses. Officers also deserve to be afforded the tools and opportunities to overcome those limitations.

Symbolic tasks that are assigned without expectations, assessment, or feedback are not likely to succeed in developing personnel. These processes place an additional burden on supervising officers. Leadership development is hard work. Leaders who delegates tasks to make their lives easier and workloads lighter are not developing personnel. As with many things in life, leadership development is a long-term investment. Officers need a strong foundation to serve as a basis as they are beginning to develop their leadership skills. "Set expectations, values, ethical standards, model appropriate behaviors, values, demand professionalism & production. Set goals & objectives" (lieutenant major county agency). Officers need someone who will "work with them . . . and help them learn from their decisions (good and bad)" (chief deputy small county agency).

Much like a field training experience, leadership development ideally will include "classroom" learning (training, education, reading, etc.), experiential learning, and mentoring. Officers require a foundation of knowledge about leadership, organizational dynamics, communication, interpersonal relations, ethics, and skills related to their advancement as increasingly competent police personnel. Training and education are not enough, by themselves, to impart knowledge as "some things cannot be taught—they must be experienced" (lieutenant medium county agency). Much as a rookie officer is paired with a series of FTOs, many National Academy respondents advocated for paired mentoring for leadership development. It was repeatedly expressed as important for officers to have mentorship "with formal & informal leaders" in their organization (lieutenant major state agency). Much like an FTO, this mentor should be emphasizing "corrective action . . . not punitive [action] unless merited" (commander mid-size county agency). Working with others in a quasi-official relationship ensures those being developed are receiving feedback and exposure to the logic and decisions of a range of different leadership styles (just as the rookie officer benefits from seeing different policing styles in application by various

FTOs). In this way, mentoring can "challenge [officers] to help them develop the leadership skills" necessary for success and efficacy within the organization (lieutenant medium municipal agency).

Leadership development is a process that requires continual work and attention, but it does not have to cost large amounts of money. Agencies can take advantage of free and reduced-cost training or rely on assigned readings, experiential tasks, and mentoring. What matters most is that agencies pay attention to efforts aimed at improving the leadership potential of their workforce, including (but not limited to) those already in formal positions of authority. Agencies and executives ought to create cultures and systems that encourage employees to pursue continual improvement. Ray Kroc, founder of the McDonald's Corporation, is famously credited with having a quote from President Calvin Coolidge posted on the wall in his office throughout much of his career. This commentary on leadership is very instructive not only of the systems that help leaders advance their skills, but also the ideal temperament leaders should have in pursuing growth and development of their followers, their unit, and themselves.

> Nothing in the world can take the place of persistence.
> Talent will not; nothing is more common than unsuccessful men with great talent.
> Genius will not; unrewarded genius is almost a proverb.
> Education will not; the world is full of educated derelicts.
> Persistence, determination alone are omnipotent.

Ultimately the police profession has to create a culture of continuous improvement and development . . . of personnel, of processes, and of leaders. Effective processes and programs must be developed, validated, and institutionalized to ensure the continuous creation of leaders who are adaptable, flexible, innovative, and effective. It is not enough to develop leaders who are competent only in narrow contexts, at finite tasks, or in contemporary realities. The profession needs to be able to develop leaders who can evolve and change to meet new challenges, constraints, and opportunities. To do any less is to create leaders who will be irrelevant and unprepared for the systems and environments of tomorrow.

Suppose We Were Really Serious About Developing American Police Leadership

Many police supervisors and executives might think themselves effective leaders, yet that presumption is not always completely accurate. Even where leaders might be characterized as effective, the attributes they think make them effective are not always consistent with what followers and subordinates perceive (Stamper 1992). Leaders can have "blind spots" that prevent them from seeing when and how they are less effective than they would like to imagine. A given leader might think his charisma and interpersonal skills are what motivates and inspires followers. The latter might truthfully find him to be a bit phony, but respect and appreciate the fact that he uses participatory decision making, is willing to make difficult decisions, and demonstrates strong communication skills. A lot is known about what leaders and followers report are important elements of good leadership. Far less is known about whether and when leaders actually live up to the expectations and desires of their followers (Vito and Higgins 2010) and what leadership approaches actually achieve desired leadership outcomes.

The argument can be made that the policing profession (and many other career fields) is not entirely serious about developing and enhancing leaders and leadership (see Geller 1997). Those who have formal positions of authority are presumed to routinely and consistently demonstrate leadership. Difficult questions are rarely asked about whether those leaders might in some way enhance their efficacy, skills, or impact. Clean distinctions are not made between the ability of an individual to attend to administrative tasks and supervisory functions as opposed to exhibiting leadership influence. At best, most agencies relegate leadership development to a short burst of classroom instruction. Otherwise potential leaders are expected to teach themselves, learn by osmosis, or to have been "born that way." Until the profession recognizes the importance of cultivating leaders and leadership through intentional developmental efforts, displays of leadership will remain ad hoc and ad hominem rather than systematic, ingrained, and widespread.

As addressed throughout the book, much in the prevailing structural and operational approaches found in American police departments actively (though perhaps unintentionally) works against leadership. This sentiment is not unique to policing environs. Leadership scholar John Kotter once addressed this same pattern in the corporate world.

> Despite the increasing importance of leadership to business success, the on-the-job experiences of most people actually seem to undermine the development of the attributes needed for leadership. (Kotter 1990, 3)

When organizations say they emphasize and value "leadership" they are often referring to something else, such as directive management and supervisory approaches. Too often leadership is empty rhetoric; it is an abstract idea rather than a clear and courageous pattern driving organizational behavior and outcomes. Despite all that is known and written about leadership, most who are in positions to demonstrate leadership are, at best, competent managers.

Despite this daunting situation, circumstances do not have to be arrayed in this manner. It is possible for police officials and organizations to take leadership more seriously. Accomplishing this will require that both leaders (current and aspiring) and leadership scholars answer a number of important questions and consider a number of central issues. The following sections consider some of the questions and issues leaders and scholars should be discussing if there is to be hope that police leadership can truly be enhanced and developed within the profession. Some questions are rhetorical, but others (particularly many of the research questions) need serious dialog, discussion, and *action*. The historical and present state of leadership in American policing does not have to be a prologue to the future. The profession can do better. Pursuing that outcome is something police officials owe themselves, their officers, their agencies, and their communities.

Issues for Leaders to Consider

Police professionals who are or aspire to become leaders in their organizations should consider a number of significant questions about leadership. Some of these questions are directed inward and are matters for leaders to contemplate as they reflect upon their own leadership style and approaches. Other questions are issues leaders ought to be asking about how leadership development is handled within their organizations and policing in general. Even where leaders feel they are doing well as individuals, there is always room for continued improvements. Even in organizations where leadership development seems to be working well, those charged with that process might pursue further enhancements and perhaps share information about their successes with others.

Though they might not always realize it, effective leaders with any degree of experience have likely experienced "crucibles" over the course of their career (Bennis and Thomas 2002; Thomas 2008). These crucibles are transformative experiences that allowed the leader to grow in that role and more broadly as a person. Recognizing this situation, leaders should consider what crucibles they can present to their own employees and followers. The implication is not to place needless or symbolic barriers in front of an employee. What accomplished leaders note, however, is "experience is their best teacher" (Thomas 2008, 215). In studying the crucible experiences of leaders in the corporate world, Thomas found common themes emerging when he asked leaders to reflect on these transformative experiences.

> These were critical events and experiences, times of testing and trial, failure more often than grand success, that grabbed them by the lapels and demanded to know "what do you stand for?" and "What are *you* going to *do*?" (Thomas 2008, 215, emphasis in original).

Leaders should be thinking about the crucible moments they could offer to followers, whether or not those followers are being developed as leaders.[5] In addition, even accomplished leaders should recognize the crucibles are opportunities that will arise throughout their personal and professional life. It might be leading an organization through a period of scandal or the death of an officer in the line of duty. It might be the veteran police chief who, despite years of success, suddenly finds she or he is no longer in the good graces of city leaders and is asked to step aside. Effective leaders will recognize when they are in these challenging times and ask themselves what they can learn, how they can develop, and how they can grow through that difficult experience.

Leaders should know themselves, their followers, and their current context (Tannenbaum and Schmidt 1958). Few leaders are truly excellent and it is possible many are only adequate. A true leader seeks ways to improve their approaches, to build on existing strengths, and to shore up deficiencies. Perfection may be impossible, but its pursuit should be constant.[6] Leaders expect the same of their followers and employees, so how could they ask any less of themselves? Leaders ought to seek to understand those they seek to influence. What do employees want from the work environment and its leaders? What do external followers (i.e., city leaders, other government employees, members of the community) want from the police department and what are they willing to do to support the pursuit of public safety in the community? How do organizational circumstances, objectives, opportunities, and constraints change over time to necessitate different leadership approaches? There are many questions leaders would have to answer as they move into new assignments. Even when they are in stable positions, leaders should strive to be sensitive to change in the leadership environment that may necessitate different approaches or may afford new opportunities.

---

5. In tactical units it is common to "debrief" after an incident to discuss what happened, what can be learned, and what units and members might do better in the future. How often do those seeking to develop leaders ask similar questions? Crucible moments are only of value if they are recognized and result in learning.

6. Leaders must balance having self-confidence in their own decisions with the realization they are never perfect, never infallible, and must seek continual self-improvement. Ego and arrogance can undo a leader's standing and reputation very quickly.

Leaders will be well served to think not only about themselves, but also about the workforce in which they operate. It is important that leaders do more than just influence the day-to-day and short-term aspects of the unit or organization for which they are responsible. The long-term advancement of the policing profession also requires that leaders work to develop followers and followership. Through training, education, socialization, and (in some cases) redefining organizational culture, leaders seek to cultivate an organizational environment in which continued growth and development are valued and pursued (Burns and Shuman 1988; Geller 1997; Schafer, Myers, Buerger, Jensen, and Levin 2012). This is not just about creating opportunities to develop leadership skills in employees. What is also required to advance policing is reorientation of the profession and its constituent organizations to the points where continued change is viewed as a vital attribute and where Big Hairy Audacious Goals (see Haberfeld 2006) are viewed with excitement and potential, rather than as heretical visions to be quashed, resisted, and destroyed.

Followership is a pivotal, but oft-overlooked, aspect of leadership. Even high ranking officials will be in situations where they are expected to listen, follow instructions, and allow someone else to set the direction and pace. A good leader will know when to switch roles and seek to be a good follower. This can be as simple as a sergeant allowing a patrol officer to have operational command at a call for service. In other situations (such as the Broken Arrow Police Department example from Chapter Five) it can be a more involved and sustained process of a leader ceding certain authority to others. Leaders ought to think about how they might cultivate good followership, which is different from cultivating a compliant or submissive workforce. Ultimately followers tell us something about a leader's worth and acumen though their behavior and outputs.

Leaders should continually work to understand themselves. What is their drive? What are their values? Are their current approaches, objectives, and workplace relationships optimal? Are they holding themselves and their followers to an appropriate standard? Too often those in positions of leadership do not engage in sufficient self-reflection and honest introspection. Leaders are continually being assessed and evaluated by followers and others. While they should not become overly obsessed with indicators of popularity or develop a need for excessive external validation, leaders must make it a point to give regular attention to their own performance in the workplace. This includes consideration not only of what is being achieved, but how those achievements are being realized.

Issues for Scholars to Consider

Leadership research, particularly in the context of policing, remains in relative infancy. Scholars have tended to focus on perceptions, opinions, and beliefs, while less is understood about the possible causal relationships between leadership behavior and various follower and organizational outcomes. Scholars have an understanding of what types of leadership styles officers would prefer from their supervisors, but far less is known about how those styles translate into tangible workforce, workplace, or community outputs. Engel's studies of management styles (2001, 2002) are exceptions to this limitation, though she used traditional policing outcomes to measure supervisory influence. Her work focused on influence at the front line of police organizations; far less is known about influence in higher levels of organizations (Densten 2003). This situation does not emerge because policing scholars lack intelligence, insight, or work ethic. Rather, studying the outcomes of leadership in policing (as in most other contexts) is quite difficult (Mastrofksi 2006; National Research Council 2004). Outcomes are multifaceted and diffuse, making easy measurement complex. Further, accepting leadership is situational means it is challenging to quantify a leader's approaches because uniform classification is an appreciable challenge. "What works" at one level of an organization or even in a given agency might not have the same influence across levels, tasks, and personnel (Densten 2003). Variation also might exist in terms of the approaches, experiences, and competencies of leaders based on a variety of factors, including race, ethnicity, education, training, and sex (c.f. Livingston, Rosette, and Washington 2012; Silvestri 2006).

Steven Murphy and Edward Drodge offered an articulate assessment of the challenges they perceive in the systematic study of police leaders and leadership. The crux of their argument is that leadership is not simply a commodity that can be easily quantified and then produced in an organization. Instead, they framed leadership as "an emergent, dynamic social process dependent upon numerous variables that are also in a state of constant flux" (2004, 1). This led them to suggest too many leadership studies and recommendations are "superficial prescriptions" (1) with little hope of curing complex social processes and problems. Murphy and Drodge reinforced the view that leadership success and influence are situationally defined. While they considered a leader's attributes as largely "static markers" those attributes are applied in "environments [that] ebb and flow requiring different competencies or varying amounts of a given competency to meet the demands of the complex personal and social worlds" (7) that define policing and communities. To be sure, this perspective paints a challenging view of not only the study of policing, but also of the prospects for enhancing police leadership.

James Meindl (1990) offered a similarly challenging assessment of how scholars have historically conceived of and understood leadership. He suggested society, as a whole, has tended to romanticize the idea and influence of leadership. In essence, he argued that the "effect size" of leadership is often overstated and that groups or systems perhaps only benefit modestly when a leader is "good." The diffuse nature of police supervision (in which managers and leaders often have limited direct contact with assigned personnel) might be expected to further restrict the "effect size" of leaders and leadership, though scholars have yet to produce strong data to support or refute this conclusion. Meindl does not suggest that leadership is irrelevant, but merely that leadership is one of a number of causal forces that influence whether a group or system will end up on a successful path. The empirical understanding of this situation is compounded by the fact that most policing research is cross-sectional in nature. At best most research establishes correlations between leadership and desired outcomes, while determining causality remains elusive (Shackleton 1995).

These are not simply academic questions of relevance for those breathing the rarified air of ivory towers. Though addressing these types of methodological issues and fundamental questions about studying human interactions are removed from the realities and challenges of policing, the implications and outcomes of these processes are salient for policing and leadership development. While it is expected that leaders have an easy and direct ability to influence followers, the existence, strength, and nature of that relationship remains largely a mystery. While there is a clear belief (expressed in the previous section of this chapter) that experiential leadership development matters, it remains unclear how much it matters, what types of experiences are most helpful, and what leadership curriculum aspiring leaders should study. It is known that leader self-efficacy enhances outcomes (Pillai and Williams 2004) but it is not clear how to develop such beliefs within leaders. It is difficult for the profession to develop and enhance effective leadership practices when so many aspects of leadership remain romanticized ideals rather than proven relationships and realities.

Paths Forward

By working faithfully eight hours a day you may eventually get to be boss and work twelve hours a day.

—Robert Frost

A number of additional observations can be offered for the enhancement of leadership in police organizations. These ideas emerge from the professional and academic literature, the National Academy data, and innumerable conversations (both formal interviews and, far more often, casual interactions) between the author and police officers of all ranks from agencies of all sizes across the country.[7] These are ideas and observations the author has derived through more than a quarter-century of working in, studying, thinking about, and researching policing, police officers, and police organizations. While not entirely derived with the same systematic approach as the other parts of the book, the author believes the observations retain relevance for thinking about the future of police leadership.

The term "leader" ought to be used based upon the actions exhibited by police personnel. It cannot simply be a rank or office to which an officer is anointed or appointed. It should be evident in an individual's behavior and not presumed because of their position in the organization. Leaders are those in the organization who demonstrate leadership aptitude through their actions, regardless of rank and formal position. A leader is not someone who has simply demonstrated promotability or the ability to survive within the organization while others around them implode. Organizations or units who fail to see leaders in their midst when promotion decisions are made have most likely failed to develop future leaders among existing employees. Though there are periodically extenuating circumstances that create leadership vacuums, too often organizations use this as an excuse to mask the failure to develop personnel.

Policing needs to reorient itself in how it thinks about organizational processes. Policing tends to stress means over ends. More emphasis is placed on how officers perform their duties rather than what efforts actually accomplish.[8] This situation causes numerous problems at the level of patrol operations that have been well documented by policing scholars (Goldstein 1977; Klockars 1985; Manning 1997). The means-ends tension can be seen to operate in parallel to conflicts that exist in the process of administering police organizations. There is a tension between means (management) and ends (leadership). Supervisory personnel are selected, trained, and evaluated based on their attention to means and processes. All too often, being considered a supervisor is a function of the control and oversight directed at subordinate personnel. In describing these patterns and

---

7. There is danger in anecdotal evidence, even when it is a recurring pattern. The comments in this section arise from a wide range of experiences the author has had as a volunteer, unsworn employee, consultant, researcher, and trainer. The generalizability and veracity of the comments offered here cannot always be established. At the same time, existing policing literature has not yet given the author a reason to be disabused from the ideas offered in this passage.

8. The means-ends tension cannot be easily resolved in policing. Both are of importance in a democratic society. Officers must perform their duties within legal parameters that maintain Constitutional rights, civil liberties, trust, and legitimacy. The point here is that policing has tended to extend its emphasis on means to structure and define too many other aspects of police behavior and operations. Too many policies exist that tell officers how to perform their duties when discretion and empowerment could be afforded without compromising citizens' rights or public interests.

trends in a variety of organizational contexts Philip Selznick observed that a "cult of efficiency in administrative theory and practice is a modern way of overstressing means and neglecting ends" (1957, 135). Demonstrating leadership or achieving meaningful outcomes is not necessary in many organizational contexts in which means are heavily stressed. For the police profession to advance there needs to be a balanced consideration of means, ends, outcomes, and leadership.

This does not imply that ethics, civil rights, due process, policies, or other restrictions should be subverted, ignored, or removed. Rather, the profession needs to recognize that the majority of situations attended to by officers of all ranks and assignments do not require extensive policies, protocols, or rules. The majority of control mechanisms imposed by police organizations are elective. It is amazing that so many dedicated officers achieve good outcomes *in spite of* all the policies, procedures, and other barriers their workplace imposes. Likewise, it is astounding that in many organizations leaders are able to achieve positive influence and change, *in spite of* all the agency's restrictions, culture, and expectations that supervisors should emphasize being a proficient manager and not attempt to be an effective leader. Too often good outcomes are achieved in spite of, rather than because of, operational and cultural aspects of police organizations and their prevailing supervisory and administrative systems.

Leadership must become an attribute that is nurtured, developed, and encouraged throughout an organization. It is not something that should be centralized in higher offices or exclusively tied to formal rank structures. One of the greatest barriers to organizational development and innovation is the various structures and obstacles that work to prevent motivated and bright employees from pursuing innovative ideas. In addition, organizations of all types link financial rewards and internal status with promotions (Wilson 1968). Too often competent and intelligent personnel rise to higher positions not because they desire new challenges or opportunities, but because they seek greater reward and validation. This does not suggest personnel should not have ambitions, but the primary driving ambition should be to improve the organization, not to increase one's paycheck or pension (Murphy 2006). Personnel need to be promoted because they possess the skills and desire to lead for the right reasons (i.e., a desire to serve and make a difference) not because of financial gain or personal glory (Guyot 1979). The countervailing tension is a system that provides pay incentives and extensive overtime opportunities for unranked personnel. Promoting above being an entry-level supervisor often moves one into a salaried position.[9] This can create a ceiling beyond which people do not want to rise because advancement costs too much. Personnel may have to endure higher levels of stress and greater professional demands while being paid less to do so.

Leaders have to rise up to the many challenges in modern American policing. The safety and allure of simply being a manager are profound and understandably seductive.

---

9. Media accounts frequently capture this situation, noting that the highest paid employees in many cities and many police departments are front-line police officers, fire fighters, and corrections personnel. In larger agencies there are often a handful of "rate buster" officers who work extensive amounts of overtime and, as a result, earn as much or more than top executives in a given calendar year (see Ryan and Carroll 2012; Sweigart and Magan 2011; Yusko 2012). In defense of officers, high earners are willing to work extra hours, are operating within existing rules, and at times are under pressure to do so when overtime pay is used to offset hiring freezes, layoffs, and other personnel shortages. This criticism is not directed at officers, but at a system that incentives staying in lower ranks because that is where (if one is willing to put in the time) the greatest financial rewards can be realized.

Management and supervision will not, however, serve the future needs of police personnel, police organizations, or the communities being policed. In communities around the country and throughout the profession there is a demand for leaders who will pursue professional excellence and encourage that in those around them. They must do so with a commitment to service of others (followers, organizations, citizens) and not service to self. They must embrace the challenges of the future and have the courage to lead with integrity, commitment, and honor in difficult times and circumstances. It is not a demand for the faint of heart.

Conclusions

Jim Isenberg (2010) conducted a series of interviews with police executives to learn their perspectives on how to lead and influence police organizations. Based on these discussions Isenberg developed a series of recommendations that tend to reinforce the traits and habits expressed by the National Academy participants. Fundamentally, leadership is about having the vision, courage, will, and understanding to bring about growth, change, and innovation. In order to pursue and achieve these outcomes leaders must attend to a number of important factors. Leaders must develop and articulate a vision for the future that advances the unit or organization toward greater efficacy, efficiency, and equity in serving relevant consumers. They must manage culture and resistance while pursuing the implementation of that vision. Leaders would be wise to recognize the importance of first-line supervisory personnel in exercising influence and leveraging change (see also Trojanowicz 1980). Leaders do not have all the answers, but they learn to ask the right questions. They take time to consider their approaches and decisions, while encouraging others to do the same.

Personnel need to be empowered and delegated responsibilities, but they also must be held accountable for how and what they produce. Leaders must recognize the importance of relationships with external entities, constituents, and sovereigns (Hennessy 1993; Isenberg 2010). Leaders must understand context and circumstances as they are implementing change. They must communicate, pursue growth, and understand what motivates followers. Leaders make decisions with incomplete information and exist in an imperfect world. They cannot always wait to have all issues and possibilities clarified. But they recognize that sometimes not making a choice can be worse than making the wrong choice. One of the most insightful comments in Isenberg's interviews was offered by Robert Olson, former chief of Minneapolis (MN) and Yonkers (NY). In describing the change process, Olson noted:

> The job of the police chief is to take a stick of wood and make it into an arch. If you work with the wood, you take a stick and plant it firmly, which is traditional policing, and you grab hold of the top and rub it with lemon seed oil and you have to keep constant pressure on it. Leadership is about applying pressure. As you're applying pressure, you have to listen to its creaks and groans, knowing full well that if you don't put enough pressure on it, it's not going to bend and if you put too much pressure on it, it's going to break. You listen and you rub and you listen and you rub and you end up with an arch! I made some mistakes in Corpus Christi [Texas] because I was naïve; I had been deputy chief and I moved too fast for the culture. What I was doing was right, but how I was doing it was

wrong. I didn't listen to the creaks and groans as I should have and I broke it. (Isenberg 2010, 117)

There is no "magic bullet" in leadership. No one style is always optimal, effective, or right for the situation and objectives at hand. No one leader is right for all circumstances and contexts (Bouza 1990; Cragg and Spurgeon 2007). Some approaches are, however, more promising than others. Transformational approaches and situational perspectives generated considerable support from the National Academy participants. Effective leaders need to have a good dose of emotional intelligence, interpersonal skills, and the ability to regulate their own emotional impulses (Drodge and Murphy 2002). Leaders who have broad cognitive and social skills are likely better able to see distinctions in various situations, actors, and circumstances (Hooijberg, Hunt, and Dodge 1997). This allows the leader to interpret the situation at hand and approach matters in a way that will maximize the likelihood of favorable outcomes. The traits and habits described in this book are not a mandate. Leadership efficacy does not require emulating all of these attributes in all situations, while avoiding ineffective behaviors. Rather, effective leaders would be well served to reflect many of these traits and habits in most of their day-to-day work, recognizing that situations will often require a variable balance of these and other elements of leadership.

Perhaps most importantly, leaders recognize that effective leadership is hard work. To be effective requires that leaders continually reflect on their performance. It demands that they seek ways to enhance their skills and influence. It necessitates that leaders never allow themselves to become complacent in believing they have achieved the best possible outcomes for themselves and their followers. Individual leaders, those they seek to influence, and the organizations they oversee can always find ways to improve. Leaders and followers should celebrate the accomplishments and achievements of today, while maintaining the perspective that the objective for tomorrow is to find new and additional ways to improve the efficacy, efficiency, and equity of police operations, services, and leadership. That is the challenge true police leaders will accept and embrace.

Appendix A

Project Methodology

From 2006 to 2008 the author served as a visiting researcher with the Behavioral Science Unit at the FBI Academy in Quantico, VA. The primary purpose of this appointment was to complete a research project studying effective police leadership. Specifically, the FBI National Academy program was identified as providing a purposive sample of mid-career police supervisors who would be able to offer insights into effective police leadership. The National Academy program was established in 1935 to provide police supervisors with an opportunity for education and career development. National Academy participants come to the FBI Academy to complete a ten-week residential experience similar to attending college for an academic quarter. They enroll in and complete a schedule of academic courses selected from a catalog of offerings in behavioral sciences, leadership, law, communications, and other disciplines. FBI staff teaches all courses and participants receive academic credit (graduate or undergraduate) from the University of Virginia.

The National Academy is designed as a residential experience because it seeks to provide participants with a break from the "noise" and demands of their everyday professional environment. It is a sabbatical of sorts for the attendees in that it provides them with a break from the pressure and strains of their job while they are given the chance to learn and experience. Participants are exposed to a range of other professional development and personal enrichment experiences that are both physical and cognitive, as well as individual and group-based. The experience also provides leaders with a chance to network with and learn from peers from across the country and the world. The program is supposed to target "up and coming" police leaders who might eventually lead their own or some other agency. Many medium and large agencies require completion of the National Academy or a similar program as a condition of eligibility to apply for chief executive positions.

The FBI Behavioral Science Unit serves a range of missions, including serving academic needs in the National Academy and research needs in furtherance of FBI priorities and interests. A series of survey instruments was developed and administered to participants in eight sessions of the National Academy. The first four waves of surveys used open-ended questions to assess: the definition and measurement of effective police leadership; the traits and habits of effective and ineffective police leaders; the prevalence and nature of effective police leadership; leadership in policing versus other occupational/organization contexts; and leadership development. Given the evolving nature of the research project and the broad focus of the project, several iterative surveys were administered across and within the sessions, though all focused on a common core set of research themes. Participants in NA sessions 226–229 (July 2006–June 2007) were given the opportunity to complete one of these open-ended surveys. Of the 1097 officers attending the National Academy during this timeframe, 769 (70.1 percent) participated in the survey. The data used in this book were primarily taken from this first wave of the research project.

The second phase of the project converted the first year of data into a set of ranking items. Respondents were presented with a list of the twelve most frequently identified traits and habits of effective leaders from the first phase of the project. They were asked to rank the top five elements from this list. Respondents were also given the opportunity to specify other traits and habits, though this did not produce a clear pattern suggesting missing elements from the twelve core behaviors. The closed ended ranking items were part of a survey administered to officers attending National Academy sessions 232–235 (January–December 2008). Of the 1107 attendees in these four sessions, 1044 (94.3 percent) participated in the survey. Across all eight sessions of the National Academy, surveys were administered in large groups (generally around 50 officers). Institutional review boards at Southern Illinois University Carbondale and the FBI Academy approved survey instruments and protocols.

Findings reported and discussed in this book are derived from these two survey projects. Survey insights are occasionally augmented with comments derived from interviews and focus groups; due to a variety of constraints these methodologies were not employed in all NA sessions or in a systematic manner. Statements in quotes are verbatim responses provided by participating supervisors. In many quotes the respondent used the male pronoun. This wording and various spelling and grammar errors have been retained in the quoted passages. Where quotes are included, basic contextual data (respondent rank, agency size,[1] and agency type) are included. Additional demographic information (sex, age, race/ethnicity) were not obtained. The average National Academy student across these eight sessions had 20 years of policing experience and 10 years of supervisory experience. The sample was reasonably well educated. Over ninety-five percent had completed some college; almost eighty percent had at least an associate's degree and over one-third had completed some post-graduate coursework. One-quarter had served in the military. Over ninety percent were American. Though the rank distribution was not systematically compiled, it appeared the most common rank of the students was lieutenants. The National Academy also tends to over-represent medium, mid-size, and large agencies, as well as state-level agencies.[2]

Though the participants were not drawn using conventional sampling, the overall responses still offer a reasonable degree of generalizability. National Academy participants represent a broad cross-section of American policing. They come from agencies of all types, sizes, and locales, though the agencies represented by any given class do not mirror the distribution of American policing, nor is that the intent. While the findings here do not achieve statistically validated generalizability, the consistency of the findings and the large number of participants lend credence to the inductive outcomes of the research project. The National Academy provides a selection of American police supervisors that is unavailable through any other cost-effective process. As a group they are also likely to have given leaders and leadership consideration and have experiences that make them well-suited to reflect on these matters in modern policing.

---

1. Respondents reported the number of sworn officers employed by their agency. For the purpose of this book agency size is categorized as small (0–50), medium (51–100), mid-size (101–250), large (251–1000), and major (1001 or more).

2. Fifty-five percent of respondents were employed by a municipal agency. Twenty percent worked for a county and almost fifteen percent worked for a state agency.

References

Adams, Richard E., William M. Rohe, and Thomas A. Arcury. "Implementing Community-Oriented Policing: Organizational Change and Street Officer Attitudes." *Crime & Delinquency* 48 (2002): 399–430.

Adlam, Robert, and Peter Villiers, eds. *Police Leadership in the Twenty-First Century: Philosophy, Doctrine and Developments.* Winchester, UK: Waterside Press, 2003.

Ahlstrom, Richard T. "Succession Planning: Mentoring Your Replacement." *Police Chief* 73, no. 1 (2006): 29–30.

Allen, David N. "Police Supervision on the Street: An Analysis of Supervisor/Officer Interaction During the Shift." *Journal of Criminal Justice* 10 (1982): 91–109.

Allen, David, and Michael Maxfield. "Judging Police Performance: Views and Behavior of Patrol Officers." In *Police at Work: Policy Issues and Analysis*, ed. Richard Bennett, 65–86. Beverly Hills, CA: Sage, 1983.

Anderson, Terry D., Kenneth D. Gisborne, and Pat Holliday. *Every Officer is a Leader: Transforming Leadership in Police, Justice, and Public Safety*, 2nd ed. Victoria, BC: Trafford Publishing, 2006.

Andreescu, Viviana, and Gennaro F. Vito. "An Exploratory Study of Ideal Leadership Behaviour: The Opinions of American Police Managers." *International Journal of Police Science & Management* 12 (2010): 567–583.

Angell, John E. "Toward an Alternative to the Classic Police Organizational Arrangements: A Democratic Model." *Criminology* 9 (1971): 185–206.

Archambeault, William G., and Charles Weirman. "Critically Assessing the Utility of Police Bureaucracies in the 1980s: Implications of Management Theory Z." *Journal of Police Science & Administration* 11 (1983): 420–429.

Argyris, Chris. *Integrating the Individual and the Organization.* New York: Wiley, 1964.

Aronson, Edward. "Integrating Leadership Styles and Ethical Perspectives." *Canadian Journal of Administrative Sciences* 18 (2001): 244–256.

Arvey, Richard D., Maria Rotundo, Wendy Johnson, Zhen Zhang, and Matt McGue. "The Determinants of Leadership Role Occupancy: Genetic and Personality Factors." *The Leadership Quarterly* 17 (2006): 1–20.

Associated Press. "AG: Review Beginning in NYPD Muslim Spying Case." 29 February 2012. Available from http://www.usatoday.com/news/washington/story/2012-02-29/justice-review-muslim-spying-nypd/53303560/1. Accessed 29 February 2012.

Auten, James H. "The Paramilitary Model of Police and Police Professionalism." *Police Studies* 2 (1981): 67–78.

Bailey, Frederick G. *Humbuggery and Manipulation: The Art of Leadership.* Ithaca, NY: Cornell University Press, 1988.

Barker, Joan C. *Danger, Duty, and Disillusion: The Worldview of LAPD Officers.* Prospect Heights, IL: Waveland, 1997.

Barras, Jonetta R. *The Last of the Black Emperors: The Hollow Comeback of Marion Barry in the New Age of Black Leaders.* Baltimore, MD: Bancroft Press, 1998.

Barker, Thomas, and David L. Carter. "Police Lies and Perjury: A Motivation-Based Taxonomy." In *Police Deviance*, 3rd ed., ed. Thomas Barker and David L. Carter, 139–152. Cincinnati, OH: Anderson, 1994.

Barling, Julian, Tom Weber, and E. Kevin Kelloway. "Effects of Transformational Leadership Training on Attitudinal and Financial Outcomes: A Field Experiment." *Journal of Applied Psychology* 81 (1996): 827–832.

Bass, Bernard M. *Leadership and Performance.* New York: Free Press, 1985.

Bass, Bernard M. *Bass & Stogdill's Handbook of Leadership: Theory, Research, & Managerial Applications*, 3rd ed. New York: Free Press, 1990.

Bayley, David H. *Policing in America: Assessment and Prospects.* Washington, DC: Police Executive Research Forum, 1998.

Bennis, Warren G. (1959). "Leadership Theory and Administrative Behavior: The Problem of Authority." *Administrative Science Quarterly* 4 (1959): 259–301.

Bennis, Warren G., and Burt Nanus. *Leaders: Strategies for Taking Charge.* New York: Harper Business, 1997.

Bennis, Warren G. and Robert J. Thomas. *Geeks & Geezers: How Era, Values, and Defining Moments Shape Leaders.* Boston: Harvard Business School Press, 2002.

Blanchard, Kenneth H., and Paul Hersey. "Great Ideas Revisited: Revisiting the Life-Cycle Theory of Leadership." *Training & Development* 40, no. 1 (1996): 42–47.

Blumstein, Alfred, and Joel Wallman, ed. *The Crime Drop in America,* 2nd ed. New York: Cambridge University Press, 2005

Bouza, Anthony V. *The Police Mystique: An Insider's Look at Cops, Crime, and the Criminal Justice System.* New York: Plenum Press, 1990.

Braiden, Chris R. "Enriching Traditional Roles." In *Police Management: Issues and Perspectives*, ed. Larry T. Hoover, 87–116. Washington, DC: Police Executive Research Forum, 1992.

Bratton, William. *The Turnaround: How America's Top Cop Reversed the Crime Epidemic.* New York: Random House, 1998.

Brewer, Neil, Carlene Wilson, and Karen Beck. "Supervisory Behavior and Team Performance Among Police Patrol Sergeants." *Journal of Occupational and Organizational Psychology* 67 (1994): 69–78.

Broderick, John J. *Policing in a Time of Change.* Prospect Heights, IL: Waveland, 1987.

Brown, Mary Maureen, and Jeffery L. Brudney. "Learning Organizations in the Public Sector? A Study of Police Agencies Employing Information and Technology to Advance Knowledge." *Public Administration Review* 63 (2003): 30–43.

Brown, Michael K. *Working the Street: Police Discretion and the Dilemmas of Reform.* New York: Russell Sage Foundation, 1988.

Buerger, Michael E. "Reenvisioning Police, Reinvigorating Policing: A Response to Thomas Cowper." *Police Quarterly* 3 (2000): 451–464.

Buerger, Michael E. *Values, Resources, and Styles of Policing: Present and Future Innovations.* Paper presented at the annual meetings of the American Society of Criminology. Washington, DC, 17 November 2011.

Burke, Ronald J. "Why Leaders Fail: Exploring the Dark Side." In *Inspiring Leaders*, ed. Ronald J. Burke and Cary L. Cooper, 237–246. London: Routledge, 2006.

Burns, Gilbert H. and I.Gayle Shuman. "Police Managers' Perception of Organizational Leadership Styles." *Public Personnel Management* 17 (1988): 145–157.

Burns, James MacGregor. *Leadership.* New York: Harper & Row, 1978.

Burruss, George W., Matthew J. Giblin and Joseph A. Schafer. "Threatened Globally, Acting Locally: Modeling Law Enforcement Homeland Security Practices." *Justice Quarterly* 27 (2010): 77–101.

Buzawa, Eve. "Determining Patrol Officer Job Satisfaction: The Role of Selected Demographic and Job-Specific Attitudes." *Criminology* 22 (1984): 61–84.

Caldero, Michael A., and John P. Crank. *Police Ethics: The Corruption of Noble Causes,* 3rd ed. Cincinnati, OH: Anderson Publishing, 2009.

Carter, David L. *Law Enforcement Intelligence: A Guide for State, Local, and Tribal Law Enforcement Agencies,* 2nd ed. Washington, DC: US Department of Justice, 2009.

Chambers, Harry E. *My Way or the Highway: The Micromanagement Survival Guide.* San Francisco: Berrett-Koehler Publishers, 2004.

Ciulla, Joan B. "Carving Leaders From the Warped Wood of Humanity." *Canadian Journal of Administrative Science* 18 (2001): 313–319.

Clements, Christine, and John B. Washbush. (1999). "The Two Faces of Leadership: Considering the Dark Side of Leader-Follower Dynamics." *Journal of Workplace Learning* 11, no. 5 (1999): 170–175.

Cohen, Bernard. "Leadership Styles of Commanders in the New York City Police Department." *Journal of Police Science and Administrations* 8 (1980): 125–138.

Cohen, Noam. "Care to Write Army Doctrine? With ID, Log On." *New York Times,* 13 August 2009. Available at http://www.nytimes.com/2009/08/14/business/14army.html. Accessed June 22, 2011.

Collins, Jim. *Good to Great: Why Some Companies Make the Leap . . . and Others Don't.* New York: Collins, 2001.

Collins, Jim. *Good to Great and the Social Sectors.* New York: Author, 2005.

Conger, Jay A. "Charismatic And Transformational Leadership in Organizations: An Insider's Perspective on These Developing Streams of Research." *The Leadership Quarterly* 10 (1999): 145–179.

Conger, Jay.A., and Beth Benjamin. *Building Leaders: How Successful Companies Develop the Next Generation.* San Francisco: Jossey-Bass, 1999.

Conger, Jay A., and Ronald E. Riggio, eds. *The Practice of Leadership: Developing the Next Generation of Leaders.* San Francisco: Jossey-Bass, 2007.

Cordner, Gary W. "Open and Closed Models of Police Organizations: Traditions, Dilemmas, and Practical Considerations." *Journal of Police Science and Administration* 6 (1978): 22–34.

Cornish, Edward. *Futuring: The Exploration of the Future.* Washington, DC: World Futures Society, 2004.

Cowper, Thomas J. "The Myth of the 'Military Model' of Leadership in Law Enforcement." *Police Quarterly* 3 (2000): 228–246.

Crank, John P. *Understanding Police Culture.* Cincinnati, OH: Anderson, 1998.

Cragg, Robert, and Peter Spurgeon. "Competencies of a Good Leader." *Clinicians in Management* 15 (2007): 109–114.

Crank, John P., and Michael Caldero. "The Production of Occupational Stress in Medium-Sized Police Agencies: A Survey of Line Officers in Eight Municipalities." *Journal of Criminal Justice* 21, (1991): 313–324.

Cunningham, Larry. "Taking on Testilying: The Prosecutor's Response to In-Court Police Deception." *Criminal Justice Ethics* 18, no. 1 (1999): 26–40.

Cyert, Richard, and James March. *Behavioral Theory of the Firm.* Oxford: Blackwell, 1963.

DeJong, Christina, Stephen D. Mastrofski, and Roger B. Parks. "Patrol Officers and Problem Solving: An Application of Expectancy Theory." *Justice Quarterly* 18 (2001): 31–61.

Delattre, Edwin J. *Character and Cops: Ethics in Policing*, 3rd ed. Washington, DC: American Enterprise Institute, 1996.

Densten, Ian L. "Senior Police Leadership: Does Rank Matter?" *Policing: An International Journal of Police Strategies & Management* 26 (2003): 400–418.

Dias, Clarissa F., and Michael S. Vaughn. (2006). "Bureaucracy, Managerial Disorganization, and Administrative Breakdown in Criminal Justice Agencies." *Journal of Criminal Justice* 24 (2006): 543–555.

Dobby, John, Jane Anscombe, and Rachel Tuffin. *Police Leadership: Expectations and Impact.* London: Home Office, 2004.

Dotlich, David L., and Peter C. Cairo. *Why CEOs Fail: The 11 Behaviors That Can Derail Your Climb to the Top- And How to Manage Them.* San Francisco: Jossey-Bass, 2003.

Douglas, Max E. "Servant-Leadership: An Emerging Supervisory Model." *Supervision* 64, no. 2 (2003): 6–9.

Drodge, Edward N. and Steven A. Murphy. "Interrogating Emotions in Police Leadership." *Human Resources Development Review* 1 (2002): 420–438.

Dvir, Taly, Dov Eden, Bruce J. Avolio, and Boas Shamir. "Impact of Transformational Leadership on Follower Development and Performance: A Field Experiment." *Academy of Management Journal* 45 (2002): 735–744.

Einarsen, Stale, Merethe S. Aasland, and Anders Skogstad. "Destructive Leadership Behavior: A Definition and Conceptual Model." *The Leadership Quarterly* 18 (2007): 207–216.

Engel, Robin S. "Supervisory Styles of Patrol Sergeants and Lieutenants." *Journal of Criminal Justice* 29 (2001): 341–355.

Engel, Robin S. "Patrol Officer Supervision in the Community Policing Era." *Journal of Criminal Justice* 30 (2002): 51–64.

Engle, Elaine M., and Robert G. Lord. "Implicit Theories, Self-Schemas, and Leader-Member Exchange." *Academy of Management Journal* 40 (1997): 988–1010.

Enter, Jack E. *Challenging the Law Enforcement Organization: Proactive Leadership Strategies.* Dacula, GA: Narrow Road Press, 2006.

Eterno, John A., and Eli B. Silverman. *The Crime Numbers Game: Management by Manipulation.* Boca Raton, FL: CRC Press, 2012.

Fast, Nathanael J. and Serena Chen. "When the Boss Feels Inadequate: Power, Incompetence, and Aggression." *Psychological Science* 20 (2009): 1406–1413.

Fiedler, Fred D. *A Theory of Leadership Effectiveness.* New York: McGraw-Hill, 1967.

Finkelstein, Sydney. *Why Smart Executives Fail: And What You Can Learn From Their Mistakes.* New York: Penguin Group, 2003.

Ford, J. Kevin. "Building Capability Throughout a Change Effort: Leading the Transformation of a Police Agency to Community Policing." *American Journal of Community Psychology* 39 (2007): 321–334.

Ford, J. Kevin, Daniel Weissbein, and Kevin Plammondon. "Distinguishing Organizational Commitment From Strategy Commitment: Linking Officer Commitment to Community Policing to Work Behaviors and Job Satisfaction." *Justice Quarterly* 20 (2003): 159–185.

Flynn, Michael T., Matt Pottinger, and Paul D. Batchelor. *Fixing Intel: A Blueprint for Making Intelligence Relevant in Afghanistan.* Washington, DC: Center for New American Security, 2010.

Frost, Dean E., Fred E. Fiedler, and Jeff W. Anderson. "The Role of Personal Risk-Taking in Effective Leadership." *Human Relations*, 36 (1983): 185–202.

Gardner, John W. *On Leadership.* New York: Free Press, 1990.

Garner, Godfrey. "Humor in Policing: Its Relationship to the Bonding Process. *Journal of Police and Criminal Psychology* 12, no. 1 (1997): 48–60.

Garrett, Terence M. "The Waco, Texas, ATF Raid and Challenger Launch Decision: Management, Judgment, and the Knowledge Analytic." *American Review of Public Administration* 31 (1999): 66–86.

Garrett, Terence M. "Whither Challenger, Wither Columbia: Management Decision Making and the Knowledge Analytic." *American Review of Public Administration* 34 (2004): 389–402.

Gascon, George, and Todd Foglesong. *Making Policing More Affordable: Managing Costs and Measuring Value in Policing (New Perspectives in Policing Series).* Washington, DC: National Institute of Justice, 2010.

Geller, William A. *Suppose We Were Really Serious About Police Departments Becoming "Learning Organizations"?* Washington, DC: National Institute of Justice,1997.

Gerth, Hans H., and C. Wright Mills. *From Max Weber: Essays in Sociology.* New York: Oxford, 1958.

Girodo, Michel. "Machiavellian, Bureaucratic, and Transformational Leadership Styles in Police Managers: Preliminary Findings of Interpersonal Ethics." *Perceptual and Motor Skills* 86 (1998): 419–427.

Glad, Betty. "Why Tyrants Go Too Far: Malignant Narcissism and Absolute Power." *Political Psychology 23* (2002): 1–37.

Goldstein, Herman. *Policing a Free Society.* Cambridge, MA: Ballinger, 1977.

Goldstein, Herman. *Problem-Oriented Policing.* Philadelphia, PA: Temple University Press, 1990.

Graen, George B. and Mary Uhl-Bien. "Relationship-Based Approach to Leadership: Development of Leader-Member Exchange (LMX) Theory of Leadership Over 25 Years: Applying a Multi-Level Multi-Domain Approach." *Leadership Quarterly* 6 (1995): 219–247.

Gray, Kelsey, Mark K. Stohr-Gillmore, and Nicholas P. Lovrich. "Adapting Participatory Management for a Paramilitary Organization: The Implementation of Teams in the Washington State Patrol." *American Journal of Police* 10, no. 4 (1991): 27–47.

Greene, Jack R., William T. Bergman, and Edward J. McLaughlin. "Implementing Community Policing: Cultural and Structural Change in Police Organizations." In *The Challenge of Community Policing: Testing the Promises*, ed. Dennis P. Rosenbaum, 92–109. Thousand Oaks, CA: Sage, 1994.

Greene, Jack R., and Stephen D. Mastrofski, ed. *Community Policing: Rhetoric or Reality.* New York: Praeger, 1988.

Greenleaf, Robert K. *Servant Leadership: A Journey Into the Nature of Legitimate Power and Greatness, 25th anniversary edition.* New York: Paulist Press, 2002.

Gulick, Luther, and L. Urwick. *Papers on the Science of Administration.* New York: Institute of Public Administration, 1937.

Guyot, Dorthy. "Bending Granite: Attempts to Change the Rank Structure of American Police Departments." *Journal of Police Science and Administration* 7 (1979): 253–284.

Haberfeld, Maki R. *Police Leadership.* Upper Saddle River, NJ: Pearson Prentice Hall, 2006.

Hackman, J. Richard, and Ruth Wageman. "Asking the Right Questions About Leadership: Discussion and Conclusions." *American Psychologist* 62 (2007): 43–47.

Hall, Peter. *Great Planning Disasters*. London: Weidenfeld and Nicolson, 1980.

Harrison, E. Frank, and Monique A. Pelletier. "Perceptions of Bureaucratization, Role Performance, and Organizational Effectiveness in a Metropolitan Police Department." *Journal of Police Science and Administration* 15 (1987): 262–270.

Hays, Kraig, Robert Regoli, and John Hewitt. "Police Chiefs, Anomia, and Leadership." *Police Quarterly* 10 (2007): 3–22.

Heifetz, Ronald. *Leadership Without Easy Answers*. Cambridge, MA: Harvard University Press, 1994.

Heifetz, Ronald A. and Donald L. Laurie. "The Work of Leadership." *Harvard Business Review* 75 no. 1 (2001): 124–134.

Heifetz, Ronald A. and Marty Linsky. "When Leadership Spells Danger." *Educational Leadership* 61, no 7 (2004): 33–37.

Hemphill, John K. *Situational Factors in Leadership*. Columbus, OH: Ohio State University Bureau of Educational Research, 1949.

Hennessy, Stephen M. *Thinking Cop, Feeling Cop: A Study in Police Personalities*. Scottsdale, AZ: Leadership, Inc., 1992.

Henry, Vincent E. *The Compstat Paradigm: Management Accountability in Policing, Business and the Public Sector*. New York: Looseleaf Law Publications. 2002.

Hersey, Paul, Kenneth H. Blanchard, and Dewey E. Johnson. *Management of Organizational Behavior: Leading Human Resources*, 9th ed. Upper Saddle River, NJ: Pearson-Prentice Hall, 2008.

Hickman, Matthew J., and Brian A. Reaves. *Local Police Departments, 2003*. Bureau of Justice Statistics: Washington, DC, 2006.

Hoffman, Melissa. "Does Sense of Humor Moderate the Relationship Between Leadership Style and Conflict Management Style?" PhD diss. University of Nebraska, 2007. ETD (AAI3284029).

Hofstede, Geert, Bram Neuijen, Denise Daval Ohayv, and Geert Sanders. "Measuring Organizational Cultures: A Qualitative and Quantitative Study Across Twenty Cases." *Administrative Science Quarterly* 35 (1990): 286–316.

Hogan, Robert, Robert Raskin, and Dan Fazzini. "The Dark Side of Charisma." In *Measures of Leadership,* ed. Kenneth E. Clark and Miriam B. Clark, 343–354. West Orange, NJ: Leadership Library of America, 1990.

Hogg, Michael A. "A Social Identity Theory of Leadership." *Personality and Social Psychology Review* 5 (2001): 184–200.

Hogg, Michael A., Robin Martin, Olga Epitropaki, Aditi Mankad, Alicia Svensson, and Karen Weeden. "Effective Leadership in Salient Groups: Revisiting Leader-Member Exchange Theory From the Perspective of the Social Identify Theory of Leadership." *Personality and Social Psychology Bulletin* 31 (2005): 991–1004.

Hogan, Joyce, and Robert Hogan. "Leadership and Sociopolitical Intelligence." In *Multiple Intelligences and Leadership*, ed. Ronald E Riggio,. Susan E. Murphy, and Francis J. Pirozzolo, 75–88. Mahwah, NJ: Lawrence Erlbaum, 2002.

Hooijberg, Robert, James G. Hunt, and George E. Dodge. "Leadership Complexity and Development of the Leaderplex Model." *Journal of Management* 23 (1997): 375–408.

Hoover, Larry T., and Edward T. Mader. "Attitudes of Police Chiefs Toward Private Sector Management Principles." *American Journal of Police* 9, no. 4 (1990): 25–37.

House, Robert J. "A Path-Goal Theory of Leader Effectiveness." *Administrative Science Quarterly* 16 (1971): 321–339.

House, Robert J., Philip M. Podsakoff. "Leadership Effectiveness: Past Perspectives and Future Directions for Research." In *Organizational Behavior: The State of the Science*, ed. Jerald Greenberg, 45–82. Hillsdale, NJ: Lawrence Erlbaum Associates, 1994.

Howard, Ann. "Best Practices in Leader Selection." In *The Practice of Leadership: Developing the Next Generation of Leaders,* ed. Jay A. Conger and Ronald E. Riggio, 11–40. San Francisco: Jossey-Bass, 2007.

Huberts, Leo W.J.C., Muel Kaptein, and Karin Lasthuizen. "A Study of the Impact of Three Leadership Styles on Integrity Violations Committed by Police Officers." *Policing: An International Journal of Police Strategies & Management* 30 (2007): - 587–607.

Hunt, Jennifer. "Police Accounts of Normal Force." *Journal of Contemporary Ethnography* 13 (1985): 315–341.

Isenberg, Jim. *Police Leadership in a Democracy: Conversations with America's Police Chiefs.* Boca Raton, FL: CRC Press, 2010.

Jackson, John, Richard Myers, and Thomas Cowper. "Leadership in the Net-Centric Organization." In *Advancing Police Leadership: Considerations, Lessons Learned, And Preferable Futures*, ed. Joseph A. Schafer and Sandy Boyd, 138–149. Washington, DC: Federal Bureau of Investigation, 2010.

Janis, Irving L. *Victims of Groupthink: A Psychological Study of Foreign-Policy Decisions and Fiascoes.* Boston: Houghton-Mifflin, 1972

Jermier, John M., and Leslie J. Berkes. "Leader Behavior in a Police Command Bureaucracy: A Closer Look at the Quasi-Military Model." *Administrative Science Quarterly* 24 (1979): 1–23.

Johnson, Richard R. "Management Influences on Officer Traffic Enforcement Productivity." *International Journal of Police Science & Management* 8 (2006): 205–217.

Johnson, Terrance A. and Raymond W. Cox III. "Police Ethics: Organizational Implications." *Public Integrity* 7, no. 1 (2004): 67–79.

Kant, Immanuel. *Perpetual Peace and Other Essays.* Translated by Ted Humphrey. Indianapolis, IN: Hackett, 1983.

Kanungo, Rabindra N. "Ethical Values of Transactional and Transformational Leaders." *Canadian Journal of Administrative Sciences* 18 (2001): 257–265.

Kellerman, Barbara. *Bad Leadership: What it is, How it Happens, Why it Matters.* Boston: Harvard Business School Press, 2004a.

Kellerman, Barbara. "Leadership: Warts and All." *Harvard Business Review* 82, no. 1 (2004b): 40–45.

Kelley, Clarence M. "Receptiveness to Change." *The Police Chief* 40, no. 12 (1973): 32–34

Kelling, George, and William Bratton. *Implementing Community Policing: The Administrative Problem.* Washington, DC: National Institute of Justice, 1993.

Kelloway, E. Kevin, Niro Sivanathan, Lori Francis, and Julian Barling. "Poor Leadership." In *Handbook of Work Stress*, ed. Julian Barling, E. Kevin Kelloway, and Michael R. Frone, 89–112. Thousand Oaks, CA: Sage, 2005.

Kets de Vries, Manfred F.R. *Leaders, Fools and Imposters: Essays on the Psychology of Leadership.* San Francisco: Jossey-Bass, 1993.

Kidd, Virginia and Rick Braziel. *COP Talk: Essential Communication Skills for Community Policing.* Lantham, MD: Rowman & Littlefield Publishers, 1999.

Kimmel, John T., and Paul Lindenmuth. "Police Chief Performance and Leadership Styles." *Police Quarterly* 4 (2001): 469–483.

King, William R. "Bending Granite Revisited: The Command Rank Structure of American Police Organizations." *Policing: An International Journal of Police Strategies and Management* 26 (2003): 208–231.

Klinger, David A. "Negotiating Order in Patrol Work: An Ecological Theory of Police Response to Deviance." *Criminology* 35 (1997): 277–306.

Klinger, David A. "Environment and Organization: Reviving a Perspective on the Police." *Annals: American Academy of Political and Social Science* 593 (2004): 119–136.

Klockars, Carl B. "The Dirty Harry Problem." *Annals: American Academy of Political and Social Science* 452 (1980); 33–47.

Klockars, Carl B. "Blue Lies and Police Placebos: The Moralities of Police Lying." *American Behavioral Scientist* 27 (1984): 529–544.

Klockars, Carl B. *The Idea of Police.* Thousand Oaks, CA: Sage, 1985.

Klockars, Carl B., Sanja K. Ivkovich, W.E. Harver, and Maki R. Haberfeld. *The Measurement of Police Integrity.* Washington, DC: National Institute of Justice, 2000.

Kobler, Arthur. "Police Homicide in a Democracy." *Journal of Social Issues* 31 (1975): 163–184.

Konkler, Gerald. "Knowledge Retention and Management." In *Advancing Police Leadership: Considerations, Lessons Learned, And Preferable Futures,* ed. Joseph A. Schafer and Sandy Boyd, 101–108. Washington, DC: Federal Bureau of Investigation, 2010.

Kotlyar, Igor and Leonard Karakowsky. (2006). "Leading Conflict? Linkages Between Leader Behaviors and Group Conflict." *Small Group Research* 37 (2006): 377–403.

Kotlyar, Igor and Leonard Karakowsky, "The Positive Side of Negative Framing: Examining a Case of Overconfidence among Decision Makers in a Hospital Merger." *Management Decision* 45 (2007): 968–981.

Kotter, John P. *A Force For Change: How Leadership Differs From Management.* New York: Free Press, 1990.

Kouzes, James M., and Barry Z. Posner. *The Leadership Challenge,* 3rd ed. San Francisco: Jossey-Bass, 2002.

Krimmel, John T., and Paul Lindenmuth. "Police Chief Performance and Leadership Styles." *Police Quarterly* 4 (2001): 469–483.

Kuykendall, Jack, and Roy R. Roberg. "Police Managers' Perceptions of Employee Types: A Conceptual Model." *Journal of Criminal Justice* 16 (1988): 131–137.

Kuykendall, Jack L., and Peter Unsinger. "The Leadership Styles of Police Managers." *Journal of Criminal Justice* 10 (1982): 311–321.

Lambert, Eric G. "A Test of a Turnover Intent Model: The Issue of Correctional Staff Satisfaction and Commitment." In *Criminal Justice Theory: Explaining the Nature and Behavior of Criminal Justice,* ed. David E. Duffee and Edward R. Maguire, 223–255. New York: Routledge, 2007

Langworthy, Robert H. "Police Cynicism: What We Know From the Niederhoffer Scale." *Journal of Criminal Justice* 15 (1987): 17–35.

Lansing, Alfred. *Endurance: Shackleton's Incredible Voyage.* London: Weidenfeld & Nicolson, 2001.

Leslie, Jean B., and Ellen Van Velsor. *A Look at Derailment Today: North America and Europe.* Greensboro, NC: Center for Creative Leadership, 1996.

Levitt, Barbara, and James G. March. "Organizational Learning." *Annual Review of Sociology* 14 (1988): 319–340.

Levy, Paul. *Industrial Organizational Psychology: Understanding the Workplace,* 3rd ed. New York: Worth, 2010.

Lindblom, Charles E. "Still Muddling, Not Yet Through." *Public Administration Review* 39 (1979): 517–526.

Lindblom, Charles E. "The Science of Muddling Through." *Public Administration Review* 19 (1959): 79–88.

Lipman-Blumen, Jean. *The Allure Of Toxic Leaders: Why We Follow Destructive Bosses and Corrupt Politicians—And How We Can Survive Them.* New York: Oxford University Press, 2005.

Lipsky, Michael. *Street-Level Bureaucracy: Dilemmas of the Individual in Public Service.* New York: Russell Sage Foundation, 1980.

Livingston, Robert W., Ashleigh Shelby Rosette, and Ella F. Washington. "Can an Agentic Black Woman Get Ahead? The Impact of Race and Interpersonal Dominance on Perceptions of Female Leaders." *Psychological Science* doi: 10.1177/0956797611428079 available online March 14, 2012.

London, Manuel, James W. Smither, and Thomas Diamante. "Best Practices in Leadership Assessment." In *The Practice of Leadership: Developing the Next Generation of Leaders,* ed. Jay A. Conger and Ronald E. Riggio, 41–63. San Francisco: Jossey-Bass, 2007.

Lord, Robert G., Christy L. De Vader, and George M. Alliger. "A Meta-Analysis of the Relation Between Personality Traits and Leadership: An Application of Validity Generalization Procedures." *Journal of Applied Psychology* 71 (1986): 402–410.

Los Angeles Police Department. *Board of Inquiry Into the Rampart Area Corruption Incident: Public Report.* Los Angeles; author, 2000.

Loveday, Barry. "Performance Management and the Decline of Leadership Within Public Services in the United Kingdom." *Policing: A Journal of Policy and Practice* 2 (2008): 120–130.

Lurigio, Arthur J. and Wesley G. Skogan. "Winning the Hearts and Minds of Police Officers: An Assessment of Staff Perceptions of Community Policing in Chicago." *Crime & Delinquency* 40 (1994): 315–330.

Maccoby, Michael. "Narcissistic leaders: The Incredible Pros, the Inevitable Cons." *Harvard Business Review* 78, no. 1 (2000): 68–77.

Manning, Peter K. "Lying, Secrecy, and Social Control." In *Policing: A View from the Street,* ed. Peter K. Manning and John Van Maanen, 238–255. Santa Monica, CA: Goodyear Publishing Co, 1978.

Manning, Peter K. *Police Work,* 2nd ed. Prospect Heights, IL: Waveland, 1997

Marks, Monique, and Jenny Fleming. " 'As Unremarkable as the Air They Breathe?' Reforming Police Management in South Africa." *Current Sociology* 52 (2004): 784–808.

Martin, R, G. Thomas, K. Charles, O. Epitropaki, and R. McNamara. (2005). "The Role of Leader-Member Exchanges in Mediating the Relationship Between Locus of Control and Work Reactions." *Journal of Occupational and Organizational Psychology* 78 (2005): 141–147.

Mastrofski, Stephen D. "Community Policing and Police Organization Structure." In *How to Recognize Good Policing: Problems and Issues*, ed. Jean Paul Brodeur, 161–189. Thousand Oaks, CA: Sage, 1998.

Mastrofski, Stephen D. "Police Organization and Management Issues for the Next Decade." Paper presented at the National Institute of Justice Police Research Workshop: Planning for the Future. Washington, DC. November 28–29, 2006.

Mastrofski, Stephen D. "The Romance of Police Leadership." In *Advances in Criminological Theory, Volume 10: Crime & Social Organization,* ed. Elin J. Warin and David Weisburd, 153–196. New Brunswick, NJ: Transaction Publishers, 2002.

Mastrofski, Stephen D., Richard R. Ritti, and Jeffrey B. Snipes. "Expectancy Theory and Police Productivity in DUI Enforcement." *Law and Society Review* 28 (1994): 113–148.

McCabe, Bill. "The Disabling Shadow of Leadership." *British Journal of Administrative Management* 46 (2005): 16–17.

McCall, Morgan W., and Michael M. Lombardo. *Off the Track: Why and How Successful Executives Get Derailed.* Greensboro, NC: Center for Creative Leadership, 1983.

McCauley, Cynthia D. "Successful and Unsuccessful Leadership." In *The Nature of Leadership,* ed. John Antonakis, Anna T. Cianciolo, and Robert J. Sternberg, 199–221. Thousand Oaks, CA: Sage, 2004.

McLean, Bethany, and Peter Elkind. *The Smartest Guys in the Room: The Amazing Rise and Scandalous Fall of Enron.* New York: Portfolio, 2003.

McGregor, Douglas. *The Human Side of Enterprise.* New York: McGraw-Hill, 1960.

Meadows, Robert J. "Decisionmaking and the Police Manager: The Application of Bounded Rationality and Perspectives for Improvement." *Journal of Police Science and Administration* 7 (1979): 236–240.

Meindl, James R. "On Leadership: An Alternative to the Conventional Wisdom." *Research in Organizational Behavior* 12 (1990): 159–203.

Meindl, James R., and Sanford B. Erlich. "The Romance of Leadership and the Evaluation of Organizational Performance." *Academy of Management Journal* 30 (1987): 91–109.

Meindl, James R., Sanford B. Ehrlich, and Janet M. Dukerich. "The Romance of Leadership." *Administrative Science Quarterly* 30 (1985): 78–102.

Merton, Robert K. "The Unanticipated Consequences of Purposive Social Action." *American Sociological Review* 1 (1936): 894–904.

Miller, Holly A., Rita J. Watkins, and David Webb. "The Use of Psychological Testing to Evaluate Law Enforcement Leadership Competencies and Development." *Police Practice and Research* 10 (2009): 49–60.

Muir, William K., Jr. *Police: Street Corner Politicians.* Chicago: University of Chicago Press, 1977.

Murphy, Steven A. "The Role of Emotions and Transformational Leadership on Police Culture: An Autoethnographic Account." *International Journal of Police Science & Management* 10 (2008): 165–178.

Murphy, Steven A. and Edward Drodge. "The Four I's of Police Leadership: A Case Study Heuristic." *International Journal of Police Science & Management* 6 (2004): 1–15.

Myers, Richard W. "From Pyramids to Networks: Police Structure and Leadership in 2020." In *Policing 2020: The Future of Crime, Communities, and Policing,* ed. Joseph A. Schafer, 487–519. Washington, DC: Federal Bureau of Investigation, 2007.

Myers, Richard and Thomas Cowper. "Net-Centric Crisis Response." In *Policing Mass Casualty Events,* ed. Joseph A. Schafer and Bernard H. Levin, 56–77. Washington, DC: Federal Bureau of Investigation, 2007.

Myers, Richard W., Joseph A. Schafer, and Bernard H. Levin. *Police Decision-Making; A Futures Perspective.* Washington, DC: Federal Bureau of Investigation, 2010.

National Research Council. *Fairness and Effectiveness in Policing: The Evidence.* Committee to Review Research on Police Policy and Practices, Committee on Law and Justice, Division on Behavioral and Social Sciences and Education. Washington, DC: The National Academies Press, 2004.

Niederhoffer, Arthur. *Behind the Shield: The Police in Urban Society.* Garden City, NY: Anchor Books, 1969.

Noblet, Andrew, John Rodwell, and Amanda Allisey. "Job Stress in the Law Enforcement Sector: Comparing the Linear, Non-Linear and Interaction Effects of Working Conditions." *Stress and Health* 25 (2009): 111–120.

Northouse, Peter G. *Leadership: Theory and Practice*, 5th ed. Thousand Oaks, CA: Sage, 2009.

Oakley, Ed, and Doug Krug. *Enlightened Leadership: Getting to the Heart of Change.* New York: Fireside, 1991.

O'Dea, Mary and John Jarvis, ed. *The Police and the Military: Future Challenges and Opportunities in Public Safety: Volume 4 of the Proceedings of the Futures Working Group.* Washington, DC: Federal Bureau of Investigation, 2008.

O'Hara, (2005). *Why Law Enforcement Organizations Fail.* Durham, NC: Carolina Academic Press.

Oliver, Willard M. "Policing for Homeland Security: Policy & Research." *Criminal Justice Policy Review* 20 (2009): 253–260.

Ortmeier, P.J., and Edwin Meese III. *Leadership, Ethics, and Policing: Challenges for the 21st Century,* 2nd ed. Upper Saddle River, NJ: Prentice Hall, 2010.

Packer, Herbert L. The Limits of Criminal Sanctions. Stanford, CA: Stanford University Press, 1968.

Pagon, Milan. "The Need for a Paradigm Shift in Police Leadership." In *Police Leadership in the Twenty-First Century: Philosophy, Doctrine and Developments,* ed. Robert Adlam and Peter Villiers, 157–168. Winchester, UK: Waterside Press, 2003.

Panzarella, Robert. "Leadership Myths and Realities." In *Police Leadership in the Twenty-First Century: Philosophy, Doctrine and Developments,* ed. Robert Adlam and Peter Villiers, 119–133. Winchester, UK: Waterside Press, 2003.

Peter, Laurence J., and Raymond Hull. *The Peter Principle.* New York: William Morrow, 1969.

Peters, Thomas J., and Robert H. Waterman. *In Search of Excellence: Lessons from America's Best Run Companies.* New York: Harper & Row, 1982.

Pfeffer, Jeffrey. "Management as Symbolic Action: The Creation and Maintenance of Organizational Paradigms." *Research in Organizational Behavior* 3 (1981): 1–52.

Pillai, Rajnandini, and Ethlyn A. Williams. "Transformational Leadership, Self-Efficacy, Group Cohesiveness, Commitment, and Performance. " *Journal of Organizational Change Management* 17 (2004): 144–159.

Police Executive Research Forum. *Is the Economic Downturn Fundamentally Changing How We Police? (Critical Issues in Policing Series).* Washington, DC: author, 2010.

Pogrebin, Mark R., and Eric D. Poole. "Humor in the Briefing Room: A Study of the Strategic Use of Humor Among Police." *Journal of Contemporary Ethnography* 17 (1988): 183–210.

Potts, Lee W. "Police Leadership: Challenges for the Eighties." *Journal of Police Science and Administration* 10 (1982): 181–188.

Pursley, Robert D. "Leadership and Community Identification Attitudes Among Two Categories of Police Chiefs: An Exploratory Inquiry." *Journal of Police Science and Administration* 2 (1974): 414–422.

Rainguet, Fred W. and Mary Dodge. "The Problems of Police Chiefs: An Examination of the Issues in Tenure and Turnover." *Police Quarterly* 4 (2001): 268–288.

Redmond, Matthew R., Michael D. Mumford, and Richard Teach. "Putting Creativity to Work: Effects of Leader Behavior on Subordinate Creativity." *Organizational Behavior and Human Decision Processes* 55 (1993): 120–151.

Regoli, Robert M. "An Empirical Assessment of Niederhoffer's Cynicism Scale." *Journal of Criminal Justice* 4 (1976): 231–241.

Regoli, Robert M., and Eric D. Poole. "Measurement of Police Cynicism: A Factor Scaling Approach." *Journal of Criminal Justice* 7 (1979): 37–51.

Reese, Renford. *Leadership in the LAPD: Walking the Tightrope.* Durham, NC: Carolina Academic Press, 2005.

Reiss, Albert J., Jr. *The Police and the Public.* New Haven, CT: Yale University Press, 1971.

Reiss, H.S. *Kant: Political Writings.* Cambridge, UK: Cambridge University Press, 1970/1996.

Reuss-Ianni, Elizabeth. *Two Cultures of Policing: Street Cops and Management Cops.* New York: Transaction Books, 1983.

Riggio, Ronald E., and Jay A. Conger. "Getting it Right: The Practice of Leadership." In *The Practice of Leadership: Developing the Next Generation of Leaders,* ed. Jay A. Conger and Ronald E. Riggio, 331–344. San Francisco: Jossey-Bass, 2007.

Ross, Darrell L. "Emerging Trends in Police Failure to Train Liability." *Policing* 23 (2000): 169–193.

Rowe, Michael. "Following the Leader: Front-Line Narratives on Police Leadership." *Policing: An International Journal of Police Strategies & Management* 29 (2006): 757–767.

Rubenstein, Jonathan. *Big City Police.* New York: Farrar, Straus, Giroux, 1973.

Ryan, Andrew, and Matt Carroll. (2012, February 10). "Officers are Hub's Top Wage Earners." *The Boston Globe,* 10 February 2012. Available at www.boston.com. Accessed March 7, 2012.

Sandler, Georgette Bennett and Ellen Mintz. "Police Organizations: Their Changing Internal and External Relationships." *Journal of Police Science and Administration* 2 (1974): 458–463.

Schackleton, Viv. *Business Leadership.* Thomson Learning: London, 1995.

Schafer, Joseph A. *Community Policing: The Challenges of Successful Organizational Change.* New York: LFB Scholarly Publishing, 2001.

Schafer, Joseph A. "The Challenge of Effective Organizational Change: Lessons Learned in Community-Policing Implementation." In *The Move to Community Policing: Making Change Happen,* ed. Merry Morash and J. Kevin Ford, 243–263. Thousand Oaks, CA: Sage, 2002.

Schafer, Joseph A. "Bureaucratic Structures and Mass Casualty Events." In *Policing and Mass Casualty Events: Volume 3 of the Proceedings of the Futures Working Group,* ed. Joseph A. Schafer and Bernard H. Levin, 24–39. Washington, DC: Federal Bureau of Investigation, 2007.

Schafer, Joseph A. "Enhancing Effective Leadership in Policing: Perils, Pitfalls, and Paths Forward." *Policing: An International Journal of Police Strategies and Management* 32 (2009): 238–260.

Schafer, Joseph A. "Effective Leaders and Leadership in Policing: Traits, Assessment, Development, and Expansion." *Policing: An International Journal of Police Strategies and Management* 33 (2010a): 644–663.

Schafer, Joseph A. "The Ineffective Police Leader." *Journal of Criminal Justice* 38 (2010b): 737–746.

Schafer, Joseph A., Michael E. Buerger, Richard W. Myers, Carl J. Jensen, and Bernard H. Levin. *The Future of Policing: A Practical Guide for Police Leaders and Managers.* Boca Raton, FL: CRC, 2012.

Schafer, Joseph A., and Thomas J. Martinelli. "First-Line Supervisor's Perceptions of Police Integrity: The Measurement of Police Integrity Revisited." *Policing: An International Journal of Police Strategies and Management* 31 (2008): 306–323.

Schein, Edgar H. "Organizational Culture." *American Psychologist* 45, no. 2 (1990): 109–119.

Sezlnick, Philip. *Leadership in Administration*. New York: Harper & Row, 1957.

Shamir, Boas and Jane M. Howell. "Organizational and Contextual Influences on the Emergence and Effectiveness of Charismatic Leadership." *Leadership Quarterly* 10 (1999): 257–283.

Shamir, Boas, Rajnandini Pillai, Michelle C. Bligh, and Mary Uhl-Bien. *Follower-Centered Perspectives on Leadership: A Tribute to the Memory of James R. Meindl*. Charlotte, NC: Information Age Publishing, 2007.

Silvestri, Marisa. " 'Doing Time': Becoming a Police Leader." *International Journal of Police Science & Management* 8 (2006): 266–281.

Silvestri, Marisa. " 'Doing' Police Leadership: Enter the 'New Smart Macho.'" *Policing & Society* 17 (2007): 38–58.

Simon, Herbert A. "Rational Choice and the Structure of the Environment." *Psychological Review* 63 (1956): 129–138.

Sinek, Simon. *Start With Why: How Great Leaders Inspire Everyone to Take Action*. New York: Portfolio, 2009.

Sklansky, David A. *Democracy and the Police*. Stanford, CA: Stanford University Press, 2007.

Skogan, Wesley G. "Community Policing: Common Impediments to Success." In *Community Policing: The Past, Present, and Future*, ed. Lorie Fridell, 159–167. Washington, DC: Police Executive Research Forum, 2004.

Skogan, Wesley G., and Susan M. Hartnett. *Community Policing, Chicago Style*. New York: Oxford University Press, 1997

Slobogin, Christopher. "Testilying: Police Perjury and What to do about it." *University of Colorado Law Review* 67 (1996): 1037–1060.

Skolnick, Jerome H. *Justice without Trial: Law Enforcement in Democratic Society*, 3rd ed. New York: Macmillan, 1994

Smith, Jeffrey A. and Roseanne J. Foti. "A Pattern Approach to the Study of Leader Emergence." *Leadership Quarterly* 9 (1998): 147–160.

Stamper, Norman H. *Removing Managerial Barriers to Effective Police Leadership: A Study of Executive Leadership and Executive Management in Big-City Police Departments*. Washington, DC: Police Executive Research Forum, 1992.

Stanton, Mike. *The Prince of Providence: The Life and Times of Buddy Cianci, America's Most Notorious Mayor, Some Wiseguys, and the Feds*. New York: Random House, 2003.

Steinheider, Brigitte, and Todd Wuestewald "From the Bottom-Up: Sharing Leadership in a Police Agency." *Police Practice and Research* 9 (2008): 145–163.

Stogdill, Ralph M. "Personal Factors Associated with Leadership: A Survey of the Literature." *Journal of Psychology* 25 (1948): 35–71.

Stogdill, Ralph M. *Handbook of Leadership: A Survey of Theory and Research*. New York: Free Press, 1974.

Sutherland, Mitti D. and Elizabeth Reuss-Ianni. "Leadership and Management." In *What Works in Policing? Operations and Administration Examined*, ed. Gary W. Cordner and Donna C. Hale, 157–177. Cincinnati, OH: Anderson, 1992.

Swartz, Mimi, and Sherron Watkins. *Power Failure: The Inside Story of the Collapse of ENRON*. New York: Doubleday, 2003.

Sweigart, Josh, and Christopher Magan. "Police at OSU Paid More Than $1M in Overtime." *Dayton Daily News*, 26 September 2011. Available at www.daytondailynews.com. Accessed March 7, 2012.

Tannenbaum, Robert. and Waren H. Schmitt. "How to Choose a Leadership Pattern." *Harvard Business Review* 36, May-June (1958): 95–101.

Thomas, Robert J. *Crucibles of Leadership: How to Learn From Experience to Become a Great Leader.* Boston: Harvard Business Press, 2008.

Trojanowicz, Robert C. *The Environment of the First-Line Police Supervisor.* Englewood Cliffs, NJ: Prentice Hall, 1980.

Trojanowicz, Robert, Victor E. Kappeler, and Larry K. Gaines. *Community Policing: A Contemporary Perspective,* 3rd ed. Cincinnati, OH: Anderson, 2002.

Tyler, Tom R. *Why People Cooperate: The Role of Social Motivations.* Princeton, NJ: Princeton University Press, 2010.

Tyler, Tom R., and Yuen J. Huo. *Trust in the Law: Encouraging Public Cooperation With the Police and Courts.* New York: Russell-Sage Foundation, 2002.

Uchida, Craig D. "The Development of the American Police: An Historical Overview." In *Critical Issues in Policing: Contemporary Readings* 6th ed, ed. Roger G. Dunham and Geoffrey P. Alpert, 17–36. Long Grove, IL: Waveland, 2010.

Van Maanen, John. "The Boss: The American Police Sergeant." In *Control in the Police Organization,* ed. Maurice Punch, 275–317. Cambridge, MA: MIT Press, 1983.

Van Maanen, John. "Making Rank: Becoming an American Police Sergeant." *Urban Life* 13 (1984): 155–176.

Villiers, Peter. "Leadership by Consent." In *Police Leadership in the Twenty-First Century: Philosophy, Doctrine and Developments,* ed. Robert Adlam and Peter Villiers, 223–236. Winchester, UK: Waterside Press, 2003.

Vito, Gennaro F. and George E. Higgins. "Examining the Validity of *The Leadership Challenge* Inventory: The Case for Law Enforcement." *International Journal of Police Science and Management* 12 (2010): 305–319.

Vroom, Victor H. *Work and Motivation.* New York: McGraw-Hill, 1964.

Vroom, Victor H., and Arthur G. Jago. *The New Leadership: Managing Participation in Organizations.* Englewood Cliffs, NJ: Prentice-Hall, 1988.

Vroom, Victor H., and Arthur G. Jago. "The Role of the Situation in Leadership." *American Psychologist* 62, no. 1 (2007): 17–24.

Vroom, Victor H., and Phillip W. Yetton. *Leadership and Decision-Making.* Pittsburgh, PA: University of Pittsburgh Press, 1973.

Walker Samuel. *A Critical History of Police Reform: The Emergence of Professionalism.* Lexington, MA: Lexington Books, 1977.

Wagner, Rodd, and James K. Harter. *12: The Elements of Great Management.* New York: Gallup Press, 2006.

Weisburd, David, Rosann Greenspan, Edwin E. Hamilton, Hubert Williams, and Kellie A. Bryant. *Police Attitudes Toward Abuse of Authority: Findings From a National Study.* Washington, DC: National Institute of Justice, 2000.

Wexler, Chuck, Mary Ann Wycoff, and Craig Fischer. *"Good to Great" Policing: Application of Business Management Principles in the Public Sector.* Washington, DC; U.S. Department of Justice, 2007.

White, Richard D. "The Micromanagement Disease: Symptoms, Diagnosis, and Cure." *Public Personnel Management* 39, no 1 (2010): 71–76.

Willis, James J., Stephen D. Mastrofski, and David Weisburd. *Compstat in Practice: An In-Depth Analysis of Three Cities.* Washington, DC: Police Executive Research Forum, 2003.

Wilson, James Q. "Dilemmas of Police Administration." *Public Administration Review* 28 (1968): 407–417.

Wilson, James Q. *Bureaucracy: What Government Agencies Do and Why They Do It*. New York: Basic, 2000.

Wilson, Orlando W. *Police Administration*. New York: McGraw-Hill, 1950.

Wilson, Orlando W. and Roy C. McLaren. *Police Administration* 3rd ed. New York: McGraw-Hill, 1977.

Witte, Jeffrey H., Lawrence F. Travis, and Robert H. Langworthy. "Participatory Management in Law Enforcement: Police Officer, Supervisor and Administrator Perceptions." *American Journal of Police* 9, no. 4 (1990): 1–23.

Worden, Robert E. "Police Officers' Belief Systems: A Framework for Analysis." *American Journal of Police* 14, no. 1 (1995): 49–81.

Wycoff, Mary Ann, and Wesley G. Skogan. "The Effect of a Community Policing Management Style on Officers' Attitudes." *Crime & Delinquency* 40 (1994): 371–383.

Yukl, Gary. *Leadership in Organizations,* 5th ed. Upper Saddle River, NJ: Prentice Hall, 2009.

Yusko, Dennis. (2012, March 6). "Spa City Overtime Jumps in 2011." *The Times Union*, 6 March 2012. Available at www.timesunion.com. Accessed March 7, 2012.

Zigarmi, Drea, Ken Blanchard, Michael O'Connor, and Carl Edeburn. *The Leader Within: Learning Enough About Yourself to Lead Others*. Upper Saddle River, NJ: Pearson-Prentice Hall, 2005.

Index

Note: *n* denotes footnotes